HAFNER PUBLISHING COMPANY
31 EAST 10th STREET
NEW YORK 3, N. Y.

THE HAFNER LIBRARY OF CLASSICS

[Number Twenty-One: Sarmiento-Argentine Republic]

Engraved by John Sartain Phil.ᵃ

D.F. Sarmiento

LIFE IN THE ARGENTINE
REPUBLIC IN THE DAYS OF
THE TYRANTS;

OR,

CIVILIZATION AND BARBARISM.

FROM THE SPANISH OF

DOMINGO F. SARMIENTO, LL. D.,

MINISTER PLENIPOTENTIARY FROM THE ARGENTINE REPUBLIC TO THE UNITED STATES.

WITH A

BIOGRAPHICAL SKETCH OF THE AUTHOR,

By MRS. HORACE MANN.

First American from the third Spanish Edition.

HAFNER PUBLISHING CO.
NEW YORK

First published in 1868

Published by
HAFNER PUBLISHING CO., INC.
31 East 10th Street
New York 3, N. Y.

Library of Congress Catalog Card Number:
60-11057

Printed in the U.S.A.
Noble Offset Printers, Inc.
New York 3, N.Y.

PREFACE.

———◆———

SINCE the translation of this work by Colonel Sarmiento was begun, the tide of events has carried its author to the proudest position before his country which any man since San Martin, the hero of its independence and of the independence of some of its sister Republics, has ever occupied. It is true that circumstances of even a trivial nature, and still more frequently of a corrupt nature, often bring a man to the chieftainship of his country, whether the office is elective or otherwise ; but in this instance such circumstances have been singularly wanting. Colonel Sarmiento, after an absence of seven years from his country, without any political party, without any pledges of policy given or required, without any of the machinery that is generally used to set in motion such important measures, has by an almost unanimous movement been made the candidate *par excellence* for the Presidency of the Argentine Republic, and the returns are already

known from the province of Buenos Ayres, which
contains one third of the population of the whole
Republic, and is by far the wealthiest, most cultivated,
and most influential part of it. In this province his
election has been complete and unanimous, and the
voice of many other provinces has long been heard
through their daily organs, so that doubtless before
these pages see the light, the favorable result will be
confirmed. Colonel Sarmiento has resisted all the
entreaties of his friends to return to his country to aid
the interests of his election. He has chosen to wait
until elected by the unbiassed will of his countrymen,
— and for wise as well as self-respecting reasons. All
who have followed the golden thread of his life through
the chaotic changes that have harassed the life of the
Republic, so determined to be free and progressive, in
spite of all the temporary reactions of the barbaric
element which has its seat in the peculiar composition
of its society, feel with him that it is only by appreciation of his motives, sympathy with his aims, and confidence in his ability to save them from the present
threatened anarchy, that he can have any assurance
of doing good from the high position now assigned
him. He has never flattered his countrymen ; he has
always recognized the barbarian tendencies which have
so often overpowered the equally persistent but vitally
permanent influences of civilization, and he has been

equally assiduous in his endeavors to arouse them from the apathy inherent, as it were, in a Spanish and at the same time priest-ridden community ; but even Cordova, the " city of priests," anchored in conservatism by the very character of its extraordinary university culture, looks to him now as the only salvation for the nation.

Although a man of decided military ability, as has been proved at various times when patriotism has called him into the field, Colonel Sarmiento is eminently a man of peace, and during a long exile of twenty years, as well as in his subsequent brilliant career as Chief of the Department of Schools, Senator, Minister of State, and Governor of his native province, in his diplomatic missions to Chili, Peru, and the United States, has had but one watchword : " The Education of the People." To his countrymen he is the very ideal type of the SCHOOLMASTER, which he has ever considered his proudest title.

By persistently keeping this idea uppermost, and opposing it to all the adverse tendencies of a community that could make money enough without it, and constantly predicting the disasters that would from time to time overwhelm it if this element of freedom were not cherished as the very ark of its liberties, he made an impression which in the hour of peril ripened quickly into a conviction, and to use an oft-repeated expression of the daily journals of the present period in South America, " his name surged spontaneously from the lips of his countrymen, and was shouted across the Cordilleras and the pampas from either border, from the eastern provinces intelligently, from the western as a cry of hope born of despair and terror, and from the interior where his beneficent labors have already borne fruit and given birth to unlimited hopes of the future." It is characteristic of that imaginative and poetical people to be powerfully swayed by a daring spirit, and a man must have self-reliance to kindle them. Colonel Sarmiento's self-reliance is founded in the nature of the principles he advocates ; and his personal courage in opposing every form of tyranny and barbarism, united with a self-respect which has prevented him from ever asking for an office or a public favor, now commands an appreciation which perhaps his countrymen would be incapable of rendering under a less powerful intellectual stimulus than that given by their present danger.

The study of education also led him to the study of legislation at home and abroad, and in those two paths he has been of incalculable benefit to his country, not only convincing its most advanced men that public education is the only basis of a republic, but aiding them essentially in modeling their government upon that of the United States, which is their prototype, and

to which they now look, rather than to Europe, for
light and knowledge.

Colonel Sarmiento, in this work offered to the
English and American public, gives no intimation of
his personal relations with the tyrants, but as his whole
life and much of the life of the Republic is connected
with these relations, it is proposed to give a short account of its many " dramatic situations," incurred by
his love and utterance of truth. These will be better
understood after than before the perusal of the main
work. A complete life of Colonel Sarmiento, with all
its interesting romantic and historical episodes, would
fill two such volumes, but it is hoped that enough has
been left untouched by the iron rules of publication to
make him known, and to show that his present un-
sought triumph is one that a truly great man may be
proud of. Constantly, from his earliest entrance into
life, sacrificing all personal considerations, rather than
swerve one iota from his principles, or deny himself the
frank utterance of his convictions, he has proved con-
clusively to those who have studied his career, that
he is incapable of any mere personal ambition, though
no one appreciates better the sympathy of his fellow-
men.

It is the cultivated cities of the Argentine Republic,
where Europeans find themselves at home in all that
constitutes civilized society, and where the high culture

of the few is painfully contrasted with the utter want
of it in the body of the people, that constitute its
difference from the other South American Republics,
Chili excepted, in which certain influences have
brought about certain elements of progress, Colonel
Sarmiento being the chief of these favorable influences.
If the chances of elections, or in this case rather the
brute prowess of the reactionary chieftains, has defeated
his election (which took place on the 12th of April),
he will return to his country and take his seat in the
Senate, to which he has of late been again chosen.
He hopes by his influence in either position to increase
the importance of his country's relations with the
United States, whose great ideas he wishes to see
planted in that hemisphere. The sources of information from which the details of his life have been gathered, are two or three small biographies, written in
Chili, Peru, and Geneva ; a short memoir in Rhode
Island, the public documents of the Argentine Republic, the " Journal of the Sessions of the Legislature,"
the " Journal of the Constitutional Convention," and
many periodical works, all containing remarkable
speeches upon various subjects. The reports of the
Chilian government on " Popular Education " may be
added to these, and a little book entitled " Recollections of a Province," which is partly an autobiography
written in 1850, while still in exile, under peculiar

circumstances best described in his own preface to it. I shall give as copious extracts from this little book as my space will allow, for it is impossible, as I have proved by repeated efforts, to convey the same impression by any method of condensation within the reach of a compiler, which is the only character in which I have the presumption to call myself Colonel Sarmiento's biographer, a task which even his countrymen are too modest to assume at this moment of so much importance to their interests. My own interest in the subject has risen both from a personal one that grew out of his peculiar relations with my husband, — in whose name Colonel Sarmiento introduced the boon of Common School Education into Chili and the Argentine Republic, making the name of Horace Mann a household word with all whom he imbued with his own views upon that subject, — and from a deep interest in the nation whose highest aspirations rather than whose actual condition he represents. I wish therefore to place before the public, the series of pictures that give it a marked individuality, and that have in the course of a few years made me cognizant of its history, so obscured to the general eye by the repeated reactions it has suffered since the days of its hardly-won independence.

The work called originally " Civilization and Barbarism," but in the American translation entitled

"Life in the Argentine Republic," was written in Chili, during the author's exile, in order to make known there the policy of Rosas. It found its way to France, and was so favorably received in the "Revue des deux Mondes," that the influence reacted upon his own country, as well as gave to European publicists an explanation of the struggle in the Argentine Republic. A work called "Rosas and the Questions of the La Plata," and many other European publications, were based upon its data and its standpoint. Rosas felt that it gave a mortal blow to his policy, yet during five years of anathemas hurled at the author by the "Gaceta Mercantil," which was his organ, the book was not named. All the author's books were proscribed, but the name of this one carefully suppressed, yet no book was more sought or more read in the Republic. It was handed about secretly, hidden away in drawers, and read at every man's peril.

The "Revue des deux Mondes" says of it: "During his residence in Santiago, which preceded his travels in Europe, Señor Sarmiento published this work full of attraction and novelty, instructive as history, interesting as a romance, brilliant with imagery and coloring. 'Civilization and Barbarism' is not only one of those rare testimonials which come to us of the intellectual life of South America, but it is an invaluable document. Doubtless passion dictated many of its vigorous pages, but even when exalted by passion, there is internal evidence of a fund of impartiality which cannot fail to be recognized, and by whose light true characteristics are given to persons, and a natural coloring to events. . . . It is no less interesting to analyze South than North America. This can only be done by the philosopher, the traveller, the poet, the historian, the painter of manners and customs, the publicist. Señor Sarmiento has succeeded in realizing this object in this work, which he has published in Chili, and which proves that if civilization has enemies in those regions it also has eloquent champions."

This work and other productions of his pen, secured to Señor Sarmiento in Europe, which he subsequently visited, the acquaintance of many prominent men : M. Guizot, M. Thiers, Cobden, then ambassador in Spain, Alexander Dumas, Gil de Zarate, Breton de los Herreros, Ventina de la Vega, Aribou, and other literary Spaniards; Baron Humboldt, and many others. Pope Pius IX., then in the meridian of his glory, sent for him as cousin of the Bishops Cuyo, Oro, and Sarmiento, whom he had known in South America. All institutions of education were thrown open to his study in the portions of Europe which he visited, and to so well-prepared a mind, everything was full of significance, even failures, both educational and political. Dr. Wappäus, Professor of Geography and Statistics in the University of Gottingen, afterwards translated and published in German Señor Sarmiento's "Memoir upon German Emigration to the La Plata," and accompanied it with one hundred and sixty-nine pages of notes and comments of his own.

When R. W. Emerson read the book, he told Colonel Sarmiento that if he would write thus for our public, he would be read ; and Mr. Longfellow suggested writing a romantic poem called the "Red Ribbon," which might be made as striking though it is to be hoped an even more exceptional picture of the peculiar customs of the country than the native poet Echevarria's "Captive," so descriptive of gaucho life.

Buenos Ayres was founded in 1535, by Don Pedro Mendoza, and in 1536 Don Juan de Aloyas, the lieutenant of Mendoza, ascended the Parana and the Paraguay, which Sebastian Cabot had visited in 1530, and founded the city of Asomption in memory of a victory gained over the Indians. This city, now the capital of Paraguay, was then the capital of the Spanish possessions in La Plata. In 1537, while Mendoza was absent in Spain, Buenos Ayres was reduced to the last extremity by the Querandi Indians. The Timbues (Indians) destroyed it entirely in 1539. It was rehabilitated in 1542, again destroyed in 1559. In 1580, Juan de Garay, lieutenant of the Governor of Paraguay, descended the river from Asomption, and on the 11th of June planted the Spanish flag on the old site. He endeavored to people this city with *Guarani* Indians, massacred the Querandis who had revolted against him, and died in 1584. Don Francisco de Zarate, chevalier of the Order of Santiago, and governor of Buenos Ayres, confirmed the foundation of the city by an act of the 10th of February, 1594, and began to construct the fortifications which are now seen on the bank of the river. In 1620, the government of Asomption was reduced in Paraguay, and Buenos Ayres became the chief city of the second government established in La Plata. In 1629, a royal decree united into a single viceroyalty the hitherto separate governments of Buenos Ayres, of Asomption, and the provinces of Charcas, Potosi, and Cochabamba. In 1640, the Portuguese carried their arms into the La Plata, but after many contests, stretching over many years, a treaty was made in 1785, by which the domain came into the possession of Spain definitively.

Until the eighteenth century there was but one viceroyalty in South America, that of Peru, which extended from the western to the eastern shore, but on account of the inconveniences of so large a territory, Spain created another in New Grenada in 1718, a capitancy in Caraccas in 1734, another in

Chili at the same time, and the viceroyalty of Buenos
Ayres, including the provinces of Upper Peru.

The viceroy was the representative of the King
and his court, and he maintained the pomp and luxury
of the court of Madrid. The viceroyalty united the
civil and military power with no other counterpoise
than the distant dependency of the Council of the
Indies, and the near but indirect inspection of the
audiencia, a court of appeal for all cases not exceed-
ing 10,000 dollars in gold. The viceroy was *ex
officio* its president. His sanction, assisted by an as-
sessor, was necessary to promulgate any sentence.

The salary of the viceroyalty, 60,000 dollars in
gold in Mexico and Peru, and 40,000 in Buenos
Ayres and New Grenada, sufficed to sustain the luxury prescribed by the royal ordinances. It generally
lasted five years, and was then obliged to render an
account of its administration, and the viceroy presented himself in person to answer to any charges
made against him. Other high functionaries were
obliged to do the same. The members of the audiencia were not paid; they must be natives of Spain,
and could not form marriage ties in South America;
they were even recommended not to contract intimate
social relations with the residents of the country; but
an exception was made in favor of creoles. The
officials of this body were a regent, three auditors,

and two fiscals, and they took command of everything but of declaring war.

The functions of subdelegates (corregidores) were the same as in the peninsula. The institution of municipalities was the best guarantee against abuses, and these are still existent and of great import. Although the individuals of these corporations were not elected popularly, they were considered by the people as their own representatives.

The ecclesiastical hierarchy formed another part of the colonial system. Ten viceroys in succession occupied Buenos Ayres from 1777 to 1806. The Marquis of Sobremonte was the King's representative in 1806, when the English invaded La Plata. The viceroy abandoned the capital on the 27th of June that year, leaving it to the occupation of General Beresford, and fled to Cordova, where he obliged the people to receive him with all the pomp due to his rank. The Governor of Montevideo, Ruiz Huidobro, and the *cabildo*[1] and population of that city, prepared to reconquer Buenos Ayres. While the expedition was in

---

[1] The cabildo was a popular assembly with officials answering to mayors and aldermen; their attributes and prerogatives were very great, especially after the downfall of the viceroyalty. This form of government was originally taken from the peninsular government, with the idea of opposing a barrier to the exactions of the territorial lords. Rivadavia, when President in 1825, suppressed this body and substituted for it the municipality which still exists.

preparation, Santiago Liniers, captain of a vessel, a Frenchman in the employ of Spain, arrived at Montevideo with the same purpose. The forces were confided to his command, and he retook Buenos Ayres on the 14th of August. The next day the principal inhabitants formed themselves into a junta which invested Liniers with the command, and created civic forces to defend the territory which was threatened with a new invasion. Sobremonte was obliged to bend before the will of the people. He confirmed Liniers in the military command, delegated his political and administrative powers to the audiencia, and retired to Montevideo.

In 1807, Sir Samuel Auchmuchty with five thousand English soldiers, took Montevideo by assault. The cabildo and the civic corps demanded the imprisonment of Sobremonte, and the audiencia, after resisting for a time, yielded to the will of the people, and took part in a second junta which decreed the arrest of the viceroy and the seizure of his papers.

Another English force under General Whitlocke, laid siege to Buenos Ayres, but was beaten in the streets of the city on the 3d of July, capitulated, and was obliged to evacuate the whole territory of La Plata. The court of Spain confirmed Liniers in the post of viceroy, and nominated Don Francesco Javier Elio governor *per interim* of Montevideo.

But from the time Sobromente was deposed, the prestige of the viceroyalty was lost, never to be restored. At this period arose two rival parties, the European and the American. Ferdinand VII. was at that time dethroned; and this trouble in Spain, added to the ideas suggested by the French revolution, increased the difficulties in South America. The 1st of January, 1809, a conspiracy, supported by the Europeans, presented themselves in the public square of Buenos Ayres, and demanded the deposition of the viceroy and the establishment of a governmental junta for the whole viceroyalty. This met with opposition, of course, but the idea of independence had taken possession of the people, and the result was that a junta was formed, and three persons were put in power. After the fall of this junta, and the establishment of other similar ones, the government was placed in 1814, in the hands of a single person, called Supreme Director of the United Provinces of the La Plata. From the beginning of this supreme directory, especially after the return of Ferdinand VII. to the throne, there was supposed to be a strong tendency in Buenos Ayres towards submitting to the royal authority. But if this desire had existed in any force among those who directed affairs, or guided public opinion, no opportunity or pretext could have offered more favorable to it than the incessant solicitations and propositions of the Princess Carlota, who asked to reign there independently, but which in effect were always utterly powerless in Buenos Ayres. General Alvear, appointed Director in 1815, had already made submission to the King, but this reaction caused a revolution in April, at the head of which stood the cabildo. The assembly was dissolved, and the Director displaced and exiled. On the 24th of March, 1816, a general congress opened its sessions at Tucuman. It declared the independence of the provinces on the 9th of July, since observed in the Republic as the 4th of July in North America, and Don Juan Martin Puyrredon was appointed Director. He assumed the power on the 29th of July. Three years after, General Rondeau was appointed Director in Puyrredon's place.[1]

[1] When Colonel Sarmiento was in France in 1867, at the awarding of prizes in the Exposition, the Argentine Minister to France, who is the son-in-law of General San Martin, the most remarkable Argentine hero of independence, gave an official banquet to the legation, on which occasion Colonel Sarmiento had the pleasure of relating an historic fact, until then unknown, namely: that General San Martin, by his counsels to the Congress of Tucuman in 1816, at which time Independence was declared, was the moving spirit of that act of the Congress, for which the Deputies were not at that time prepared. To Colonel Sarmiento, also, the public is indebted for the details of the famous interview between San Martin and Bolivar in Guayaquil, which resulted in San Martin's noble self-abnegation and renunciation, not only of his place in the activity of that period, but in the lifelong misunderstanding of his contemporaries, all of which Colonel Sarmiento took from the lips of the grand old man when he

In the mean time, the province of Montevideo had rebelled, and the place had been taken by General Alvear on the 23d of June, 1814. General Artigas, one of the country commandants, who coöperated in the siege, had early given tokens of insubordination, and General Alvear undertook to pursue him with the forces that had occupied Montevideo. Master of the Banda Oriental, and of all its resources, Artigas displayed his resentment towards Buenos Ayres. He not only took the Oriental province from the Argentine community, but his personal influence and that of his system, extended over Corrientes, Entrerios, Santa Fé, and Cordova. No treaties were accepted by either side. One of the effects of his influence was the invasion of the province of Buenos Ayres by the troops of Santa Fé and Entrerios, and in February 1820, the Director Rondeau was beaten at La Cañada de Cepeda. The conquerors entered Buenos Ayres with their troops, dissolved the Congress and the Directory, and reduced its power to Buenos Ayres alone. Some authors, in speaking of the revolution of 1810, have attributed to the landed proprietors considered as a class, an influence, an ambition, and political views which never had an existence. They declared them-

visited him in his self-imposed exile at Grandbourg in France, in 1846. Party passions had obscured the subject till that revelation was made from so authentic a source.

selves for their country, as many other classes did,
purely from a sentiment of patriotism, and nothing
more. During the first ten years of the revolution,
when the existence of the Federal and Unitario parties was an old story, the rural districts of most of
the provinces, and that of Buenos Ayres particularly,
were indifferent and even strangers to those questions
and those parties. That multitude of changes in the
government which took place in the cities in favor of
one or the other party, were of no importance or
interest in the campagna. It was not till 1815 that it
was called upon to give its opinion, conjointly with
that of the city, not only upon the validity of a government, but even upon the proposed reform of a
provisory State, which was never realized. The rural
districts never made a movement which revealed a
political idea, and they never misunderstood any government. It is true that the gauchos, a peculiar race
of men that is seen in the pampas, and holds a middle
place between the European and the aboriginal inhabitant, followed certain partisans of that epoch, but it
was because those partisans were the immediate authority which they recognized; they followed them
from personal affection and from the habit of obedience, but from no political conviction, nor from any
desire to make any system prevail for their interest as
a class. The chieftainship (caudillage) did not ap-

pear till 1829. The rural districts, passively obedient, knew neither " Unitarianism " nor " Federalism." If the Congress of 1826 had proclaimed a federation, the chiefs that then represented the federation would have cried *unity ;* the opposition was against men, not against things, which were but a pretext.

In 1820, in the absence of the Governor of the Province, Don Manuel Dorrego, who had offended and gone to fight the Governor of Sante Fé, Don Martin Rodriguez was put in his place. The cabildo protested against this ; the city was thrown into agitation, and Rodriguez had to flee to the country. He returned to the city with Juan Manuel Rosas, commander of the militia or country forces, called the Colorados (or red soldiers) of La Conchas — a man of a Buenos Ayres family, but who, rejecting education, had gone into the country to enjoy more license for his vices than the customs of the city would allow. By the help of Rosas, Rodriguez was reëstablished. Happily, Rodriguez chose Rivadavia for his prime minister, and the country appeared to breathe a free breath under the wise and enlightened administration of this truly great man.

When the Revolution of Independence began, the grand fractions of the viceroyalty, now its separate States, proposed to separate and form private governments. When the struggle with Spain ended, this was effected. Rivadavia, who was the chief of the Unitarios, began by introducing into Buenos Ayres the complete system of a Republic for this province alone, with legislature, government, revenues, etc., like the North American States, and advised the other provinces to do the same, each for itself. This was *Unitarianism*. The foundations of federal system were thus unconsciously laid by the Unitarios themselves, though at that time they opposed federation. What Rivadavia wished at that moment was to give to the actual governments regular form ; but he, San Martin and Bolivar, had the same horror of the idea of federation that the French had in the time of the Girondines. Rodriguez was succeeded in 1824 by General Don Juan Gregorio las Heras. Under his administration a general Congress was convoked, which created a general government under a President, independent of the government of Buenos Ayres. The seat of both the provincial and general governments was the city of Buenos Ayres, and grave inconveniences were the consequence. The provincial government and its representatives were dissolved, and Rivadavia was made President-General on the 8th of February, 1826. He kept that office but one year. The opposition to him in Congress was in the majority, and he resigned. Dr. Don Vicente Lopez was put in his place. When Congress dissolved, the representatives, the majority of whom were Federals, nominated Don Manuel Dorrego, who began to rule in August, 1827. He was driven out by Juan Lavalle in December of this year. Dorrego fled to the country, but was beaten and shot by Lavalle. Rosas, partisan of Dorrego, fled to Santa Fé, from whence he returned with Lopez, its governor. Lavalle was beaten by Lopez, at the Puente del Marques, in 1828. Don J. José Viemont was appointed Governor, and in 1829 was succeeded by Rosas. The Unitario forces, who, with their leaders, had emigrated from Buenos Ayres, occupied the Province of Cordoba, under the orders of General Paz, who was caught by a lasso at the head of his army, and thus made prisoner. Facundo Quiroga triumphed over Castillo, another Unitario chief, and this was the occasion of his appearing on the general scene of action. He was the most celebrated of all those chiefs, representing no party, but a *gaucho of gauchos;* his characteristics brought him an influence, baleful though it was, which made him aspire to the first place in the Republic. Rosas, whose most distinguishing traits were his atrocious cruelty and malice, was jealous of him, and caused his assassination at Barranca-yaco. All the accomplices of the crime were subsequently arrested and executed. Lopez died soon after under circumstances that pointed almost unmistakably to poison. Cullen, Governor of Santa Fé, who had bathed his hands in the conspiracy against Quiroga, and who had letters in his possession that would have compromised Rosas, was shot by Rosas' order at the Arroyo del Medio, a little river between the Provinces of Buenos Ayres and Santa Fé, to which place he was transported for that purpose. The character of Rosas was as stupidly misunderstood abroad, at the time of his supremacy, as that of Lopez of Paraguay at the present time. When he was appointed Governor by the Congress, he was crowned by the women ; the city was illuminated, bands of music paraded, the people were in a state of exultation, and the universal cry was " Death to the Unitarios ! " On the 18th day of the same month the House of Representatives, " in order to reward the worthy citizen, Don Juan Manuel Rosas, and his country companions, for having stifled the scandalous military insurrection of the 1st of December, 1828," voted for a law declaring all publications printed since the 1st of December, 1828, against the former governor, Dorrego, or Colonel Rosas, or the provincial governors and respectable patriots who had served the cause of order, to be infamous libels, and disgraceful to public morals and honor. It also declared him " the restorer of the laws and institutions of the Province of Buenos Ayres. The rank of Brigadier-General of this province shall be given him, and the legislature charges itself with making him known in this character throughout the Republic. He shall be decorated with a sword and a golden medal ornamented with the symbols of law, justice, and courage ; the medal shall be garnished with brilliants on one side, and shall have a crown of laurels and an olive branch as an emblem of gratitude, with these words : *Buenos Ayres to the Restorer of the Laws.* The reverse shall have his bust in cement, with utensils of agriculture and trophies of war, and the device : *He cultivated his fields and defended his country.*"

But their hopes were sadly disappointed. For more than twenty years he held them in abject terror, such as Colonel Sarmiento has described. The rigor of his rule deceived the world, which gives the meed to success rather than to merit. When Colonel Sarmiento visited the United States in 1847, and saw the working of federal institutions, his views of government underwent a great change. He had been a Unitario from education, and antagonism of ideas to Rosas and the *caudillos,* or country chiefs, and from 1827 had taken arms against the Federal party, which was identified with them. Forty years of separation of the provinces, during which each had had its own government, had broken every national tie, and they could not easily unite under a federal government, such as the caudillos had proposed in opposition to Rivadavia.

Rosas had continued to triumph over all the forces which the Republic had united to free itself from his horrible tyranny, and the Unitario chiefs and emigrants were driven into Montevideo, where Rosas besieged them. In 1848, while still in Chili, Colonel Sarmiento established a periodical called " The Cronica," and advocated a *federal* government, like that of the United States, as the only means of continuing the Republic. In this manner he could attract the provinces to their party, accepting the federation, which existed, in fact. After he had established that semi-annual periodical, he founded another weekly one, called " Sud Amercia," which lasted till 1850, in which he unfolded the constituent principles of federation, and promoted the free navigation of the rivers in order to give seaports to the provinces. Another object of it was to encourage emigration. His endeavors were crowned with the most complete success. In 1850, he wrote a pamphlet proposing a Congress, and preparing the way to form a union and alliance of the Unitario chiefs and the Federal caudillos. This pamphlet was called " Argiropolis," and his plan was to found another capital in the island of *Martin Garcia.* This pamphlet was very effective, and ruined Rosas among his own supporters. Bompland, the celebrated naturalist, the companion of Humboldt, presented himself before Urquiza, the principal chieftain under Rosas, and refused obedience to the latter, and proposed a federal constitution and the alliance of the Unitarios, who had collected for mutual defense at Montevideo. This plan was accepted. Colonel Sarmiento, the present President Mitré, and General Paunero, now candidate for the Vice-Presidency, left Chili and went to Buenos Ayres, round Cape Horn, to join Urquiza. They conquered Rosas at Caseros. Thus the Unitarian party itself agreed to give the country a federal constitution. Colonel Sarmiento began the movement alone, but was finally joined by his friends. But General Urquiza proved incapable, through his ignorance and his gaucho habits, of comprehending the significance of the thing he had done himself, and endeavored to continue the old arbitrary rule. The biographical sketch in this volume recounts the self-banishment of Colonel Sarmiento at this time, and his subsequent return and labors in the Province of Buenos Ayres in a private capacity. Buenos Ayres succeeded in resisting Urquiza at this time, and constituted itself again a separate State while Urquiza governed the provinces. When Colonel Sarmiento was elected Deputy to the legislature of Buenos Ayres, before his release from Chili in 1855, he refused the office, and addressed a letter to the electors, reproaching them for having separated from the Republic. He was then appointed Deputy from Tucuman, and refused that also, because

Tucuman had constituted itself independent of Buenos Ayres. When he went to Buenos Ayres in 1856, all his efforts and writings had for their object the Union. His oration at that time over the ashes of Rivadavia, which he gave at the request of the municipality when they were received from Europe at the port of Buenos Ayres, was an appeal to the national sentiment for this Union. In 1859, the Convention, called at the instigation of himself and friends, met at Buenos Ayres to amend the Constitution, and Colonel Sarmiento proposed such amendments as made it resemble that of the United States, and in the National Convention was chiefly instrumental in ratifying these and bringing about the Union which now exists.

When Governor of San Juan, he labored to amend the State government, but was opposed by his Unitario friends, who feared that he would give the provinces too much power. The disastrous history of the last few years has proved that he was in the right, and his countrymen, by the light of the conflagration of civil war, have at last seen that he was their best guide, and the only prominent man that has clearly mastered the situation. Their wild cry of agony now summons him to their aid.

MARY MANN.

CONTENTS.

CHAPTER I.

PHYSICAL CONTENTS OF THE REPUBLIC.

CHAPTER II.

ORIGINALITY AND PECULIARITIES OF THE PEOPLE.

CHAPTER III.

ASSOCIATION.

CONTENTS.

CHAPTER XII.

SOCIAL WAR.

CHAPTER XIII.

BARRANCA-YACO!!!

CHAPTER XIV.

FRIAR JOSÉ FELIX ALDAO, BRIGADIER-GENERAL AND GOVERNOR.

—◆—

BIOGRAPHICAL SKETCH OF THE AUTHOR.

CONTENTS.

LIFE IN THE ARGENTINE REPUBLIC.

CHAPTER I.

PHYSICAL ASPECT OF THE ARGENTINE REPUBLIC, AND
THE FORMS OF CHARACTER, HABITS, AND IDEAS INDUCED
BY IT.

"The extent of the Pampas is so prodigious that they are bounded on the north
by groves of palm-trees and on the south by eternal snows." — *Head*.

THE Continent of America ends at the south in a
point, with the Strait of Magellan at its southern extremity. Upon the west, the Chilian Andes run parallel to the coast at a short distance from the Pacific.
Between that range of mountains and the Atlantic is
a country whose boundary follows the River Plata up
the course of the Uruguay into the interior, which was
formerly known as the United Provinces of the River
Plata, but where blood is still shed to determine
whether its name shall be the Argentine Republic or
the Argentine Confederation. On the north lie Paraguay, the Gran Chaco, and Bolivia, its assumed boundaries.

The vast tract which occupies its extremities is altogether uninhabited, and possesses navigable rivers as
yet unfurrowed even by a frail canoe. Its own extent

is the evil from which the Argentine Republic suffers ; the desert encompasses it on every side and penetrates its very heart ; wastes containing no human dwelling, are, generally speaking, the unmistakable boundaries between its several provinces. Immensity is the universal characteristic of the country : the plains, the woods, the rivers, are all immense ; and the horizon is always undefined, always lost in haze and delicate vapors which forbid the eye to mark the point in the distant perspective, where the land ends and the sky begins. On the south and on the north are savages ever on the watch, who take advantage of the moonlight nights to fall like packs of hyenas upon the herds in their pastures, and upon the defenseless settlements. When the solitary caravan of wagons, as it sluggishly traverses the pampas, halts for a short period of rest, the men in charge of it, grouped around their scanty fire, turn their eyes mechanically toward the south upon the faintest whisper of the wind among the dry grass, and gaze into the deep darkness of the night, in search of the sinister visages of the savage horde, which, at any moment, approaching unperceived, may surprise them. If no sound reaches their ears, if their sight fails to pierce the gloomy veil which covers the silent wilderness, they direct their eyes, before entirely dismissing their apprehensions, to the ears of any horse standing within the firelight, to see if they are pricked up or turned carelessly backwards. Then they resume their interrupted conversation, or put into their mouths the half-scorched pieces of dried beef on which they subsist. When not fearful of the approach of the savage, the plainsman has equal cause to dread the keen eyes of the tiger, or the viper beneath his feet. This constant insecurity of life outside the towns, in my opinion, stamps upon the Argentine character a certain stoical resignation to death by violence, which is regarded as one of the inevitable probabilities of existence. Perhaps this is the reason why they inflict death or submit to it with so much indifference, and why such events make no deep or lasting impression upon the survivors.

The inhabited portion of this country — a country unusually favored by nature, and embracing all varieties of climates — may be divided into three sections possessing distinct characteristics, which cause differences of character among the inhabitants, growing out of the necessity of their adapting themselves to the physical conditions which surround them.

In the north, an extensive forest, reaching to the Chaco, covers with its impenetrable mass of boughs a space whose extent would seem incredible if there could be any marvel too great for the colossal types of Nature in America.

In the central zone, lying parallel to the former, the plain and the forest long contend with each other for the possession of the soil ; the trees prevail for some distance, but gradually dwindle into stunted and thorny bushes, only reappearing in belts of forest along the banks of the streams, until finally in the south, the victory remains with the plain, which displays its smooth, velvet-like surface unbounded and unbroken. It is the image of the sea upon the land ; the earth as it appears upon the map — the earth yet waiting for the command to bring forth every herb yielding seed after its kind. We may indicate, as a noteworthy feature in the configuration of this country, the aggregation of navigable rivers, which come together in the east, from all points of the horizon, to form the Plata by their union, and thus worthily to present their mighty tribute to the Ocean, which receives it, not without visible marks of disturbance and respect. But these immense canals, excavated by the careful hand of Nature, introduce no change into the national customs. The sons of the Spanish adventurers who colonized the country hate to travel by water, feeling themselves imprisoned when within the narrow limits of a boat or a pinnace. When their path is crossed by a great river, they strip themselves unconcernedly, prepare their horses for swimming, and plunging in, make for some island visible in the distance, where horse and horseman take breath, and by thus continuing their course from isle to isle, finally effect their crossing.

Thus is the greatest blessing which Providence bestows upon any people disdained by the Argentine gaucho, who regards it rather as an obstacle opposed to his movements, than as the most powerful means of facilitating them; thus the fountain of national growth, the origin of the early celebrity of Egypt, the cause of Holland's greatness, and of the rapid development of North America, the navigation of rivers, or the use of canals, remains a latent power, unappreciated by the inhabitants of the banks of the Bermejo, Pilcomayo, Parana, and Paraguay. A few small vessels, manned by Italians and adventurers, sail up stream from the

Plata, but after ascending a few leagues, even this navigation entirely ceases. The instinct of the sailor, which the Saxon colonists of the north possess in so high a degree, was not bestowed upon the Spaniard. Another spirit is needed to stir these arteries in which a nation's life-blood now lies stagnant. Of all these rivers which should bear civilization, power, and wealth, to the most hidden recesses of the continent, and make of Santa Fé, Entre Rios, Corrientes, Cordova, Saltas, Tucuman, and Jujui, rich and populous states, the Plata alone, which at last unites them all, bestows its benefits upon the inhabitants of its banks. At its mouth stand two cities, Montevideo and Buenos Ayres, which at present reap alternately the advantages of their enviable position. Buenos Ayres is destined to be some day the most gigantic city of either America. Under a benignant climate, mistress of the navigation of a hundred rivers flowing past her feet, covering a vast area, and surrounded by inland provinces which know no other outlet for their products, she would ere now have become the Babylon of America, if the spirit of the Pampa had not breathed upon her, and left undeveloped the rich offerings which the rivers and provinces should unceasingly bring. She is the only city in the vast Argentine territory which is in communication with European nations; she alone can avail herself of the advantages of foreign commerce; she alone has power and revenue. Vainly have the provinces asked to receive through her, civilization, industry, and European population; a senseless colonial policy made her deaf to these cries. But the provinces had their revenge when they sent to her in Rosas the climax of their own barbarism.

Heavily enough have those who uttered it, paid for the saying, "The Argentine Republic ends at the Arroyo del Medio." It now reaches from the Andes to the sea, while barbarism and violence have sunk Buenos Ayres below the level of the provinces. We ought not to complain of Buenos Ayres that she is great and will be greater, for this is her destiny. This would be to complain of Providence and call upon it to alter physical outlines. This being impossible, let us accept as well done what has been done by the Master's hand. Let us rather blame the ignorance of that brutal power which makes the gifts lavished by Nature upon an erring people of no avail for itself or for the provinces. Buenos Ayres, instead of sending to the interior, light, wealth, and prosperity, sends only chains, exterminating hordes, and petty subaltern tyrants. She, too, takes her revenge for the evil inflicted upon her by the provinces when they prepared for her a Rosas!

I have indicated the circumstance that the position of Buenos Ayres favors monopoly, in order to show that the configuration of the country so tends to centralization and consolidation, that even if Rosas had uttered his cry of "Confederation or Death!" in good faith, he would have ended with the consolidated system which is now established. Our desire, however, should be for union in civilization, and in liberty, while there has been given us only union in barbarism and in slavery. But a time will come when business will take its legitimate course. What it now concerns us to know is, that the progress of civilization must culminate only in Buenos Ayres; the pampa is a very bad medium of transmission and distribution through the provinces, and we are now about to see what is the result of this condition of things.

But above all the peculiarities of special portions of the country, there predominates one general, uniform, and constant character. Whether the soil is covered with the luxuriant and colossal vegetation of the tropics, or stunted, thorny, and unsightly shrubs bear witness to the scanty moisture which sustains them ; or whether finally the pampa displays its open and monotonous level, the surface of the country is generally flat and unbroken — the mountain groups of San Luis and Cordova in the centre, and some projecting spurs of the Andes toward the north, being scarcely an interruption to this boundless continuity.

We have, in this fact, a new element calculated to consolidate the nation which is hereafter to occupy these great solitudes, for it is well known that mountains and other natural obstacles interposed between different districts, keep up the isolation and the primitive peculiarities of their inhabitants. North America is destined to be a federation, not so much because its first settlements were independent of each other, as on account of the length of its Atlantic coast, and the various routes to the interior afforded by the St. Lawrence in the north, the Mississippi in the south, and the immense system of canals in the centre. The Argentine Republic is " one and indivisible."

Many philosophers have also thought that plains prepare the way for despotism, just as mountains furnish strongholds for the struggles of liberty. The boundless plain which permits the unobstructed passage of large

and weighty wagons by routes upon which the hand
of man has only been required to cut away a few trees
and thickets, and which extend from Salta to Buenos
Ayres, and thence to Mendoza, a distance of more than
seven hundred leagues, constitutes one of the most
noteworthy features of the internal conformation of the
Republic. The exertions of the individual, aided by
what rude nature has done already, suffice to provide
ways and means of communication ; if art shall offer
its assistance, if the forces of society shall attempt to
supply the strength lacking in the individual, the colossal dimensions of the work will repel the most enterprising, and insufficiency of labor will be an obstacle.
Thus in the matter of roads, untamed nature will long
have control, and the action of civilization will continue weak and inoperative.

Moreover, these outstretched plains impart to the
life of the interior a certain Asiatic coloring, which we
may even call very decided. I have often mechanically saluted the moon, as it rose calmly and brightly,
with these words of Volney in his description of the
Ruins : " La pleine lune à l'Orient s'élévait sur un
fond bleuâtre aux plaines rives de l'Euphrate." There
is something in the wilds of the Argentine territory
which brings to mind the wilds of Asia ; the imagination discovers a likeness between the pampa and the
plains lying between the Euphrates and the Tigris ;
some affinity between the lonely line of wagons which
crosses our wastes, arriving at Buenos Ayres after a
journey lasting for months, and the caravan of camels
which takes its way toward Bagdad or Smyrna. The
wagons which make such journeys among us, consti-

tute, so to speak, squadrons of little barks, the crews of which have a peculiar dress, dialect, and set of customs, which distinguish them from their fellow-countrymen, just as the sailor differs from the landsman. The head of each party is a military leader, like the chief of an Asiatic caravan; this position can be filled only by a man of iron will, and daring to the verge of rashness, that he may hold in check the audacity and turbulence of the land pirates who are to be directed and ruled by himself alone, for no help can be summoned in the desert. On the least symptom of insubordination, the captain raises his iron *chicote*, and delivers upon the mutineer blows which make contusions and wounds; if the resistance is prolonged, before resorting to his pistols, the help of which he generally scorns, he leaps from his horse, grasps his formidable knife, and quickly reëstablishes his authority by his superior skill in handling it. If any one loses his life under such discipline, the leader is not answerable for the assassination, which is regarded as an exercise of legitimate authority.

From these characteristics arises in the life of the Argentine people the reign of brute force, the supremacy of the strongest, the absolute and irresponsible authority of rulers, the administration of justice without formalities or discussion. The caravan of wagons is provided, moreover, with one or two guns to each wagon, and sometimes the leading one has a small piece of artillery on a swivel. If the train is attacked by the savages, the wagons are tied together in a ring, and a successful resistance is almost always opposed to the blood-thirsty and rapacious plunder of the assailants. Defenseless droves of pack-mules often fall into the hands of these American Bedouins, and muleteers rarely escape with their lives.   In these long journeys, the lower classes of the Argentine population acquire the habit of living far from society, of struggling single-handed with nature, of disregarding privation, and of depending for protection against the dangers ever imminent upon no other resources than personal strength and skill.

The people who inhabit these extensive districts, belong to two different races, the Spanish and the native ; the combinations of which form a series of imperceptible gradations.   The pure Spanish race predominates in the rural districts of Cordova and San Luis, where it is common to meet young shepherdesses fair and rosy, and as beautiful as the belles of a capital could wish to be.   In Santiago del Estero, the bulk of the rural population still speaks the Quichua dialect, which plainly shows its Indian origin.   The country people of Corrientes use a very pretty Spanish dialect. " Dame, general, una chiripà," said his soldiers to La-valle.   The Andalusian soldier may still be recognized in the rural districts of Buenos Ayres ; and in the city foreign surnames are the most numerous.   The negro race, by this time nearly extinct (except in Buenos Ayres), has left, in its zambos and mulattoes, a link which connects civilized man with the denizen of the woods.   This race mostly inhabiting cities, has a tendency to become civilized, and possesses talent and the finest instincts of progress.

With these reservations, a homogeneous whole has resulted from the fusion of the three above-named families.   It is characterized by love of idleness and incapacity for industry, except when education and the exigencies of a social position succeed in spurring it out of its customary pace. To a great extent, this unfortunate result is owing to the incorporation of the native tribes, effected by the process of colonization. The American aborigines live in idleness, and show themselves incapable, even under compulsion, of hard and protracted labor. This suggested the idea of introducing negroes into America, which has produced such fatal results. But the Spanish race has not shown itself more energetic than the aborigines, when it has been left to its own instincts in the wilds of America. Pity and shame are excited by the comparison of one of the German or Scotch colonies in the southern part of Buenos Ayres and some towns of the interior of the Argentine Republic; in the former the cottages are painted, the front-yards always neatly kept and adorned with flowers and pretty shrubs; the furniture simple but complete; copper or tin utensils always bright and clean; nicely curtained beds; and the occupants of the dwelling are always industriously at work. Some such families have retired to enjoy the conveniences of city life, with great fortunes gained by their previous labors in milking their cows, and making butter and cheese. The town inhabited by natives of the country, presents a picture entirely the reverse. There, dirty and ragged children live, with a menagerie of dogs; there, men lie about in utter idleness; neglect and poverty prevail everywhere; a table and some baskets are the only furniture of wretched huts remarkable for their general aspect of barbarism and carelessness.

This wretched manner of life of a people already on

the decrease, and belonging to the pastoral districts, doubtless gave rise to the words which spite and the humiliation of the English arms drew from Sir Walter Scott: "The vast plains of Buenos Ayres," he says, "are inhabited only by Christian savages known as Guachos" (gauchos, he should have said), "whose furniture is chiefly composed of horses' skulls, whose food is raw beef and water, and whose favorite pastime is running horses to death. Unfortunately," adds the good foreigner, "they prefer their national independence to our cottons and muslins." [1]

It would be well to ask England to say at a venture how many yards of linen and pieces of muslin she would give to own these plains of Buenos Ayres!

Upon the boundless expanse above described stand scattered here and there fourteen cities, each the capital of a province. The obvious method of arranging their names would be to classify them according to their geographical position: Buenos Ayres, Santa Fé, Entre Rios, and Corrientes, on the banks of the Paraná; Mendoza, San Juan, Rioja, Catamarca, Tucuman, Salta, and Jujui, being on a line nearly parallel to the Chilian Andes; with Santiago, San Luis, and Cordova, in the centre. But this manner of enumerating the Argentine towns has no connection with any of the social results which I have in view. A classification adapted to my purpose must originate in the ways of life pursued by the country people, for it is this which determines their character and spirit. I have stated above that the proximity of the rivers makes no difference in this respect, because the extent to which they

---

[1] *Life of Napoleon Bonaparte*, vol. ii., chap. 1.

are navigated is so trifling as to be without influence upon the people.

All the Argentine provinces, except San Juan and Mendoza, depend on the products of pastoral life ; Tucuman avails itself of agriculture also, and Buenos Ayres, besides raising millions of cattle and sheep, devotes itself to the numerous and diversified occupations of civilized life.

The Argentine cities, like almost all the cities of South America, have an appearance of regularity. Their streets are laid out at right angles, and their population scattered over a wide surface, except in Cordova, which occupies a narrow and confined position, and presents all the appearance of a European city, the resemblance being increased by the multitude of towers and domes attached to its numerous and magnificent churches. All civilization, whether native, Spanish, or European, centres in the cities, where are to be found the manufactories, the shops, the schools and colleges, and other characteristics of civilized nations. Elegance of style, articles of luxury, dress-coats, and frock-coats, with other European garments, occupy their appropriate place in these towns. I mention these small matters designedly. It is sometimes the case that the only city of a pastoral province is its capital, and occasionally the land is uncultivated up to its very streets. The encircling desert besets such cities at a greater or less distance, and bears heavily upon them, and they are thus small oases of civilization surrounded by an untilled plain, hundreds of square miles in extent, the surface of which is but rarely interrupted by any settlement of consequence.

The cities of Buenos Ayres and Cordova have succeeded better than the others in establishing about them subordinate towns to serve as new foci of civilization and municipal interests ; a fact which deserves notice. The inhabitants of the city wear the European dress, live in a civilized manner, and possess laws, ideas of progress, means of instruction, some municipal organization, regular forms of government, etc. Beyond the precincts of the city everything assumes a new aspect; the country people wear a different dress, which I will call South American, as it is common to all districts ; their habits of life are different, their wants peculiar and limited. The people composing these two distinct forms of society, do not seem to belong to the same nation. Moreover, the countryman, far from attempting to imitate the customs of the city, rejects with disdain its luxury and refinement ; and it is unsafe for the costume of the city people, their coats, their cloaks, their saddles, or anything European, to show themselves in the country. Everything civilized which the city contains is blockaded there, proscribed beyond its limits ; and any one who should dare to appear in the rural districts in a frock-coat, for example, or mounted on an English saddle, would bring ridicule and brutal assaults upon himself.

The whole remaining population inhabit the open country, which, whether wooded or destitute of the larger plants, is generally level, and almost everywhere occupied by pastures, in some places of such abundance and excellence, that the grass of an artificial meadow would not surpass them. Mendoza, and especially San Juan, are exceptions to this general absence of tilled fields, the people here depending chiefly on the products of agriculture. Everywhere else, pasturage being plenty, the means of subsistence of the inhabitants — for we cannot call it their occupation — is stock-raising. Pastoral life reminds us of the Asiatic plains, which imagination covers with Kalmuck, Cossack, or Arab tents. The primitive life of nations — a life essentially barbarous and unprogressive — the life of Abraham, which is that of the Bedouin of to-day, prevails in the Argentine plains, although modified in a peculiar manner by civilization. The Arab tribe which wanders through the wilds of Asia, is united under the rule of one of its elders or of a warrior chief; society exists, although not fixed in any determined locality. Its religious opinions, immemorial traditions, unchanging customs, and its sentiment of respect for the aged, make altogether a code of laws and a form of government which preserves morality, as it is there understood, as well as order and the association of the tribe. But progress is impossible, because there can be no progress without permanent possession of the soil, or without cities, which are the means of developing the capacity of man for the processes of industry, and which enable him to extend his acquisitions.

Nomad tribes do not exist in the Argentine plains; the stock-raiser is a proprietor, living upon his own land; but this condition renders association impossible, and tends to scatter separate families over an immense extent of surface. Imagine an expanse of two thousand square leagues, inhabited throughout, but where the dwellings are usually four or even eight leagues apart, and two leagues, at least, separate the nearest neighbors. The production of movable property is not impossible, the enjoyments of luxury are not wholly incompatible with this isolation; wealth can raise a superb edifice in the desert. But the incentive is wanting; no example is near; the inducements for making a great display which exist in a city, are not known in that isolation and solitude. Inevitable privations justify natural indolence; a dearth of all the amenities of life induces all the externals of barbarism. Society has altogether disappeared. There is but the isolated self-concentrated feudal family. Since there is no collected society, no government is possible; there is neither municipal nor executive power, and civil justice has no means of reaching criminals. I doubt if the modern world presents any other form of association so monstrous as this. It is the exact opposite of the Roman municipality, where all the population were assembled within an inclosed space, and went from it to cultivate the surrounding fields. The consequence of this was a strong social organization, the good results of which have prepared the way for modern civilization. The Argentine system resembles the old Slavonic Sloboda, with the difference that the latter was agricultural, and therefore more susceptible of government, while the dispersion of the population was not so great as in South America. It differs from the nomad tribes in admitting of no social reunion, and in a permanent occupation of the soil. Lastly, it has something in common with the feudal system of the Middle Ages, when the barons lived in their strongholds, and thence made war on the cities, and laid waste the country in the vicinity; but the baron and the feudal castle are wanting. If power starts up in the country, it lasts only for a moment, and is democratic; it is not inherited, nor can it maintain itself, for want of mountains and strong positions. It follows from this, that even the savage tribe of the pampas is better organized for moral development than are our country districts.

But the remarkable feature of this society, viewed in its social aspect, is its affinity to the life of the ancients — to the life of the Spartans or Romans; but again a radical dissimilarity appears when the subject is considered from another side. The free citizen of Sparta or of Rome threw upon his slaves the weight of material life, the care of providing for his subsistence, while he lived, free from such cares, in the forum or in the public place of assembly, exclusively occupied with the interests of the State — peace, war, and party contests. The stock-raiser has his share of the same advantages, and his herds fulfill the degrading office of the ancient Helot. Their spontaneous multiplication constitutes and indefinitely augments his fortune; the help of man is superfluous; his labor, his intelligence, his time, are not needed to the preservation and increase of the means of life. But though he needs none of these forces for the supply of his physical wants, he is unable to make use of them, when thus saved, as the Roman did. He has no city, no municipality, no intimate associations, and thus the basis of all social development is wanting. As the land-owners are not brought together, they have no public wants to satisfy; in a word, there is no *res publica*.

Moral progress, and the cultivation of the intellect, are here not only neglected, as in the Arab or Tartar tribe, but impossible. Where can a school be placed for the instruction of children living ten leagues apart in all directions ? Thus, consequently, civilization can in no way be brought about. Barbarism is the normal condition,[1] and it is fortunate if domestic customs preserve a small germ of morality. Religion feels the consequences of this want of social organization. The offices of the pastor are nominal, the pulpit has no audience, the priest flees from the deserted chapel, or allows his character to deteriorate in inactivity and solitude. Vice, simony, and the prevalent barbarism penetrate his cell, and change his moral superiority into the means of gratifying his avarice or ambition, and he ends by becoming a party leader. I once witnessed a scene of rural life worthy of the primitive ages of the world, which preceded the institution of the priesthood. In 1838 I happened to be in the Sierra de San Luis, at the house of a proprietor whose two favorite occupations were saying prayers and gambling. He had built a chapel where he used to pray through the rosary on Sunday afternoons, to supply the want of a priest, and of the public divine service of which the place had been destitute for many years. It was a Homeric picture: the sun declining to the west ; the sheep returning to the fold, and rending the air with their confused bleatings ; the service conducted by the master of the house, a man of sixty,

---

[1] In 1826, during a year's residence at the Sierra de San Luis, I taught the art of reading to six young people of good families, the youngest of whom was twenty-two years old.

with a noble countenance, in which the pure European race was evident in the white skin, blue eyes, and wide and open forehead ; while the responses were made by a dozen women and some young men, whose imperfectly broken horses were fastened near the door of the chapel. After finishing the rosary, he fervently offered up his own petitions. I never heard a voice fuller of pious feeling, nor a prayer of purer warmth, of firmer faith, of greater beauty, or better adapted to the circumstances, than that which he uttered. In this prayer he besought God to grant rain for the fields, fruitfulness for the herds and flocks, peace for the Republic, and safety for all wayfarers. I readily shed tears, and wept even with sobs, for the religious sentiment had been awakened in my soul to intensity, and like an unknown sensation, for I never witnessed a more religious scene. I seemed to be living in the times of Abraham, in his presence, in that of God, and of the nature which reveals Him. The voice of that sincere and pure-minded man made all my nerves vibrate, and penetrated to my inmost soul.

To this, that is, to natural religion, is all religion reduced in the pastoral districts. Christianity exists, like the Spanish idioms, as a tradition which is perpetuated, but corrupted; colored by gross superstitions and unaided by instruction, rites, or convictions. It is the case in almost all the districts which are remote from the cities, that when traders from San Juan or Mendoza arrive there, three or four children, some months or a year old, are presented to them for baptism, confidence being felt that their good education will enable them to administer the rite in a valid manner ; and on the arrival of a priest, young men old enough to break a colt, present themselves to him to be anointed and have baptism *sub conditione* administered to them.

In the absence of all the means of civilization and progress, which can only be developed among men collected into societies of many individuals, the education of the country people is as follows: The women look after the house, get the meals ready, shear the sheep, milk the cows, make the cheese, and weave the coarse cloth used for garments. All domestic occupations are performed by women ; on them rests the burden of all the labor, and it is an exceptional favor when some of the men undertake the cultivation of a little maize, bread not being in use as an ordinary article of diet. The boys exercise their strength and amuse themselves by gaining skill in the use of the lasso and the bolas, with which they constantly harass and pursue the calves and goats. When they can ride, which is as soon as they have learned to walk, they perform some small services on horseback. When they become stronger, they race over the country, falling off their horses and getting up again, tumbling on purpose into rabbit [1] burrows, scrambling over precipices, and practicing feats of horsemanship. On reaching puberty, they take to breaking wild colts, and death is the least penalty that awaits them if their strength or courage fails them for a moment. With early manhood comes complete independence and idleness.

Now begins the public life of the gaucho, as I may say, since his education is by this time at an end.

[1] Viscachas.

These men, Spaniards only in their language and in the confused religious notions preserved among them, must be seen, before a right estimate can be made of the indomitable and haughty character which grows out of this struggle of isolated man with untamed nature, of the rational being with the brute. It is necessary to see their visages bristling with beards, their countenances as grave and serious as those of the Arabs of Asia, to appreciate the pitying scorn with which they look upon the sedentary denizen of the city, who may have read many books, but who cannot overthrow and slay a fierce bull, who could not provide himself with a horse from the pampas, who has never met a tiger alone, and received him with a dagger in one hand and a poncho rolled up in the other, to be thrust into the animal's mouth, while he transfixes his heart with his dagger.

This habit of triumphing over resistance, of constantly showing a superiority to Nature, of defying and subduing her, prodigiously develops the consciousness of individual consequence and superior prowess. The Argentine people of every class, civilized and ignorant alike, have a high opinion of their national importance. All the other people of South America throw this vanity of theirs in their teeth, and take offense at their presumption and arrogance. I believe the charge not to be wholly unfounded, but I do not object to the trait. Alas, for the nation without faith in itself! Great things were not made for such a people. To what extent may not the independence of that part of America be due to the arrogance of these Argentine gauchos, who have never seen anything beneath the sun superior to themselves in wisdom or in power? The European is in their eyes the most contemptible of all men, for a horse gets the better of him in a couple of plunges.[1]

If the origin of this national vanity among the lower classes is despicable, it has none the less on that account some noble results; as the water of a river is no less pure for the mire and pollution of its sources. Implacable is the hatred which these people feel for men of refinement, whose garments, manners, and customs, they regard with invincible repugnance. Such is the material of the Argentine soldiery, and it may easily be imagined what valor and endurance in war are the consequences of the habits described above. We may add that these soldiers have been used to slaughtering cattle from their childhood, and that this act of necessary cruelty makes them familiar with bloodshed, and hardens their hearts against the groans of their victims.

Country life, then, has developed all the physical but none of the intellectual powers of the gaucho. His moral character is of the quality to be expected from his habit of triumphing over the obstacles and the forces of nature; it is strong, haughty, and energetic. Without instruction, and indeed without need of any, without means of support as without wants, he is happy in the midst of his poverty and privations, which are not such to one who never knew nor wished for greater pleasures than are his already. Thus if the disorgani-

[1] General Mansilla said, in a public meeting during the French blockade, " What have we to apprehend from those Europeans, who are not equal to one night's gallop? " and the vast plebeian audience drowned the speaker's voice with thunders of applause.

zation of society among the gauchos deeply implants
barbarism in their natures, through the impossibility
and uselessness of moral and intellectual education, it
has, too, its attractive side to him. The gaucho does not
labor; he finds his food and raiment ready to his hand.
If he is a proprietor, his own flocks yield him both; if
he possesses nothing himself, he finds them in the house
of a patron or a relation. The necessary care of the
herds is reduced to excursions and pleasure parties;
the branding, which is like the harvesting of farmers,
is a festival, the arrival of which is received with trans-
ports of joy, being the occasion of the assembling of
all the men for twenty leagues around, and the opportunity for displaying incredible skill with the lasso.
The gaucho arrives at the spot on his best steed, riding
at a slow and measured pace; he halts at a little distance and puts his leg over his horse's neck to enjoy
the sight leisurely. If enthusiasm seizes him, he slowly
dismounts, uncoils his lasso, and flings it at some bull,
passing like a flash of lightning forty paces from him;
he catches him by one hoof, as he intended, and quietly
coils his leather cord again.

CHAPTER II.

ORIGINALITY AND PECULIARITIES OF THE ARGENTINE PEOPLE.

" Ainsi que l' ocean, les Steppes remplessent l'esprit du sentiment de l'infini." — *Humboldt.*

" Like the ocean, the Pampas fill the mind with the impression of the infinite." — *Humboldt.*

IF from the conditions of pastoral life, such as colonization and neglect have constituted it, rise serious obstacles in the way of creating any political organization, and much more for the introduction of European civilization and institutions, as well as their natural results, wealth, and liberty, it cannot be denied, on the other hand, that this state of things has its poetic side, and possesses aspects worthy of the pen of the romancer. If any form of national literature shall appear in these new American societies, it must result from the description of the mighty scenes of nature, and still more from the illustration of the struggle between European civilization and native barbarism, between mind and matter — a struggle of imposing magnitude in South America, and which suggests scenes so peculiar, so characteristic, and so far outside the circle of ideas in which the European mind has been educated, that their dramatic relations would be unrecognized machinery, except in the country in which they are found.

The only North American novelist who has gained a European reputation is Fenimore Cooper, and he succeeded in doing so by removing the scene of the events he described from the settled portion of the country to the border land between civilized life and that of the savage, the theatre of the war for the possession of the soil waged against each other, by the native tribes and the Saxon race.

It was in this manner that our young poet Echevarria succeeded in attracting the attention of the literary world of Spain by his poem entitled " The Captive." The subjects of " Dido and Argea " which his predecessors the Varelas had treated with classic art and poetic fire, but without success and ineffectively, because they added nothing to the stock of European ideas, were abandoned by this Argentine bard, who turned his eyes to the desert. In its immeasurable and boundless spaces, in its wastes traversed by wandering savages, in the distant belt of flame which the traveller sees approaching when a fire has broken out upon the plains, he found the inspiration derived by the imagination from the sight of such natural scenery as is solemn, imposing, unusual, and mysterious; and from this the echo of his verses resounded, and was applauded even in the Spanish Peninsula.

A fact which explains many of the social phenomena of nations deserves a passing notice. The natural peculiarities of any region give rise to customs and practices of a corresponding peculiarity, so that where the same circumstances reappear, we find the same means of controlling them invented by different nations.

Thus, in my opinion, is to be explained the use of bows and arrows among all savage nations, whatever may be their race, their origin, and their geographical position. When I came to the passage in Cooper's " Last of the Mohicans," where Hawkeye and Uncas lose the trail of the Mingos in a brook, I said to myself : " They will dam up the brook." When the trapper in " The Prairie " waits in irresolute anxiety while the fire is threatening him and his companions, an Argentine would have recommended the same plan which the trapper finally proposes, — that of clearing a space for immediate protection, and setting a new fire, so as to be able to retire upon the ground over which it had passed beyond the reach of the approaching flames. Such is the practice of those who cross the pampa when they are in danger from fires in the grass.

When the fugitives in " The Prairie " arrive at a river, and Cooper describes the mysterious way in which the Pawnee gathers together the buffalo's hide, " he is making a *pelota*," said I to myself, — " it is a pity there is no woman to tow it," — for among us it is the women who tow *pelotas* across rivers with lassos held between their teeth. The way in which a buffalo's head is roasted in the desert is the same which we use for cooking [1] a cow's head or a loin of veal. I omit many other facts which prove the truth that analogies in the soil bring with them analogous customs, resources, and expedients. This explains our finding in Cooper's works accounts of practices and customs which seem plagiarized from the pampa ; thus, too, we find reproduced among American herdsmen, the serious coun-

[1] Batear.

tenance, the hospitality, and the very garments of the Arab.

The country consequently derives a fund of poetry from its natural circumstances and the special customs resulting from them. To arouse the poetic sense (which, like religious feeling, is a faculty of the human mind), we need the sight of beauty, of terrible power, of immensity of extent, of something vague and incomprehensible; for the fables of the imagination, the ideal world, begin only where the actual and the commonplace end.

Now, I inquire, what impressions must be made upon the inhabitant of the Argentine Republic by the simple act of fixing his eyes upon the horizon, and seeing nothing? — for the deeper his gaze sinks into that shifting, hazy, undefined horizon, the further it withdraws from him, the more it fascinates and confuses him, and plunges him in contemplation and doubt. What is the end of that world which he vainly seeks to penetrate? He knows not! What is there beyond what he sees? The wilderness, danger, the savage, death! Here is poetry already; he who moves among such scenes is assailed by fantastic doubts and fears, by dreams which possess his waking hours.

Hence it follows that the disposition and nature of the Argentine people are poetic. How can such feelings fail to exist, when a black storm-cloud rises, no one knows whence, in the midst of a calm, pleasant afternoon, and spreads over the sky before a word can be uttered? The traveller shudders as the crashing thunder announces the tempest, and holds his breath in the fear of bringing upon himself one of the thousand bolts which flash around him. The light is followed by thick darkness ; death is on every side ; a fearful and irresistible power has instantaneously driven the soul back upon itself, and made it feel its nothingness in the midst of angry nature ; made it feel God himself in the terrible magnificence of his works. What more coloring could the brush of fancy need ? Masses of darkness which obscure the sun ; masses of tremulous livid light which shine through the darkness for an instant and bring to view far distant portions of the pampa, across which suddenly dart vivid lightnings, symbols of irresistible power. These images must remain deeply engraved on the soul. When the storm passes by, it leaves the gaucho sad, thoughtful, and serious, and the alternation of light and darkness continues in his imagination, as the disk of the sun long remains upon the retina after we have been looking at it fixedly.

Ask the gaucho, " Whom does the lightning prefer to kill ? " and he will lead you into a world of moral and religious fancies, mingled with ill-understood facts of nature, and with superstitious and vulgar traditions. We may add that if it is certain that the electric fluid enters into the economy of human life and is the same as the so-called nervous fluid, the excitement of which rouses the passions and kindles enthusiasm, imaginative exertion ought to be well suited to the temper of a people living under an atmosphere so highly charged with electricity that one's clothes sparkle when rubbed, like a cat's fur stroked the wrong way.

How can he be otherwise than a poet who witnesses these impressive scenes ?

" Jira en vano, reconcentra
Su inmensidad, i no encuentra
La vista en su vivo anhelo
Dó fijar su fugaz vuelo,
Como el pájaro en la mar.
Doquier campo i heredades
Del ave i bruto guaridas;
Doquier cielo i soledades
De Dios solo conocidas,
Que él solo puede sondear." — *Echevarria.*

Or he who thus sees Nature in her gala dress?

" De las entrañas de América
Dos raudales se desatan;
El Paraná, faz de perlas,
I el Uruguai, faz de nácar.
Los dos entre bosques corren
O entre floridas barrancas,
Como dos grandes espejos
Entre marcos de esmeraldas.
Salúdanlos en su paso
La melancólica pava,
El picaflor i jilguero,
El zorzal i la torcaza.
Como ante reyes se inclinan
Ante ellos seibos i palmas,
I le arrojan flor del aire,
Aroma i flor de naranja.
Luego en el Guazú se encuentran
I reuniendo sus aguas,
Mezclando nácar i perlas,
Se derraman en el Plata." — *Dominguez.*

But this is cultivated poetry, the poetry of the city. There is another poetry which echoes over the solitary plains — the popular, natural, and irregular poetry of the gaucho.

Music, too, is found among our people. It is a national taste recognized by all our neighbors. When

an Argentine is first introduced to a Christian family,
they at once invite him to the piano, or hand him a
guitar, and if he excuses himself on the ground that
he does not know how to play, they express wonder
and incredulity, saying, "An Argentine, and not
understand music!" This general supposition bears
witness to our national habits. It is the fact, that the
young city people of the better classes, play the piano,
flute, violin, or guitar; the half-breeds devote themselves
almost wholly to music, and many skillful composers
and players have sprung up among them. Guitars are
constantly heard at the shop-doors on summer evenings; and late in the night, one's sleep is pleasantly
disturbed by serenades and peripatetic concerts.

The country people have songs peculiar to themselves. The "Ariste," prevalent among the people of
the northern districts, is a fugue melody expressive
of lamentation, such as Rousseau considers natural to
man in his primitive state of barbarism.

The "Vidalita" is a popular song with a chorus,
accompanied by the guitar and tabor, in the refrain of
which the bystanders join, and the number and volume
of the voices increase. I suppose this melody originated with the aborigines, for I once heard it at an
Indian festival at Copiapo, held to celebrate Candle-
mas. As a religious song it must be very old, and the
Indians of Chili can hardly have adopted it from the
Spaniards of the Argentine Republic.

The "Vidalita" is the popular measure for songs
about the topics of the day, or for warlike odes; the
gauchos compose the words which they sing, and trust
to the associations which the song arouses, to make

them understood by the people. Thus, then, amidst the rudeness of the national customs, two arts which embellish civilized life and give vent to many generous passions, are honored and favored, even by the lowest classes, who exercise their uncultured genius in lyrical and poetic composition.

In 1840, Echevarria, then a young man, lived some months in the country, where the fame of his verses upon the pampa had already preceded him ; the gauchos surrounded him with respect and affection, and when a new-comer showed symptoms of the scorn he felt for the little minstrel,[1] some one whispered, " He is a poet," and that word dispelled every prejudice.

It is well known that the guitar is the popular instrument of the Spanish race; it is also common in South America. The *majo* or troubadour, the type of a large class of Spaniards, is still found there, and in Buenos Ayres especially. He is discoverable in the gaucho of the country, and in the townsman of the same class. The *cielito*, the dance of the pampas, is animated by the same spirit as the Spanish *jaleo*, the dance of Andalusia ; the dancer makes castañets of his fingers ; all his movements disclose the *majo ;* the action of his shoulders, his gestures, all his ways, from that in which he puts on his hat, to his style of spitting through his teeth, all are of the pure Andalusian type.

From these general customs and tastes are developed remarkable peculiarities, which will hereafter embellish the national dramas and romances, and give them an original shade of color. I propose at present only to notice a few of these special developments, in order to

---

[1] *Cajeteija*, little musical box.

complete the idea of the customs of the country, and so to explain subsequently the nature, causes, and effects of its civil wars.

THE RASTREADOR.

The most conspicuous and extraordinary of the occupations to be described, is that of the Rastreador, or track-finder. All the gauchos of the interior are Rastreadores. In such extensive plains, where paths and lines of travel cross each other in all directions, and where the pastures in which the herds feed are unfenced, it is necessary often to follow the tracks of an animal, and to distinguish them among a thousand others, and to know whether it was going at an easy or a rapid pace, at liberty or led, laden or carrying no weight.

This is a generally understood branch of household knowledge. I once happened to turn out of a by-way into the Buenos Ayres road, and my guide, following the usual practice, cast a look at the ground. "There was a very nice little Moorish mule in that train," said he, directly. "D. N. Zapata's it was — she is good for the saddle, and it is very plain she was saddled this time ; they went by yesterday." The man was travelling from the Sierra de San Luis, while the train had passed on its way from Buenos Ayres, and it was a year since he had seen the Moorish mule, whose track was mixed up with those of a whole train in a path two feet wide. And this seemingly incredible tale only illustrates the common degree of skill ; — the guide was a mere herdsman, and no professional Rastreador.

The Rastreador proper is a grave, circumspect personage, whose declarations are considered conclusive evidence in the inferior courts. Consciousness of the knowledge he possesses, gives him a certain reserved and mysterious dignity. Every one treats him with respect ; the poor man because he fears to offend one who might injure him by a slander or an accusation ; and the proprietor because of the possible value of his testimony. A theft has been committed during the night ; no one knows anything of it ; the victims of it hasten to look for one of the robber's footprints, and on finding it, they cover it with something to keep the wind from disturbing it. They then send for the Rastreador, who detects the track and follows it, only occasionally looking at the ground as if his eyes saw in full relief the footsteps invisible to others. He follows the course of the streets, crosses gardens, enters a house, and pointing to a man whom he finds there, says, coldly, " That is he ! " The crime is proved, and the criminal seldom denies the charge. In his estimation, even more than in that of the judge, the Rastreador's deposition is a positive demonstration ; it would be ridiculous and absurd to dispute it. The culprit accordingly yields to a witness whom he regards as the finger of God pointing him out. I have had some acquaintance myself with Calibar, who has practiced his profession for forty consecutive years in one province. He is now about eighty years old, and of venerable and dignified appearance, though bowed down by age. When his fabulous reputation is mentioned to him, he replies, " I am good for nothing now ; there are the boys." The " boys," who have studied under so famous a master, are his sons. The story is that his best horse-trappings were once stolen while he was absent on a journey to Buenos Ayres. His wife covered one of the thief's footprints with a tray. Two months afterwards Calibar returned, looked at the footprint, which by that time had become blurred, and could not have been made out by other eyes, after which he spoke no more of the circumstance. A year and a half later, Calibar might have been seen walking through a street in the outskirts of the town with his eyes on the ground. He turned into a house, where he found his trappings, by that time blackened by use and nearly worn out. He had come upon the trail of the thief nearly two years after the robbery.

In 1830, a criminal under sentence of death having escaped from prison, Calibar was employed to search for him. The unhappy man, aware that he would be tracked, had taken all the precautions suggested to him by the image of the scaffold, but they were taken in vain. Perhaps they only assured his destruction; for as Calibar's reputation was hazarded, his jealous self-esteem made him ardent in accomplishing a task which would demonstrate the wonderful sharpness of his sight, though it insured the destruction of another man. The fugitive had left as few traces as the nature of the ground would permit; he had crossed whole squares on tiptoe; afterwards he had leaped upon low walls; he had turned back after crossing one place; but Calibar followed without losing the trail. If he missed the way for a moment, he found it again, exclaiming, "Where are you?" Finally, the trail entered a water-course in the suburbs, in which the fugitive had sought to elude the Rastreador. In vain! Calibar went along the bank without uneasiness or hesitation. At last he stops, examines some plants, and says, " He came out here; there are no footprints, but these drops of water on the herbage are the sign ! " On coming to a vineyard, Calibar reconnoitered the mud walls around it, and said, " He is in there." The party of soldiers looked till they were tired, and came back to report the failure of the search. " He has not come out," was the only answer of the Rastreador, who would not even take the trouble to make a second investigation. In fact, he had not come out, but he was taken and executed the next day.

In 1831, some political prisoners were planning an escape ; all was ready, and outside help had been secured. On the point of making the attempt, " What shall be done about Calibar? " said one. " To be sure, Calibar ! " said the others, in dismay. Their relations prevailed upon Calibar to be ill for four full days after the escape, which was thus without difficulty effected.

What a mystery is this of the Rastreador! What microscopic power is developed in the visual organs of these men ! How sublime a creature is that which God made in his image and likeness !

THE BAQUEANO, OR PATH-FINDER.

Next to the Rastreador comes the Baqueano, a personage of distinction, and one who controls the fate of individuals and of provinces. The Baqueano is a grave and reserved gaucho, who knows every span of twenty thousand square leagues of plain, wood, and

mountain ! He is the most thorough topographer, the
only map which a general consults in directing the
movements of his campaign. The Baqueano is always
at his side. Modest and mute as a garden-wall, he is
in possession of every secret of the campaign ; the
fate of the army, the issue of a battle, the conquest of
a province, all depend upon him. The Baqueano
almost always discharges his duty with fidelity, but
the general does not place full confidence in him.

Conceive the situation of a commander condemned
to be attended by a traitor, from whom he has to
obtain the information without which he cannot succeed. A Baqueano finds a little path crossing the
road which he is following ; he knows to what distant
watering-place it leads. If he finds a thousand such
paths, some of them even a hundred leagues apart, he
is acquainted with each, and knows whence it comes
and whither it goes. He knows the hidden fords of a
hundred rivers and streams, above or below the ordinary places of crossing. He can point out a convenient
path through a hundred distinct and extensive swamps.

In the deepest darkness of the night, surrounded
by boundless plains or by forests, while his companions
are astray and at a loss, he rides round them inspect-
ing the trees ; if there are none, he dismounts and
stoops to examine the shrubs, and satisfies himself of
his points of compass. He then mounts, and reassures
his party by saying, " We are in a straight line from
such a place, so many leagues from the houses ; we
must travel southwards." And he sets out in the direction he has indicated, without uneasiness, without
hurrying to confirm his judgment by arriving at the

town, and without answering the objections suggested
to the others by fear or bewilderment.

If even this is insufficient, or if he finds himself upon
the pampa in impenetrable darkness, he pulls up herbs
from different places, smells their roots and the earth
about them, chews their foliage, and by often repeating
this proceeding, assures himself of the neighborhood of
some lake or stream, either of salt or of fresh water,
of which he avails himself, upon finding it, to set himself exactly right. It is said that General Rosas knows
the pasturage of every estate in the south of Buenos
Ayres by its taste.

If the Baqueano belongs to the pampa, where no
roads exist, and a traveller asks him to show the way
straight to a place fifty leagues off, he pauses a moment,
reconnoitres the horizon, examines the ground, fixes
his eyes upon some point, and gallops off straight as
an arrow, until he changes his course for reasons known
only to himself, and keeps up his gallop day and night
till he arrives at the place named.

The Baqueano also announces the approach of the
enemy; that is, that they are within ten leagues; and
he also detects the direction in which they are approaching by means of the movements of the ostriches, deer,
and guanacos, which fly in certain directions. At
shorter distances he notices the clouds of dust, and es-
timates the number of the hostile force by their density.
" They have two thousand men," he says; " five hundred," " two hundred; " and the commander acts
upon this assumption, which is almost always infallible.
If the condors and crows are wheeling in circles through
the air, he can tell whether there are troops hidden

thereabouts, or whether a recently abandoned camp, or simply a dead animal is the attractive object. The Baqueano knows how far one place is from another, the number of days and hours which the journey requires, and besides, some unknown by-way through which the passage may be made in half the time, so as to end in a surprise; and expeditions for the surprise of towns fifty leagues away are thus undertaken, and generally with success, by parties of peasants. This may be thought an exaggeration. No! General Rivera, of the Banda Oriental, is a simple Baqueano, who knows every tree that grows anywhere in the Republic of Uruguay. The Brazilians would not have occupied that country if he had not aided them; nor, but for him, would the Argentines have set it free.

This man, at once general and Baqueano, overpowered Oribe, who was supported by Rosas, after a contest of three years; and at the present day, were he in the field against it, the whole power of Buenos Ayres, with its numerous armies, which are spread all over Uruguay, might gradually fade away by means of a surprise to-day, by a post cut off to-morrow, by some victory which he could turn to his own advantage by his knowledge of some route to the enemy's rear, or by some other unnoticed or trifling circumstance.

General Rivera began his study of the ground in 1804, when making war upon the government as an outlaw; afterwards he waged war upon the outlaws as a government officer; next, upon the king as a patriot; and later upon the patriots as a peasant; upon the Argentines as a Brazilian chieftain; and upon the Brazilians, as an Argentine general; upon Lavalleja,

as President ; upon President Oribe, as a proscribed
chieftain ; and, finally, upon Rosas, the ally of Oribe,
as a general of Uruguay ; in all which positions he has
had abundance of time to learn something of the art
of the Baqueano.

THE GAUCHO OUTLAW.

The example of this type of character, to be found
in certain places, is an outlaw, a squatter, a kind of
misanthrope. He is Cooper's Hawkeye or Trapper,
with all the knowledge of the wilderness possessed by
the latter ; and with all his aversion to the settlements
of the whites, but without his natural morality or his
friendly relations with the savages. The name of
gaucho outlaw is not applied to him wholly as an un-
complimentary epithet. The law has been for many
years in pursuit of him. His name is dreaded —
spoken under the breath, but not in hate, and almost
respectfully. He is a mysterious personage ; his abode
is the pampa ; his lodgings are the thistle fields ; he
lives on partridges and hedgehogs, and whenever he is
disposed to regale himself upon a tongue, he lassos a
cow, throws her without assistance, kills her, takes his
favorite morsel, and leaves the rest for the carrion
birds. The gaucho outlaw will make his appearance
in a place just left by soldiers, will talk in a friendly
way with the admiring group of good gauchos around
him ; provide himself with tobacco, yerba maté, which
makes a refreshing beverage, and if he discovers the
soldiers, he mounts his horse quietly and directs his
steps leisurely to the wilderness, not even deigning to
look back. He is seldom pursued ; that would be

killing horses to no purpose, for the beast of the gaucho
outlaw is a bay courser, as noted in his own way as
his master.   If he ever happens to fall unawares into
the hands of the soldiers, he sets upon the densest masses
of his assailants, and breaks through them, with the
help of a few slashes left by his knife upon the faces
or bodies of his opponents ; and lying along the ridge
of his horse's back to avoid the bullets sent after him,
he hastens towards the wilderness, until, having left
his pursuers at a convenient distance, he pulls up and
travels at his ease.   The poets of the vicinity add this
new exploit to the biography of the desert hero, and
his renown flies through all the vast region around.
Sometimes he appears before the scene of a rustic festival with a young woman whom he has carried off,
and takes a place in the dance with his partner, goes
through the figures of the *cielito*, and disappears, unnoticed.   Another day he brings the girl he has
seduced, to the house of her offended family, sets her
down from his horse's croup, and reckless of the
parents' curses by which he is followed, quietly betakes
himself to his boundless abode.

This white-skinned savage, at war with society and
proscribed by the laws, is no more depraved at heart
than the inhabitants of the settlements.   The reckless
outlaw who attacks a whole troop, does no harm to the
traveller.   The gaucho outlaw is no bandit, or highwayman ; murderous assaults do not suit his temper,
as robbery would not suit the character of the *churri-
ador* (sheep-stealer).   To be sure, he steals ; but this is
his profession, his trade, his science.   He steals horses.
He arrives, for instance, at the camp of a train from the

interior ; its master offers to buy of him a horse of some unusual color, of a particular shape and quality, with a white star on the shoulder. The gaucho collects his thoughts, considers a moment, and replies, after a short silence : " There is no such horse alive." What thoughts have been passing through the gaucho's mind ? In that moment his memory has traversed a thousand estates upon the pampa ; has seen and examined every horse in the province, with its marks, color, and special traits, and he has convinced himself that not one of them has a star on its shoulder ; some have one on their foreheads, others have white spots on their haunches. Is this power of memory amazing ? No ! Napoleon knew two hundred thousand soldiers by name, and remembered, when he saw any one of them, all the facts relating to him. Therefore, if nothing impossible is required of him, the gaucho will deliver upon a designated day and spot, just such a horse as has been asked for, and with no less punctuality if he has been paid in advance. His honor is as sensitive upon this point as that of a gambler about his debts.

Sometimes he travels to the country about Cordova or Santa Fé. Then he may be seen crossing the pampa behind a small body of horses ; if any one meets him, he follows his course without approaching the new comer unless he is requested to do so.

THE CANTOR (THE MINSTREL).

And now we have the idealization of this life of resistance, civilization, barbarism, and danger. The gaucho Cantor corresponds to the singer, bard, or troubadour of the Middle Ages, and moves in the same scenes, amidst the struggles of the cities with provincial feudalism, between the life which is passing away and the new life gradually arising. The Cantor goes from one settlement to another "de tapera en galpon," singing the deeds of the heroes of the pampa whom the law persecutes, the lament of the widow whose sons have been taken off by the Indians in a recent raid, the defeat and death of the brave Ranch, the final overthrow of Facundo Quiroga, and the fate of Santos Perez.

The Cantor is performing in his simple way the same labor of recording customs, history, and biography, which was performed by the mediæval bard, and his verses would hereafter be collected as documents and authorities for the future historian, but that there stands beside him another more cultivated form of society with a knowledge of events superior to that displayed by this less favored chronicler in his artless rhapsodies. Two distinct forms of civilization meet upon a common ground in the Argentine Republic : one, still in its infancy, which, ignorant of that so far above it, goes on repeating the crude efforts of the Middle Ages ; the other, disregarding what lies at its feet, while it strives to realize in itself the latest results of European civilization ; the nineteenth and twelfth centuries dwell together — one inside the cities, the other without them.

The Cantor has no fixed abode ; he lodges where night surprises him ; his fortune consists in his verses and in his voice. Wherever the wild mazes of the *cielito* are threaded, wherever there is a glass of wine to drink, the Cantor has his place and his particular part in the festival. The Argentine gaucho only drinks when excited by music and verse,[1] and every grocery has its guitar ready for the hands of the Cantor who perceives from afar where the help of his " gay science " is needed, by the group of horses about the door.

The Cantor intersperses his heroic songs with the tale of his own exploits. Unluckily his profession of Argentine bard does not shield him from the law. He can tell of a couple of stabs he has dealt, of one or two *misfortunes* (homicides!) of his, and of some horse or girl he has carried off.

In 1840, a Cantor was sitting on the ground, cross-legged, on the banks of the majestic Paraná, in the midst of a group of gauchos whom he was keeping in eager suspense by the long and animated tale of his labors and adventures. He had already related the abduction of his love, with the difficulties overcome on the occasion ; also his *misfortune* and the dispute that led to it ; and was relating his encounter with the soldiery, and the stabs with which he defended himself, when the noisy advance and the shouts of a body of troops made him aware that this time he was sur-

[1] Without wandering from our subject, we may here call to mind the noteworthy resemblance between the Argentines and the Arabs. In Algiers, Oran, Mascara, and the desert encampments, I constantly saw the Arabs collected in coffee-shops — strong drink being forbidden them, — closely crowded about the singer, or more usually two singers, who accompany themselves with guitars in a duet, and recite national songs of a mournful character like our *tristes* before mentioned. The Arabian bridle is of plaited leather thongs, continued into a whip-lash like ours; the bit which we use is that of the Arabs, and many of our customs show the intercourse of our ancestors with the Moors of Andalusia. I have met some Arabs whom I could have sworn I had seen in my own country.

rounded.   The troops had, in fact, closed up in the
form of a horseshoe, open towards the Paraná, the
steep banks of which rose twenty yards above the water.
The Cantor, undismayed by the outcry, was mounted
in an instant, and after casting a searching look at the
ring of soldiers and their ready pieces, he wheeled his
horse towards the river's bank, covered the animal's
eyes with his poncho, and drove his spurs into him.
A few moments after, the horse, freed from his bit so
that he could swim more easily, emerged from the
depths of the Paraná, the minstrel holding him by the
tail, and looking back to the scene on shore which he
had quitted, as composedly as if he had been in an
eight-oared boat.   Some shots fired by the troops did
not hinder him from arriving safe and sound at the
first island in sight.

To conclude, the original poetry of the minstrel is
clumsy, monotonous, and irregular, when he resigns
himself to the inspiration of the moment.   It is occupied rather with narration than with the expression of
feeling, and is replete with imagery relating to the
open country, to the horse, and to the scenes of the
wilderness, which makes it metaphorical and grandiose.
When he is describing his own exploits or those of
some renowned evil-doer, he resembles the Neapolitan
improvisatore, his style being unfettered, commonly
prosaic, but occasionally rising to the poetic level for
some moments, to sink again into dull and scarcely
metrical recitation.   The Cantor possesses, moreover,
a repertory of popular poems in octosyllabic lines vari-
ously combined into stanzas of five lines, of ten, or of
eight.   Among them are many compositions of merit
which show some inspiration and feeling.

To these original types might be added many others of equal peculiarity, but they would not, like the former, illustrate the national customs, a knowledge of which is necessary for the right comprehension of our political personages and of the primitive and American nature of the bloody strife which distracts the Argentine Republic. In the course of this narrative the reader will himself discover where are to be met the Track-viewer, Path-finder, Gaucho-outlaw, and Minstrel. He will see in the chieftains whose fame has passed the Argentine frontiers, and even in those who have filled the world with the horror of their names, the vivid reflection of the internal condition, customs, and organization of the country.

CHAPTER III.

ASSOCIATION.

"The gaucho lives on privations, but his luxury is freedom. Proud of an unrestricted independence, his feelings, though wild as his life, are yet noble and good." — *Head.*

LA PULPERIA (THE COUNTRY STORE).

In the first chapter we left the Argentine rustic, at the moment of his arrival at maturity, in the possession of such a character as had resulted from the natural circumstances about him, and from his want of any true society. We have seen that he is a man independent of every want, under no control, with no notion of government, all regular and systematic order being wholly impossible among such people. With these habits of heedlessness and independence he enters on another step of rural life, which, commonplace as it is, is the starting-point of all the great events which we are shortly to describe.

It is to be remembered that I am speaking of the essentially pastoral part of the people, and that I select for consideration only their fundamental characteristics, neglecting the accidental modifications they receive, the partial effects of which will be indicated separately. I am speaking of the combination of landed proprietaries which cover the surface of a province, four leagues, more or less, being occupied by each.

The society of the agricultural districts is also much subdivided and dispersed, but on a smaller scale. One laborer assists another, and the implements of tillage, the numerous tools, stores, and animals employed, the variety of products and the various arts which agriculture calls to its aid, establish necessary relations between the inhabitants of a valley and make it indispensable for them to have a rudiment of a town to serve as a centre. Moreover, the cares and occupations of agriculture require such a number of hands that idleness becomes impossible, and the men of an estate are compelled to remain within its limits. The exact contrary takes place in the singular society we are describing. The bounds of ownership are unmarked ; the more numerous the flocks and herds the fewer hands are required ; upon the women devolve all the domestic duties and manufactures ; the men are left without occupations, pleasures, ideas, or the necessity of application. Home life is wearisome and even repulsive to them. They need, then, factitious society to remedy this radical want of association. Their early acquired habit of riding gives them an additional incentive to leave their houses.

It is the children's business to drive the horses to the corral before the sun has quite risen ; and all the men, even the lads, saddle their horses, even when they have no object in view. The horse is an integral part of the Argentine rustic ; it is for him what the cravat is to an inhabitant of the city. In 1841, El Chacho, a chieftain of the Llanos, emigrated to Chili. " How are you getting on, friend ? " somebody asked him. " How should I be getting on ? " returned he, in

tones of distress and melancholy. " Bound to Chili,
and on foot ! " Only an Argentine gaucho can appreciate all the misfortune and distress which these two
phrases express.

Here again we have the life of the Arab or Tartar.
The following words of Victor Hugo might have been
written in the pampas : —

" He cannot fight on foot ; he and his horse are but one person. He lives on horseback ; he trades, buys, and sells on horseback ; drinks, eats, sleeps, and dreams on horseback." — *Le Rhin.*

The men then set forth without exactly knowing
where they are going. A turn around the herds, a
visit to a breeding-pen or to the haunt of a favorite
horse, takes up a small part of the day ; the rest is
consumed in a rendezvous at a tavern or grocery store.
There assemble inhabitants of the neighboring par-
ishes ; there are given and received bits of information
about animals that have gone astray ; the traces of the
cattle are described upon the ground ; intelligence of
the hunting-ground of the tiger or of the place where
the tiger's tracks have been seen, is communicated.
There, in short, is the Cantor ; there the men frater-
nize while the glass goes round at the expense of those
who have the means as well as the disposition to pay
for it.

In a life so void of emotion, gambling exercises the
enervated mind, and liquor arouses the dormant imagination. This accidental reunion becomes by its daily
repetition a society more contracted than that from
which each of its individual members came ; yet in
this assembly, without public aim, without social interest, are first formed the elements of those characters

which are to appear later on the political stage. We
shall see how. The gaucho esteems skill in horsemanship and physical strength, and especially courage,
above all other things, as we have said before. This
meeting, this daily club, is a real Olympic circus where
each man's merit is tested and assayed.

The gaucho is always armed with the knife inherited from the Spaniard. More fully even than in
Spain is here realized that peninsular peculiarity, that
cry, characteristic of Saragossa — *war to the knife*.
The knife, besides being a weapon, is a tool used for
all purposes ; without it, life cannot go on. It is like
the elephant's trunk, arm, hand, finger, and all. The
gaucho boasts of his valor like a trooper, and every
little while his knife glitters through the air in circles,
upon the least provocation, or with none at all, for the
simple purpose of comparing a stranger's prowess with
his own ; he plays at stabbing as he would play at
dice. So deeply and intimately have these pugnacious
habits entered the life of the Argentine gaucho that
custom has created a code of honor and a fencing
system which protect life. The rowdy of other lands
takes to his knife for the purpose of killing, and he
kills ; the Argentine gaucho unsheathes his to fight,
and he only wounds. To attempt the life of his
adversary he must be very drunk, or his instincts must
be really wicked, or his rancor very deep. His aim is
only to *mark* his opponent, to give him a slash in the
face, to leave an indelible token upon him. The
numerous scars to be seen upon these gauchos, accordingly, are seldom deep. A fight is begun, then, for the
sake of shining, for the glory of victory, for the love

of fame. A close ring is made around the combatants, and excited and eager eyes follow the glitter of the knives which do not cease to move. When blood flows in torrents the spectators feel obliged to stop the fight. If a *misfortune* has resulted, the sympathies are with the survivor; the best horse is available for his escape to a distant place where he is received with respect or pity. If the law overtakes him he often shows fight, and if he rushes through soldiers and escapes, he has from that time a wide-spread renown. Time passes, the judge in place has been succeeded by another, and he may again show himself in the township without further molestation: he has a full discharge.

Homicide is but a misfortune, unless the deed has been so often repeated that the perpetrator has gained the reputation of an assassin. The landed proprietor, Don Juan Manuel Rosas, before being a public man, had made his residence a sort of asylum for homicides without ever extending his protection to robbers; a preference which would easily be explained by his character of gaucho proprietor, if his subsequent conduct had not disclosed affinities with evil which have filled the world with terror.

With respect to equestrian sports, it will suffice to point out one of the many which are practiced, that the reader may judge what daring is required of those who engage in them. A gaucho rides at full speed before his comrades. One of them flings a set of *bolas* at him so as to shackle the horse in the midst of his career. Issuing from the whirlwind of dust raised by his fall, appears the rider at a run, followed by the horse, the latter carried on by the impulse of his interrupted career according to the laws of physics. In this pastime, life is staked, and sometimes lost.

Will it be believed that these displays of valor or skill and boldness in horsemanship are the basis of the great exploits which have filled the Argentine Republic with their name and changed the face of the country? Nothing is more certain, however. I do not mean to assert that assassination and crime have always been a ladder by which men have risen. Thousands of daring men have remained in the position of obscure bandits; but those who owe their position to such deeds are to be counted by larger numbers than hundreds. In all despotic societies, great natural gifts tend to lose themselves in crime; the Roman *genius* which could conquer the world is to-day the terror of the Pontine Marshes, and the Spanish Zumalacarreguis and Minas are to be met by hundreds in Sierra Morena. Man's need of developing his strength, capacity, and ambition, requires him, upon the failure of legitimate means, to frame a world, with its own morality and laws, where he shows complacently that he was born to be a Napoleon or a Cæsar.

In this society, then, where mental culture is useless or impossible, where no municipal affairs exist, where, as there is no public, the public good is a meaningless word, the man of unusual gifts, striving to exert his faculties, takes with that design the means and the paths which are at hand. The gaucho will be a malefactor or a military chief, according to the course which things are taking at the moment when he attains celebrity.

Such customs need vigorous methods of repression, and to restrain hardened men, judges still more hardened are required. What I said at the outset, of the captain of the freight-carts, is exactly applicable to the country justice. He wants bravery more than anything else; the terror of his name is more powerful than the punishments he inflicts. The justice is naturally some one of former notoriety recalled to orderly life by old age and his family ties. Of course, the law he administers is altogether arbitrary; his conscience or his passions determine it, and his decrees are final. Sometimes justices officiate during their whole lives, and are remembered with respect. But the consciousness of these methods of administration and the arbitrary nature of the attendant penalties, produce among the people ideas of judicial authority which will have their effects hereafter. The justice secures obedience by his reputation for formidable boldness, by his force of character, his informal decisions, his decree, the announcement "such are my commands," and the forms of punishment which he invents himself. From this disorder, perhaps long since inevitable, it follows that the military commander who reaches distinction during rebellions possesses a sway, undisputed and unquestioned by his followers, equal to the wide and terrible power now only to be found among the nations of Asia. The Argentine chieftain is a Mohammed who might change the prevailing religion, if such were his whim, and contrive another. He has power in all its forms; his injustice is a misfortune for his victim, but no abuse on his part; for he may be unjust, — still more, he must be unjust, — for he has been a lawless man all his life.

These remarks are also applicable to the
commandant. This personage is of more im
than the former, and requires in a higher de
combination of the reputation and anteceden
distinguish him. Far from being lessened, the evil is
even aggravated by an additional circumstance. The
title of country commandant is conferred by the rulers
of the cities ; but as the city is destitute of power,
influence, and supporters in the country, the administration lays hold of the men it most fears, and confers
this office upon them in order to retain their obedience — a well known procedure of all weak governments, which put off the evil of the moment only to
allow it to appear later in colossal dimensions. Thus
the Papal government has dealings with banditti, to
whom it gives offices in Rome, encouraging brigand-
age by this means, and making its continuance certain;
thus did the Sultan grant Mehemet Ali the rank of
Pacha of Egypt, having afterwards to purchase the
continuance of his own reign by recognizing his vas-
sal's title to an hereditary throne. It is singular that
all the chieftains of the Argentine revolutionary movement were country commandants: Lopez and Ibarra,
Artigas and Guemes, Facundo and Rosas. This is
the constant starting-point of ambition. When Rosas
had made himself master of the city, he exterminated
all the commandants to whom he owed his elevation,
intrusting with this influential position commonplace
men, who could only follow the path he had traced.
Pajarito, Celarragan, Arbolito, Pancho el ñato, Molina,
were among the commandants of whom Rosas cleared
the country.

I assign so much importance to these lesser points, because they will serve to explain all our social phenomena, and the revolution which has been taking place in the Argentine Republic. The features of this revolution are distorted because described in words from the political dictionary, which disguise and hide them by the mistaken ideas they call up. In the same way that of the Spaniards gave familiar European names to the new animals they encountered upon landing in America; saluting with the terrible name of lion, which calls up the notion of the magnanimity and strength of the king of beasts, a wretched cat called the puma, which runs at the sight of the dogs, and naming the jaguar of our woods the tiger. Evidence will soon be brought to show the firm and indestructible nature of the foundations upon which I assert the civil war to be based, however unstable and ignoble they may appear. The life of the Argentine country people as I have exhibited it is not a mere accident; it is the order of things, a characteristic, normal, and in my judgment unparalleled system of association, and in itself affords a full explanation of our revolution.

Before 1810, two distinct, rival, and incompatible forms of society, two differing kinds of civilization existed in the Argentine Republic: one being Spanish, European, and cultivated, the other barbarous, American, and almost wholly of native growth. The revolution which occurred in the cities acted only as the cause, the impulse, which set these two distinct forms of national existence face to face, and gave occasion for a contest between them, to be ended, after lasting many years, by the absorption of one into the other.

I have pointed out the normal form of association, or want of association, of the country people, a form worse, a thousand times, than that of the nomad tribe. I have described the artificial associations formed in idleness, and the sources of fame among the gauchos — bravery, daring, violence, and opposition to regular law, to the civil law, that is, of the city. These phenomena of social organization existed in 1810, and still exist, modified in many points, slowly changing in others, and yet untouched in several more. These foci, about which were gathered the brave, ignorant, free, and unemployed peasantry, were found by thousands through the country. The revolution of 1810 carried everywhere commotion and the sound of arms. Public life, previously wanting in this Arabico-Roman society, made its appearance in all the taverns, and the revolutionary movement finally brought about provincial, warlike associations, called *montoneras*, legitimate offspring of the tavern and the field, hostile to the city and to the army of revolutionary patriots. As events succeed each other, we shall see the provincial montoneras headed by their chiefs; the final triumph, in Facundo Quiroga, of the country over the cities throughout the land; and by their subjugation in spirit, government, and civilization, the final formation of the central consolidated despotic government of the landed proprietor, Don Juan Manuel Rosas, who applied the knife of the gaucho to the culture of Buenos Ayres, and destroyed the work of centuries — of civilization, law, and liberty.

CHAPTER IV.

THE REVOLUTION OF 1810.

" When the battle opens, the Tartar utters a terrible cry, closes, vanishes, and returns like a flash of lightning." — Victor Hugo.

I HAVE been obliged to traverse the whole of the route hitherto pursued, in order to reach the point at which our drama begins. It is needless to consider at length the character, object, and end, of the Revolution of Independence.

They were the same throughout America, and sprang from the same source, namely, the progress of European ideas. South America pursued that course because all other nations were pursuing it. Books, events, and the impulses given by these, induced South America to take part in the movement imparted to France by North American demands for liberty, and to Spain by her own and by French writers. But what my object requires me to notice, is, that the revolution — except in its external symbolic independence of the king — was interesting and intelligible only to the Argentine cities, but foreign and unmeaning to the rural districts. Books, ideas, municipal spirit, courts, laws, statutes, education, all the points of contact and union existing between us and the people of Europe, were to be found in the cities, where there was a basis of organization, incomplete and comparatively evil,

perhaps, for the very reason it was incomplete, and had
not attained the elevation which it felt itself capable of
reaching, but it entered into the revolution with enthusiasm. Outside the cities, the revolution was a problem-
atical affair, and so far as shaking off the king's authority was shaking off judical authority, it was acceptable.
The pastoral districts could only regard the question
from this point of view. Liberty, responsibility of
power, and all the questions which the revolution was
to solve, were foreign to their mode of life and to their
needs. But they derived this advantage from the
revolution, that it tended to confer an object and an
occupation upon the excess of vital force, the presence
of which among them has been pointed out, and was
to add a broader base of union than that to which
throughout the country districts the men daily resorted.
These Spartan constitutions, that warlike nature hitherto ill-satisfied by the free use of the dagger, that
Roman-like idleness which could only be exchanged
for the activity of a battle-field, that utter impatience
of judicial control, were all to have at last a fit sphere
of action in the world.

Revolutionary movements then began in Buenos
Ayres, and the call met with a decided response from
all the interior cities. The pastoral districts became
unsettled and joined in the movement. Tolerably disciplined armies were raised in Buenos Ayres to be sent
to Upper Peru and Montevideo, where the Spanish
forces under General Vigodet were stationed. General Rondeau laid siege to Montevideo with a disciplined army, and Artigas, a noted chieftain, took part
in the siege with some thousands of gauchos. Artigas

had been a formidable outlaw till 1804, when the civil authorities of Buenos Ayres succeeded in bringing him over and inducing him to undertake the duties of country commandant, as a supporter of the same authorities upon whom he had, till then, made war. If the reader has not forgotten the baqueano, and the general requisites of a country commandant, he will readily understand the character and feelings of Artigas. After a time, Artigas and his gauchos withdrew from General Rondeau, and began to make war upon him.

The latter's position was the same as Oribe's when he conducted the siege of Montevideo while taking care of another enemy at his rear. The only difference between the cases is that Artigas was hostile at once to patriots and royalists. It is not my purpose to determine with precision the causes or pretexts which occasioned this rupture, and I am as little disposed to apply to it any designation from the language of politics, for none such would be appropriate. When a nation engages in a revolution, it is begun by the conflict of two opposing interests, the revolutionary and the conservative ; among us the names of patriots and royalists were applied to the corresponding parties. It is natural for the victors, after their triumph, to separate into moderate and extreme factions, one set wishing to carry out all the consequences of the revolution, while their opponents seek to restrain it within certain bounds. It is also characteristic of revolutions for the originally conquered party to renew its organization, and to find a means of success in the dissensions of its conquerors. But when one of the parties called to

the aid of a revolution, immediately loses its connection
with the others, forms a third entity, and shows hostility indiscriminately to both combatants (royalists
and patriots), this detached party is heterogeneous,
not having been conscious of existence until that time,
the revolution having served to develop it and make
it known.

This was the element set in motion by the renowned
Artigas. It was a blind tool, but a tool full of life and
of instincts hostile to European civilization and to all
regular organization ; opposed to monarchy as to republicanism, because both came from the city and possessed already order and reverence for authority.
This tool was employed by the various parties, prin-
cipally by that least revolutionary, in the civilized
cities, until in the course of time the very men who
had summoned it to their aid, yielded to it ; and with
them fell the city, its ideas, its literature, its colleges,
its tribunals, its civilization !

This spontaneous movement of the pastoral districts
was so ingenuous in its first manifestations, so full of
genius and expression in its spirit and tendencies, that
its adoption and baptism by the parties of the cities,
with the political names which divided them, makes
the sincerity of the latter appear in the most unfavor-
able light. The force which supported Artigas in
Entre Rios, did the same for Lopez in Santa Fé, for
Ibarra in Santiago, for Facundo in the Llanos. Its
essence was individual action ; its exclusive weapon,
the horse ; its stage, the vast pampas. The Bedouin
hordes which in our day disturb the Algerian frontier
by their war-cries and depredations, gives an exact idea

of the Argentine montonera, which has been made use of by men of sagacity, as well as by noted desperadoes. In Africa, at the present day, there exists the same struggle between civilization and barbarism ; the *goom* and the montonera are distinguished by the same characters, the same spirit, the same undisciplined strategy. Immense masses of horsemen wander in each case over the wilderness, offering battle to the disciplined forces of the cities, if they feel themselves the stronger party; dispersing in all directions like clouds of Cossacks, if the fight is even, to unite again and fall unexpectedly upon their sleeping foes, snatch away their horses, and kill their laggards and advanced parties. Ever at hand, but too much scattered to be successfully attacked, impotent in battle, but powerful and invincible in an extensive region, they finally decimate and overpower an organized force by means of skirmishes, surprises, fatigues, and privations.

The montonera, as it appeared under the command of Artigas in the early days of the Republic, already showed that character of brutal ferocity and the promise of a reign of terror, which it was reserved for the immortal bandit, the Buenos Ayres land-owner, to convert into a legislative system applied to a civilized society, and to present to the contemplation of Europe, to the shame and disgrace of America. Rosas invented nothing ; his talent was only that of copying his predecessors and combining the brutal instincts of the ignorant masses into a coolly planned system.

The thongs made of Colonel Maciel's skin, and by command of Rosas converted into a pair of manacles, have been actually seen by foreign officials, an outrage not without its precedent, under the rule of Artigas and the other barbarous and Tartaric chiefs of the time. The montonera of Artigas *waistcoated* its enemies ; that is, sewed them up in an envelope of raw hide, and left them in the fields in this condition.

The reader may imagine all the horrors of this slow death, and this horrible punishment was repeated in 1836, in the case of a colonel in the army. The infliction of death by cutting the throat with a knife instead of by shooting, is the result of the butcherly instinct which led Rosas to encourage cruelty, to give executions a more barbarous form which he thought would give pleasure to the assassins ; in other words, he changed the legal punishments recognized by civil society, for others which he called American, and in the name of which he invited his fellow-Americans to come forward in his defense when the sufferings of Brazil, Paraguay, and Uruguay invoked the aid of the European powers to assist in their liberation from the cannibal, who was even then overrunning them with his sanguinary hordes. It is impossible to maintain the calmness needed to investigate historic truth when we are forced to remember at every step that America and Europe have been so long successfully deluded by a system of assassination and cruelty, scarcely tolerated in the African provinces of Ashantee or Dahomey.

Such is the character presented by the montonera from its first appearance ; a singular kind of warfare and civil polity, unprecedented except among the tribes of the Asiatic plains, and not to be confounded with the habits, ideas, and customs of the Argentine cities, which were, like all South American cities, a continuaon of European civilization, and especially that of Spain.

The only explanation of the montonera is to be discovered by the examination of the society from which it proceeded. Artigas, the baqueano and outlaw, at war with the authorities of the city, but bought over as provincial commandant and chief of equestrian bands, presents a type reproduced with little change in each provincial commandant who came to be a partisan leader. Like all civil wars in which deep differences of education, belief, and motives divide the parties engaged in them, the internal warfare of the Argentine Republic was long and obstinate, until one of the elements of the strife was victorious. The Argentine Revolutionary War was twofold: 1st, a civilized warfare of the cities against Spain ; 2d, a war against the cities on the part of the country chieftains with the view of shaking off all political subjection and satisfying their hatred of civilization. The cities overcame the Spaniards, and were in their turn overcome by the country districts. This is the explanation of the Argentine Revolution, the first shot of which was fired in 1810, and the last is still to be heard.

I will not enter into all the details of this contest. The struggle was of various duration in different places ; some cities yielded at first, others later. The life of Facundo Quiroga will afford us an opportunity of displaying this strife in all its naked deformity. What I have now to notice is that the triumph of these chiefs involved the disappearance of all civil order, even as it existed among the Spaniards. In some places it has totally disappeared ; in others only in part, but it

is clearly on its way to destruction. The mass of men
are incapable of distinctly comparing one epoch with
another ; the present moment is the only one embraced
by their observation ; and for this reason no one has
yet observed this destruction and decadence of the
cities ; just as the visible progress of the people of the
interior to total barbarism escapes notice. Buenos
Ayres has so many of the elements of European civilization that it will end by educating Rosas and repress-
ing his bloody and barbarous instincts. The high
position which he occupies, his relations with European
governments, the necessity of respecting strangers and
of denying through the press the atrocities he has committed, in order to escape universal reprobation, all
combine to check his outrages, — a perceptible advantage.

Four cities have already been annihilated by the
rule of the partisan supporters of Rosas : Santa Fé,
Santiago del Estero, San Luis, and La Rioja. Santa
Fé, situated at the junction of the Paraná and another
navigable river, the mouth of which is close by the
town, is one of the most favored spots of South America, and yet contains less than two thousand souls;
San Luis, the capital of a province with a population
of fifty thousand, in which it is the only city, contains
less than fifteen hundred.

To make the ruin and decadence of civilization and
the rapid progress of barbarism perceptible to the reader, I must select two cities — one already annihilated,
the other insensibly proceeding towards barbarism —
La Rioja and San Juan. La Rioja was formerly a
city of some account, but its own sons would fail to

recognize it in its present condition. When the revolution of 1810 began, it contained a large number of capitalists, and men of note, who have figured in a distinguished manner in arms, at the bar, on the bench, or in the pulpit. From Rioja came Dr. Castro Barros, deputy to the Congress of Tucuman, and a celebrated divine; General Davila, who freed Copiapo from the Spanish power in 1817; Gabriel Ocampo, one of the most noted members of the Argentine bar; and a large number of advocates of the families Ocampo, Davila, and Garcia, at present scattered over the Chilian territory, as well as various priests of much learning, among whom is Dr. Gordillo, actual curate of Huasco.

The ability of a province to produce in a given epoch so many eminent and illustrious men, proves the diffusion of learning among a greater number of individuals, and that it was respected and desired. If such was the case in the early days of the revolution, what an increase of enlightenment, wealth, and population, might we not expect to find now, if a fearful retrogression towards barbarism had not checked the development of that unfortunate people! What Chilian city, however insignificant, is there, in which no progress has been made during a period of ten years, in enlightenment, wealth, and elegance, even if we include among these such as have been destroyed by earthquakes?

Let us now look at the condition of La Rioja, as exhibited by the answers given to one of the many inquiries I have instituted for the purpose of gaining a thorough knowledge of the facts on which I base my theories. These are the statements of a reliable person, who was unacquainted with my object in investigating his memory of matters which must have been fresh in his mind, for it was only four months before that he left Rioja.[1]

1. What is about the actual amount of the population of Rioja city ?

Ans. About fifteen hundred souls. It is said that only fifteen adult males reside in the city.

2. How many persons of note live in it ?

Ans. Six or eight in the city.

3. How many lawyers' offices are open there ?

Ans. None.

4. How many men wear dress-coats ?

Ans. None.

5. How many young men from La Rioja are studying at Cordova or Buenos Ayres ?

Ans. I know of only one.

6. How many schools are there, and how many children attend them ?

Ans. None.

7. Are there any public charitable institutions ?

Ans. None, nor any means for the simplest instruction. The only Franciscan ecclesiastic of the place has given instruction to some children.

8. How many of the churches are in ruins ?

Ans. Five; the Matriz is the only one at all serviceable.

9. Are new houses building ?

[1] Dr. Don Manuel Ignacio Castro Barros, canon of the Cordova Cathedral.

Ans. Not one, nor are people making any of the needed repairs.

10. Are the existing houses going to ruins ?

Ans. Almost all, owing to the frequency with which the streets are flooded.

11. How many priests in orders are there ?

Ans. Only two young men in the city : one is a secular curate, the other an ecclesiastic of Catamarca. There are four others in the province.

12. Are there any fortunes of fifty thousand dollars ? and how many of twenty thousand ?

Ans. None ; all the people are extremely poor.

13. Has the population increased or diminished ?

Ans. It has diminished by more than one half.

14. Is there any feeling of terror prevalent among the people ?

Ans. A very strong one ; there is a fear of uttering even harmless words.

15. Is the money coined of full value ?

Ans. That of the province is debased.

These facts speak with all their sad and fearful severity. The only example of so rapid a decline towards barbarism is presented by the history of the Mohammedan conquests of Greece. And this happens in America, and in the nineteenth century, and is the work of but twenty years !

What is true of La Rioja is equally so of Santa Fé, San Luis, and Santiago del Estero, which have become skeletons of cities, decrepit and devastated, mere apologies for towns. In San Luis there has been but one priest for ten years past, and for the same period it has contained no school, nor any person who wears a dress-coat. But let us judge by San Juan the fate of the cities which have escaped destruction, but in which barbarism is insensibly increasing.

San Juan is an exclusively agricultural and commercial province. Its want of open country has long kept it free from the rule of the provincial chieftains. Whatever party was in power, its governor and officials were taken from the educated part of its population until 1833, when Facundo Quiroga placed a man of the lower class in possession of the government. This person, unable to avoid the influence of the civilized usages, went over to the party of culture and yielded to their dictations, until he was overthrown by Brizuela, chief of La Rioja. Brizuela was succeeded by General Benavides, whose power has lasted nine years, and has come to seem rather his own property than a magistracy held for a term. San Juan has grown in population,—owing to the progress of agriculture there, and to the emigrants driven by hunger and wretchedness from La Rioja and San Luis, — and its buildings have sensibly increased in number ; facts which prove the natural wealth of the region, and the progress that might be made under a government which cared to foster education and culture, the sole methods of elevating a nation.

The despotism of Benavides is mild and pacific, so that men's minds are kept quiet and calm. He is the only subordinate of Rosas who has not reveled in blood ; but this does not lessen the tendency to barbarism inherent in the present system.

All the courts are held by men destitute of the slightest knowledge of law, worthless in every sense. There is no military man who has served in regular armies outside the Republic.[1] Is it credible that such an inferior position is naturally that of a city of the interior? No, the past proves the contrary. Twenty years ago San Juan was one of the most civilized towns of the interior; and what must be the decline and prostration of a South American city which has to look back twenty years for its time of prosperity!

In 1831 two hundred heads of families, youths, educated men, advocates, soldiers, and other of its citizens, emigrated to Chili, Copiapo, Coquimbo, Valparaiso; and other parts of that Republic are still full of these noble victims of proscription, among whom are capitalists, intelligent miners, merchants, farmers, lawyers, and physicians. As at the Babylonian dispersion, none of them have yet been able to return to see the promised land. A second set of emigrants left the city in 1840, never to return.

San Juan had been, before these days, rich enough in distinguished men to give to the celebrated Congress of Tucuman a President of the capacity and rank of Dr. Laprida, who was afterwards assassinated by the Aldaos; a prior to the Recoleta Dominica of Chili, in the person of the distinguished sage and patriot Oro,

---

[1] From 1845, when this book was written, to the present date, a salutary reaction occurred in the province of San Juan. It now contains one male and one female academy, and the Honorable House of Representatives has just proclaimed primary education for both sexes a public institution of the province. More than twenty youths are studying in Buenos Ayres, Cordova, and Chili, for the professions of law or medicine. Music and drawing have become quite frequent accomplishments for both sexes, and the artisans and other grades of society dress by preference in civilized costume, which is a sign of a satisfactory direction of the public mind to the improvement of its condition.

afterwards Bishop of San Juan. An illustrious patriot, Don Ignacio de la Rosa, who, in conjunction with San Martin, prepared the expedition to aid Chili, and who scattered through his country the seeds of the *equality of classes* promised by the Revolution, was also a citizen of San Juan ; as were a minister of the government of Rivadavia, Dr. Carril ; a minister of the Argentine Legation, Don Domingo Oro, whose diplomatic talents are yet insufficiently appreciated ; a deputy to the Congress of 1826, the enlightened priest Vera ; a deputy to the convention of Santa Fé, in the presbyter Oro, an orator of note ; one to that of Cordova, Don Rudecindo Rojo, as eminent for his talents and genius for industrial pursuits as for his great learning ; and, among others, General Rojo, a soldier in the army, who saved two provinces by suppressing conspiracies, which he did solely by his quiet determination of character, and of whom General Paz, a competent judge of such matters, said, that he bade fair to be one of the first generals of the Republic. San Juan then possessed a theatre and a permanent company of actors.

There are still in existence the remains of six or seven private libraries, which comprised the most valuable books of the eighteenth century, and translations of the best Greek and Latin works. I had no other instruction up to 1836 than that afforded me by these rich, though partially destroyed libraries. San Juan had so many illustrious men in 1825 that the House of Representatives contained six noted orators. Let the wretched peasants who now [1] disgrace the House of Representatives of San Juan, within which have been

---

[1] 1845.

heard such eloquent speeches and such elevated sentiments, turn from the record of those times and flee
abashed at the profanation of that august sanctuary by
their diatribes !

The judicial chairs and the administrative offices
were then occupied by educated men, and a sufficient
number remained to plead the causes of others.

The elegance of manners, the refinement of customs, the cultivation of literature, the great commercial interests, the public spirit which animated the
people, — all announced to foreigners the existence of
a society of culture advancing rapidly to the attainment
of a distinguished rank, and justified the following estimate of San Juan given to America and Europe
through the London press : —

" They are showing the strongest inclination to advance in
civilization, and this city is regarded at present as only second
to Buenos Ayres in the progress of social reform. Various institutions lately established in Buenos Ayres have been adopted at
San Juan on a scale proportionate to its size, and the people have
made extraordinary progress in ecclesiastical reform, incorporat-
ing all the monastic orders with the secular clergy, and suppressing the convents of the latter."

But the state of primary education will give the best
idea of the culture of the period we are considering.
No portion of the Argentine Republic has been more
distinguished by its anxiety for the diffusion of knowledge than San Juan, nor have more complete results
been obtained elsewhere. The government, not satisfied with the capacity of the men of the province for
the fulfillment of so important a duty, sent in 1815 for
a person uniting competent learning and high morals

from Buenos Ayres. Some gentlemen of the name of Rodriguez accordingly came to San Juan. These were three brothers worthy of ranking with the first families of the country, with whom they became connected, such was their merit, and such were the many excellent qualities they possessed. My present profession as superintendent of primary education, and my study of such subjects, enable me to say that if ever any parallel to the celebrated Dutch schools described by M. Cousin, occurred in Spanish America, it was in the school of San Juan. The moral and religious instruction was perhaps superior to the elementary teaching given there; and to this cause I attribute the small number of crimes committed in San Juan, and the moderate conduct of Benavides himself, who like most of the present citizens of San Juan, was educated in that famous school, where the pupils were indoctrinated into the precepts of morality with special care.

If these pages reach the hands of Don Ignacio and Don Roque Rodriguez, I trust they will accept this feeble homage, due, as I believe, to the eminent service done to the culture and morality of a whole city, in connection with their late brother, Don José. [1]

Such is the history of the Argentine cities. They can all claim past glory, civilization, and distinction. For the present they are borne down to the level of barbarism, and this barbarism of the interior has succeeded in penetrating even to the streets of Buenos Ayres.

[1] A detailed account of the system and organization of this public educational establishment will be found in *Popular Education*, a special work devoted to that subject, and the fruit of my journey to Europe and the United States, undertaken by order of the Chilian government.

From 1810 to 1840 the provinces which contained such civilized cities, were yet sufficiently barbarous to destroy by their propensities the colossal work of the Revolution of Independence! Now that nothing is left of what men, enlightenment, and institutions they once held, what will become of them? Ignorance and its consequence, poverty, are waiting like carrion birds for the last gasp of the cities of the interior to devour their prey, and to convert them into fields and pastures. Buenos Ayres may again become what it was; for there European civilization has such strength that it must maintain itself in spite of the brutality of the government. But what can the provinces depend upon? Two centuries will not suffice for their restoration to the path they have abandoned, if the present generation shall educate their children in the barbarism which they have reached. Are we now asked for what we are contending? We are contending for the restoration of their former life, and the promise of improvement to the cities.

CHAPTER V.

LIFE OF JUAN FACUNDO QUIROGA.

"Moreover these traits belong to the original character of the human race. The man of nature who has not yet learned to restrain or disguise his passions, displays them in all their energy, and gives himself up to their impetuosity." — *Aléx. History of the Ottoman Empire.*

HIS INFANCY AND YOUTH.

BETWEEN the cities of San Luis and San Juan, lies an extensive desert, called the Travesia, a word which signifies *want of water*. The aspect of that waste is mostly gloomy and unpromising, and the traveller coming from the east does not fail to provide his *chifles* with a sufficient quantity of water at the last cistern which he passes as he approaches it. This Travesia once witnessed the following strange scene. The consequences of some of the encounters with knives so common among our gauchos had driven one of them in haste from the city of San Luis and forced him to escape to the Travesia on foot, and with his riding gear on his shoulder, in order to avoid the pursuit of the law. Two comrades were to join him as soon as they could steal horses for all three. Hunger and thirst were not the only dangers which at that time awaited him in the desert ; a tiger that had already tasted human flesh had been following the track of those who crossed it for a year, and more than eight persons had already been the victims of this preference.

In these regions, where man must contend with this animal for dominion over nature, the former sometimes falls a victim, upon which the tiger begins to acquire a preference for the taste of human flesh, and when it has once devoted itself to this novel form of chase, the pursuit of mankind, it gets the name of *man-eater*. The provincial justice nearest the scene of his depredations calls out the huntsmen of his district, who join, under his authority and guidance, in the pursuit of the beast, which seldom escapes the consequences of its outlawry.

When our fugitive had proceeded some six leagues, he thought he heard the distant roar of the animal, and a shudder ran through him. The roar of the tiger resembles the screech of the hog, but is prolonged, sharp, and piercing, and even when there is no occasion for fear, causes an involuntary tremor of the nerves as if the flesh shuddered consciously at the menace of death. The roaring was heard clearer and nearer. The tiger was already upon the trail of the man, who saw no refuge but a small carob-tree at a great distance. He had to quicken his pace, and finally to run, for the roars behind him began to follow each other more rapidly, and each was clearer and more ringing than the last. At length, flinging his riding gear to one side of the path, the gaucho turned to the tree which he had noticed, and in spite of the weakness of its trunk, happily quite a tall one, he succeeded in clambering to its top, and keeping himself half concealed among its boughs which oscillated violently. Thence he could see the swift approach of the tiger, sniffing the soil and roaring more frequently in proportion to its increasing perception of the nearness of its prey. Passing beyond the spot where our traveller had left the path, it lost the track, and becoming enraged, rapidly circled about until it discovered the riding gear, which it ·dashed to fragments by a single blow. Still more furious from this failure, it resumed its search for the trail, and at last found out the direction in which it led. It soon discerned its prey, under whose weight the slight tree was swaying like a reed upon the summit of which a bird has alighted. The tiger now sprang forward, and in the twinkling of an eye, its monstrous fore-paws were resting on the slender trunk two yards from the ground, and were imparting to the tree a convulsive trembling calculated to act upon the nerves of the gaucho, whose position was far from secure. The beast exerted its strength in an ineffectual leap; it circled around the tree, measuring the elevation with eyes reddened by the thirst for blood, and at length, roaring with rage, it crouched down, beating the ground frantically with its tail, its eyes fixed on its prey, its parched mouth half open. This horrible scene had lasted for nearly two mortal hours; the gaucho's constrained attitude, and the fearful fascination exercised over him by the fixed and bloodthirsty stare of the tiger, which irresistibly attracted and retained his own glances, had begun to diminish his strength, and he already perceived that the moment was at hand when his exhausted body would fall into the capacious mouth of his pursuer. But at this moment the distant sound of the feet of horses on a rapid gallop gave him hope of rescue. His friends had indeed seen the tiger's foot-prints, and were hastening on, though without hope of saving him. The scattered fragments of the saddle directed them to the scene of action, and it was the work of a moment for them to reach it, to uncoil their lassoes, and to fling them over the tiger, now blinded by rage. The beast, drawn in opposite directions by the two lassos, could not evade the swift stabs by which its destined victim took his revenge for his prolonged torments. "On that occasion I knew what it was to be afraid," was the expression of Don Juan Facundo Quiroga, as he related this incident to a group of officers.

He too was called "the tiger of the Llanos," a title which did not ill befit him. There are, in fact, as is proved by phrenology and comparative anatomy, relations between external forms and moral qualities, between the countenance of a man and that of some animal whose disposition resembles his own. Facundo, as he was long called in the interior, — or, General Don Facundo Quiroga, as he afterwards became, when society had received him into its bosom and victory had crowned him with laurels, — was a stoutly built man of low stature, whose short neck and broad shoulders supported a well-shaped head, covered with a profusion of black and closely curling hair. His somewhat oval face was half buried in this mass of hair and an equally thick black, curly beard, rising to his cheek-bones, which by their prominence evinced a firm and tenacious will. His black and fiery eyes, shadowed by thick eyebrows, occasioned an involuntary sense of terror in those on whom they chanced to fall, for Facundo's glance was never direct, whether from habit or intention. With the design of making himself always formidable, he always kept his head bent down, to look at one from under his eyebrows, like the Ali Pacha of Monovoisin. The

image of Quiroga is recalled to me by the Cain represented by the famous Ravel troupe, setting aside the artistic and statuesque attitudes, which do not correspond
to his. To conclude, his features were regular, and
the pale olive of his complexion harmonized well with
the dense shadows which surrounded it.

The formation of his head showed, notwithstanding
this shaggy covering, the peculiar organization of a man
born to rule. Quiroga possessed those natural qualities
which converted the student of Brienne into the genius
of France, and the obscure Mameluke who fought with
the French at the Pyramids, into the Viceroy of Egypt.
Such natures develop according to the society in which
they originate, and are either noble leaders who hold
the highest place in history, ever forwarding the progress of civilization, or the cruel and vicious tyrants
who become the scourges of their race and time.

Facundo Quiroga was the son of an inhabitant
of San Juan, who had settled in the Llanos of La
Rioja, and there had acquired a fortune in pastoral
pursuits. In 1779, Facundo was sent to his father's
native province to receive the limited education, con-
sisting only of the arts of reading and writing, which
he could acquire in its schools. After a man has come
to employ the hundred trumpets of fame with the noise
of his deeds, curiosity or the spirit of investigation is
carried to such an extent as to scent out the insignificant
history of the child, in order to connect it with the biography of the hero ; and it is not seldom that the rudiments of the traits characteristic of the historical personage are met amid fables invented by flattery. The
young Alcibiades is said to have lain down at full

length upon the pavement of the street where he was playing, in order to insist that the driver of an approaching vehicle should yield the way to avoid running over him. Napoleon is reported to have ruled over his fellow-students, and to have entrenched himself in his study to resist an apprehended insult. Many anecdotes are now in circulation relating to Facundo, many of which reveal his true nature. In the house where he lodged, he could never be induced to take his seat at the family table ; in school he was haughty, reserved, and unsocial ; he never joined the other boys except to head their rebellious proceedings or to beat them. The master, tired of contending with so untamable a disposition, on one occasion provided himself with a new and stiff strap, and said to the frightened boys, as he showed it to them, " This is to be made supple upon Facundo." Facundo, then eleven years old, heard this threat, and the next day he tested its value. Without having learned his lesson, he asked the head-master to hear it himself, because, as he said, the assistant was unfriendly to him. The master complied with the request. Facundo made one mistake, then two, three, and four ; upon which the master used his strap upon him. Facundo, who had calculated everything, down to the weakness of the chair in which the master was seated, gave him a buffet, upset him on his back, and, taking to the street in the confusion created by this scene, hid himself among some wild vines where they could not get him out for three days. Was not such a boy the embryo chieftain who would afterwards defy society at large ?

In early manhood his character took a more decided

cast, constantly becoming more gloomy, imperious, and wild. From the age of fifteen years he was irresistibly controlled by the passion for gambling, as is often the case with such natures, which need strong excitement to awaken their dormant energies. This made him notorious in the city, and intolerable in the house which afforded him its hospitality ; and finally under this influence, by a shot fired at one George Peña, he shed the first rill of blood which went to make up the wide torrent that marked his way through life.

On his becoming an adult, the thread of his life disappears in an intricate labyrinth of bouts and broils among the people of the surrounding region. Sometimes lying hid, always pursued, he passed his time in gambling, working as a common laborer, domineering over everybody around him, and distributing his stabs among them.

On the Godoy farm in San Juan are shown to this day mud-walls of Quiroga's treading ; there are others in Fiambola, in La Rioja, made by him. He himself pointed out others in Mendoza, in the very place where one afternoon he had twenty-six of the officers who surrendered at Chacon dragged from their houses and shot to avenge Villifañe. He also showed some monuments of his wandering life of labor in the country districts of Buenos Ayes. What motives induced this man, brought up in a respectable family, son of a man of means and creditable life, to descend to a hireling's position, and moreover to select the dullest and most brutish kind of work, needing only bodily strength and endurance ? Was it because the labor of building these mud-walls is recompensed with double wages, and that he was in haste to get together a little money ?

The most connected account of this obscure and roaming part of his life that I can procure is as follows :

Towards 1806, he went to Chili with a consignment of grain on his parent's account. This he gambled away, as well as the animals, which had brought it, and the family slaves who had accompanied him.

He often took to San Juan and Mendoza droves of the stock on his father's estate, and these always shared the same fate ; for with Facundo, gambling was a fierce and burning passion which aroused the deepest instincts of his nature. These successive gains and losses of his must have worn out his father's generosity, for at last he broke off all amicable relations with his family.

When he had become the terror of the Republic, he was once asked by one of his parasites, " What was the largest bet you ever made in your life, General ? " " Seventy dollars," replied Quiroga, carelessly, and yet he had just won two hundred dollars at one stake. He afterwards explained that once when a young man, having only seventy dollars, he had lost them all at one throw. But this fact has its characteristic history. Facundo had been at work for a year as a laborer upon the farm of a lady, situated in the Plumerillo, and had made himself conspicuous by his punctuality in going to work, and by the influence and authority which he exercised over the other laborers. When they wanted a holiday to get drunk in, they used to apply to Facundo, who informed the lady, and gave her his word, which was always fulfilled, to have all

the men at work the next day. On this account the
laborers called him *the father*. At the end of a year
of steady work, Facundo asked for his wages, which
amounted to seventy dollars, and mounted his horse
without knowing where he was bound, but seeing a
collection of people at a grocery store, he alighted, and
reaching over the group around the card-dealer, bet
his seventy dollars on one card. He lost them, and
remounting, went on his way, careless in what direction, until after a little time a justice, Toledo by name,
who happened to be passing, stopped him to ask for his
passport. Facundo rode up as if about to give it to
him, pretended to be feeling for something in his pocket,
and stretched the justice on the ground with a stab.
Was he taking his revenge upon the judge for his
recent loss at play ? or was it his purpose to satisfy the
irritation against civil authority natural to a gaucho
outlaw, and increase, by this new deed, the splendor
of his rising fame ? Both are true explanations. This
mode of revenging himself for misfortunes upon whatever first offered itself, had many examples in his life.
When he was addressed as General, and had colonels
at his orders, he had two hundred lashes given one of
them in his house at San Juan, for having, as he said,
cheated at play. He ordered two hundred lashes to
be given to a young man for having allowed himself a
jest at a time when jests were not to his taste ; and
two hundred lashes was the penalty inflicted on a
woman in Mendoza for having said to him as he
passed, " Farewell, General," when he was going off
in a rage at not having succeeded in intimidating a

neighbor of his, who was as peaceable and judicious as Facundo was rash and gaucho-like.

Facundo reappears later in Buenos Ayres, where he was enrolled in 1810 as a recruit in the regiment of Arribeños, which was commanded by General Ocampo, a native of his own province, and afterwards president of Charcas. The glorious career of arms opened before him with the first rays of the sun of May ; and doubtless, endowed with such capacity as his, and with his destructive and sanguinary instincts, Facundo, could he have been disciplined to submit to civil authority and ennobled in the sublimity of the object of the strife, might some day have returned from Peru, Chili, or Bolivia, as a General of the Argentine Republic, like so many other brave gauchos who began their careers in the humble position of a private soldier. But Quiroga's rebellious spirit could not endure the yoke of discipline, the order of the barrack, or the delay of promotion. He felt his destiny to be to rule, to rise at a single leap, to create for himself, without assistance, and in spite of a hostile and civilized society, a career of his own, combining bravery and crime, government and disorganization. He was subsequently recruited into the army of the Andes, and enrolled in the Mounted Grenadiers. A lieutenant named Garcia took him for an assistant, and very soon desertion left a vacant place in those glorious files. Quiroga, like Rosas, like all the vipers that have thriven under the shade of their country's laurels, made himself notorious in after-life by his hatred for the soldiers of Independence, among whom both the men above named made horrible slaughter.

Facundo, after deserting from Buenos Ayres, set out for the interior with three comrades. A squad of soldiery overtook him; he faced the pursuers and engaged in a real battle with them, which remained undecided for awhile, until, after having killed four or five men, he was at liberty to continue his journey, constantly cutting his way through detachments of troops which here and there opposed his progress, until he arrived at San Luis. He was, at a later day, to traverse the same route with a handful of men, to disperse armies instead of detachments, and proceed to the famous citadel of Tucuman to blot out the last remains of Republicanism and civil order.

Facundo now reappears in the Llanos, at his father's house. At this period occurred an event which is well attested. Yet one of the writers whose manuscripts I am using, replies to an inquiry about the matter, "that to the extent of his knowledge Quiroga never attempted forcibly to deprive his parents of money," and I could wish to adopt this statement, irreconcilable as it is with unvarying tradition and general consent. The contrary is shocking to relate. It is said that on his father's refusal to give him a sum of money which he had demanded, he watched for the time when both parents were taking an afternoon nap to fasten the door of the room they occupied, and to set fire to the straw roof, which was the usual covering of the buildings of the Llanos! [1]

But what is certain in the matter is that his father

---

[1] The author afterwards learned that Facundo related this story to a company of ladies, and one of his own early acquaintances testified to his having given his father a blow on one occasion.

once requested the governor of La Rioja to arrest him in order to check his excesses, and that Facundo, before taking flight from the Llanos, went to the city of La Rioja, where that official was to be found at the time, and coming upon him by surprise, gave him a blow, saying as he did so, " You have sent, sir, to have me arrested. There, have me arrested now ! " On which he mounted his horse and set off for the open country at a gallop. At the end of a year he again showed himself at his father's house, threw himself at the feet of the old man whom he had used so ill, and succeeded amid the sobs of both, and the son's assurances of his reform in reply to the father's recriminations, in reëstablishing peace, although on a very uncertain basis.

But no change occurred in his character and disorderly habits ; races, gambling parties, and expeditions into the country were the occasions of new acts of violence, stabbings, and assaults on his part, until he at length made himself intolerable to all, and rendered his own position very unsafe. Then a great thought which he announced without shame, got hold of his mind. The deserter from the Arribeños regiment, the mounted grenadier who refused to make himself immortal at Chacabuco or Maipù, determined to join the montonera of Ramirez, the offshoot from that led by Artigas, whose renown for crime and hatred for the cities on which it was making war, had reached the Llanos, and held the provincial government in dread. Facundo set forth to join those buccaneers of the pampa. But perhaps the knowledge of his character, and of the importance of the aid which he would give to the destroyers, alarmed his fellow provincials, for they informed the authorities of San Luis, through which he was to pass, of his infernal design. Dupuis, then (1818) governor, arrested him, and for sometime he remained unnoticed among the criminals confined in the prison. This prison of San Luis, however, was to be the first step in his ascent to the elevation which he subsequently attained. San Martin had sent to San Luis a great number of Spanish officers of all ranks from among the prisoners taken in Chili. Irritated by their humiliations and sufferings, or thinking it possible that the Spanish forces might be assembled again, this party of prisoners rose one day and opened the doors of the cells of the common criminals, to obtain their aid in a general escape. Facundo was one of these criminals, and as soon as he found himself free from prison, he seized an iron bar of his fetters, split the skull of the very Spaniard who had released him, and passing through the group of insurgents, left a wide path strewn with the dead. Some say that the weapon he employed was a bayonet, and that only three men were killed by it. Quiroga, however, always talked of the iron bar of the fetters, and of fourteen dead men. This may be one of the fictions with which the poetic imagination of the people adorns the types of brute force they so much admire ; perhaps the tale of the iron bar is an Argentine version of the jaw-bone of Samson, the Hebrew Hercules. But Facundo looked upon it as a crown of glory, in accordance with his idea of excellence, and whether by bar or bayonet, he succeeded, aided by other soldiers and prisoners whom his example encouraged, in suppressing the insurrection and reconciling society to himself by this act of bravery, and placing himself under his country's protection. Thus his name spread everywhere, ennobled and cleansed, though with blood, from the stains which had tarnished it.

Facundo returned to La Rioja covered with glory, his country's creditor; and with testimonials of his conduct, to show in the Llanos, among gauchos, the new titles which justified the terror his name began to inspire; for there is something imposing, something which subjugates and controls others in the man who is rewarded for the assassination of fourteen men at one time.

Something still remains to be noticed of the previous character and temper of this pillar of the Confederation. An illiterate man, one of Quiroga's companions in childhood and youth, who has supplied me with many of the above facts, sends me the following curious statements in a manuscript describing Quiroga's early years: "His public career was not preceded by the practice of theft; he never committed robbery even in his most pressing necessities. He was not only fond of fighting, but would pay for an opportunity, or for a chance to insult the most renowned champion in any company. He had a great aversion to respectable men. He never drank. He was very reserved from his youth, and desired to inspire others with awe as well as with fear, for which purpose he gave his confidants to understand that he had the gift of prophecy, in short was a soothsayer. He treated all connected with him as slaves. *He never went to confession, prayed, or heard mass;* I saw him once at mass after he be-

came a general. He said of himself that he believed
in nothing." The frankness with which these words
are written, prove their truth.

And here ends the private life of Quiroga, in which
I have omitted a long series of deeds which only show
his evil nature, his bad education, and his fierce and
bloody instincts. The facts stated appear to me to
sum up the whole public life of Quiroga. I see in them
the great man, the man of genius, in spite of himself
and unknown to himself; a Cæsar, Tamerlane, or
Mohammed. The fault is not his that thus he was born.
In order to contend with, rule, and control the power
of the city, and the judicial authority, he is willing to
descend to anything. If he is offered a place in the
army, he disdains it, because his impatience cannot
wait for promotion. Such a position demands submission, and places fetters upon individual independence ;
the soldier's coat oppresses his body, and military tactics control his steps, all of which are insufferable!
His equestrian life, a life of danger and of strong ex-
citements, has steeled his spirit and hardened his heart.
He feels an unconquerable and instinctive hatred for
the laws which have pursued him, for the judges who
have condemned him, and for the whole society and
organism from which he has felt himself withdrawn
from his childhood, and which regards him with suspicion and contempt. With these remarks is connected
by imperceptible links the motto of this chapter, " He
is the natural man, as yet unused either to repress or
disguise his passions ; he does not restrain their energy,
but gives free rein to their impetuosity. This is the
character of the human race." And thus it appears

in the rural districts of the Argentine Republic. Facundo is a type of primitive barbarism. He recognized no form of subjection. His rage was that of a wild beast. The locks of his crisp black hair, which fell in meshes over his brow and eyes, resembled the snakes of Medusa's head. Anger made his voice hoarse, and turned his glances into dragons. In a fit of passion he kicked out the brains of a man with whom he had quarreled at play. He tore off both the ears of a woman he had lived with, and had promised to marry, upon her asking him for thirty dollars for the celebration of the wedding; and laid open his son John's head with an axe, because he could not make him hold his tongue. He violently beat a beautiful young lady at Tucuman, whom he had failed either to seduce or to subdue, and exhibited in all his actions a low and brutal yet not a stupid nature, or one wholly without lofty aims. Incapable of commanding noble admiration, he delighted in exciting fear; and this pleasure was exclusive and dominant with him to the arranging all his actions so as to produce terror in those around him, whether it was society in general, the victim on his way to execution, or his own wife and children. Wanting ability to manage the machinery of civil government, he substituted terror for patriotism and self-sacrifice. Destitute of learning, he surrounded himself with mysteries, and pretended to a foreknowledge of events which gave him prestige and reputation among the commonalty, supporting his claims by an air of impenetrability, by natural sagacity, an uncommon power of observation, and the advantage he derived from vulgar credulity.

The repertory of anecdotes relating to Quiroga, and with which the popular memory is replete, is inexhaustible ; his sayings, his expedients, bear the stamp of an originality which gives them a certain Eastern aspect, a certain tint of Solomonic wisdom in the conception of the vulgar.   Indeed, how does Solomon's advice for discovering the true mother of the disputed child differ from Facundo's method of detecting a thief in the following instances : —

An article had been stolen from a band, and all endeavors to discover the thief had proved fruitless. Quiroga drew up the troops and gave orders for the cutting of as many small wands of equal length as there were soldiers ; then, having had these wands distributed one to each man, he said in a confident voice, " The man whose wand will be longer than the others to-morrow morning is the thief." Next day the troops was again paraded, and Quiroga proceeded to inspect the wands.   There was one whose wand was, not *longer* but *shorter* than the others.   " Wretch ! " cried Facundo, in a voice which overpowered the man with dismay, " it is thou ! "   And so it was ; the culprit's confusion was proof of the fact.   The expedient was a simple one ; the credulous gaucho, fearing that his wand would really grow, had cut off a piece of it.   But to avail one's self of such means, a man must be superior in intellect to those about him, and must at least have some knowledge of human nature.

Some portions of a soldier's accoutrements having been stolen and all inquiries having failed to detect the thief, Quiroga had the troops paraded and marched past him as he stood with crossed arms and a fixed, piercing, and terrible gaze.   He had previously said,

" I know the man," with an air of assurance not to
be questioned. The review began ; many men had
passed, and Quiroga still remained motionless, like the
statue of Jupiter Tonans or the God of the Last Judgment. All at once he descended upon one man, and
said in a curt and dry voice, " Where is the saddle ? "
" Yonder, sir," replied the other, pointing to a thicket.
" Ho ! four fusileers !" cried Quiroga. What revelation was this ? that of terror and guilt made to a man
of sagacity.

On another occasion, when a gaucho was answering
to charges of theft which had been brought against
him, Facundo interrupted him with the words, " This
rogue has begun to lie. Ho, there ! a hundred lashes ! "
When the criminal had been taken away, Quiroga said
to some one present, " Look you, my master, when a
gaucho moves his foot while talking, it is a sign he is
telling lies." The lashes extorted from the gaucho the
confession that he had stolen a yoke of oxen.

At another time he was in need of a man of resolution and boldness to whom he could intrust a dangerous mission. When a man was brought to him for
this purpose, Quiroga was writing ; he raised his head
after the man's presence had been repeatedly announced, looked at him and returned to his writing
with the remark, " Pooh ! that is a wretched creature.
I want a brave man and a venturesome one ! " It
turned out to be true that the fellow was actually good
for nothing.

Hundreds of such stories of Facundo's life, which
show the man of superior ability, served effectually to
give him a mysterious fame among the vulgar, who
even attribute superior powers to him.

CHAPTER VI.

LA RIOJA.

" The sides of the mountain enlarge and assume an aspect at once more grand and more barren. By little and little, the scanty vegetation languishes and dies ; and mosses disappear, and a red burning hue succeeds." — Roussée's Palestine.

THE COUNTRY COMMANDANT.

IN a document dating as far back as 1560, I have seen recorded the name of Mendoza of the valley of La Rioja. But La Rioja proper is an Argentine province lying north of San Juan, from which it is separated by several strips of desert, although these are broken by some inhabited valleys. Its western portion is intersected in parallel lines by spurs branching off from the Andes and including in their valleys los Pueblos and Little Chili, as it was called by the Chilian miners, who frequented the rich and renowned mines of Famatina.

Further to the east stretches a sandy, barren, and sun-scorched plain, at the northern extremity of which, and near a mountain covered to its summit with rank and lofty vegetation, lies the skeleton of La Rioja, a lonely city with no suburbs, and withered away, as it were, like Jerusalem at the foot of the Mount of Olives. This sandy plain is bounded, far towards the south, by the Colorados, mountains of hardened clay, whose regular outlines take the most picturesque and fantastic forms ;

sometimes resembling a smooth wall with projecting bas-
tions; sometimes suggesting to the eye massive towers
and the battlements of ruined castles. Lastly, in the
southeast and surrounded by extensive wastes, lie the
Llanos, a broken and hilly region, in spite of its name,
forming an oasis of pasturage which formerly maintained thousands of flocks.

The general aspect of the country is desolate, its
climate torrid, its soil parched and destitute of running
streams. Reservoirs called *represas* are constructed by
the peasantry to collect rain-water for the supply of
their animals. I have always been disposed to think
that the general aspect of Palestine resembles that of
La Rioja, in the reddish or ochreous tints of the soil,
the dryness of some regions and their cisterns; also the
orange-trees, vines, and fig-trees bearing exquisite and
enormous fruits, which are raised along the course of
some turbid and confined Jordan. There is a strange
combination of mountain and plain, fruitfulness and
aridity, parched and bristling heights, and hills covered
with dark green forests as lofty as the cedars of Leba-
non.

What chiefly brings these reminiscences of the East
before my imagination is the truly patriarchal appearance of the country people of La Rioja. Thanks to
caprices of fashion, there is now nothing unusual in
seeing men with full beards, according to the immemorial practice of Eastern nations; but yet this fact would
not wholly prevent the surprise naturally occasioned
by the sight of a Spanish-speaking population among
whom full beards, frequently descending to the chest,
are, and always have been worn; a population of mel-

ancholy, silent, sedate, and crafty demeanor ; of Arabic
appearance, riding upon asses, and sometimes clothed
in goat-skins, like the hermit of En-gedi.   There are
places where the people live exclusively on wild honey
and the fruit of the carob-tree, as St. John did on lo-
custs in the desert.   The Llanista himself is alone un-
conscious of being the most unfortunate, wretched, and
barbarous of mortals, and thanks to this ignorance, he
lives contentedly and happily when hunger does not
trouble him.

I have already said that there are in Rioja some reddish mountains which bear at a distance a resemblance to towers and feudal castles in ruins ; and still
other mediæval characteristics are mingled with the
Oriental resemblances above referred to, for in Rioja
there has been a contest of a century between two
hostile families, whose enmity, rank, and celebrity find
an accurate parallel among the Ursini, Colonnas, and
Medici of Italian feuds.   The whole history of the
civilized inhabitants of La Rioja is that of the conten-
tions of the Ocampos and Dávilas.   These families,
alike ancient, rich, and noble, long strove with each
other for supremacy, and, even long before the Revolution of Independence, had divided the population
into parties like those of the Guelphs and Ghibellines.
A great number of the members of these two families
have distinguished themselves in arms, at the bar, and
in industrial pursuits ; for the Dávilas and the Ocampos
were ever attempting to surpass each other by every
method of acquiring power recognized by civilization.
The extinction of this hereditary animosity was often
an object of the policy of the patriots of Buenos Ayres.

The two families were induced by the logic of Lautaro to unite an Ocampo with a lady of the Dávila family in order to promote a reconciliation. All know that such was the Italian practice; but on this occasion the Romeo and Juliet were more fortunate. Towards 1817 the government of Buenos Ayres, also with the view of ending the hostility of these families, sent the province a governor from without, Barnachea by name, who fell ere long under the influence of the Dávila party, dependent upon the support of Don Prudencio Quiroga, a man much beloved by the inhabitants of the Llanos where he lived; he had been summoned to the city and appointed Treasurer and Alcalde. The rural districts were just beginning, although in a legitimate and noble manner, in Don Prudencio Quiroga, Facundo's father, to come into play as a political element among the civil parties. The Llanos I have stated, consist of a hilly oasis of pasture land in the midst of an extensive desert (*travesia*); their inhabitants, exclusively shepherds, lead that patriarchal and primitive life which its isolation preserves in all its purity and hostility to the cities. Hospitality is in that region a duty of general obligation. The laborer defends his master from all kinds of danger, even at the risk of his own life. These customs will of themselves furnish a partial explanation of the phenomena we are to witness.

After the event that occurred in his favor at San Luis, Facundo made his appearance on the Llanos invested with the prestige of his recent exploit, and fortified with a recommendation from the government. The parties dividing La Rioja were not slow to solicit the adhesion of a man regarded by all with the respect

and dread always felt for deeds of unusual dar
The Ocampos, who came into power in 1820, gave
the title of Sergeant Major of the Militia of the Llanos,
with the influence and authority of Commandant.

The beginning of his public career starts from this
moment. The pastoral and barbaric element of La
Rioja, the same with that third force which appears
with Artigas at the siege of Montevideo, is now to present itself at La Rioja with Quiroga, upon whom one
of the parties of the *city* had called for support. The
moment of such an action is a solemn and critical
one in the history of all the pastoral states of the
Argentine Republic; in each there comes a day when a
man of audacity is made country commandant either
because he is already dreaded, or because foreign aid
is needed. Such a man is a Grecian horse like that
which the Trojans made haste to bring into the city.

At this time occurred at San Juan the unfortunate
insurrection of the first regiment of the Andes, which
had returned from Chili for reorganization. Francisco
Aldao and Corro, foiled in the objects of the rebellion,
undertook a calamitous retreat towards the north to
join Güemes, a partisan chieftain of Salta. General
Ocampo, Governor of La Rioja, took measures to bar
their passage, and for that purpose called out all the
forces of the province and made ready for a battle.
Facundo was at hand with his Llanistas [men of the
plains]. The action began, and a few minutes were
enough to show that the First Regiment had, by rebellion, lost none of their ancient lustre on fields of battle.
Corro and Aldao moved upon the city, and their scattered antagonists betook themselves for reorganization

to the Llanos, where they could await the arrival of the troops from San Juan and Mendoza who were in pursuit of the fugitives. Facundo meanwhile, abandoning the point of reunion, fell upon the rear-guard of the victors, skirmishing with and harassing them, and killing or capturing their stragglers. Facundo was the only man endowed with a life of his own, waiting for no orders, wholly influenced by the motive power within himself. He had felt himself called to action, and waited for no impulse from without. Yet more; he spoke scornfully of the government and of the General, and declared his intention of overthrowing it and acting henceforward as his judgment might dictate. It is said that a council of the chief officers of the army urged upon General Ocampo his arrest, trial, and execution; but the General declined, perhaps less from moderation than from a feeling that Quiroga was now less a subordinate officer than a formidable ally.

A definite agreement between Aldao and the government decided that the former should return to San Luis, it not being his wish to follow Corro, and the government engaging to provide means for his passage through its territory by a route across the Llanos. Facundo was charged with the performance of this part of the stipulation, and returned with Aldao to the Llanos. Quiroga by this time was conscious of his power; and when he turned his back on La Rioja, he might have taken leave of it with the saying, " Woe to thee, O city! Verily I say unto thee that yet a little while, and there shall not be left of thee one stone upon another."

Aldao, upon his arrival at the Llanos, offered Quiroga, with whose discontent he had become acquainted, a hundred drilled soldiers, to enable him to make himself master of La Rioja, in exchange for his aid in future enterprises. Quiroga eagerly assented, set out for the city, took it, captured the officers of the government, sent them confessors, and orders to prepare themselves for death. What object had he in this revolution? None. Feeling himself powerful and stretching out his arms, he overthrew the city. Is it his fault?

Old Chilian patriots doubtless still remember the prowess of Sergeant Araya of the Mounted Grenadiers; for among those veterans the halo of glory frequently rested upon the common soldier. The priest Menéses has informed me that, after the rout of Cancha Rayada, Sergeant Araya and seven grenadiers went to Mendoza. It was heart-breaking to the patriots to see the bravest soldiers of their army passing and repassing the Andes while Las Heras still had forces at his command to face the Spaniards. The detention of Sergeant Araya was projected; but a difficulty presented itself. Who was to approach him? A detachment of seventy militia-men was at hand; but all the soldiers knew that the fugitive was Sergeant Araya, and they would have been a thousand times more ready to attack the Spaniards than this lion of the grenadiers.

Upon this, Don José Maria Menéses, alone and unarmed, followed and overtook Araya, and, intercepting him on his way, reminded him of his past glories and of the disgrace of an objectless flight. Araya was not deaf to this appeal, and yielded unresistingly to the entreaties and commands of the good neighbor. He then became enthusiastic, hastened to stop other squads of grenadiers who had preceded him in flight, and his diligence and reputation enabled him to join the army again with seventy comrades in arms, who cleared their laurels at Maipú of the momentary stain which had rested on them.

This Sergeant Araya and a man named Lorca, also known in Chili by his bravery, commanded the force placed by Aldao under Facundo's orders. The prisoners at La Rioja who were under sentence of death, among them Dr. Don Gabriel Ocampo, a former minister of government, entreated Lorca to protect them by his intercession. Facundo, feeling yet insecure in his momentary elevation, consented to grant their lives ; but this limit set to his power made him aware that he must have full control of this veteran force, in order to avoid future opposition.

Returning to the Llanos, he came to an understanding with Araya, and in pursuance of their agreement, they fell upon the rest of Aldao's force by surprise, and Facundo then found himself at the head of four hundred regulars, from whose ranks were afterwards drawn the officers of his first armies.

Remembering that Don Nicholas Dávila was in exile at Tucuman, he summoned him to take charge of the annoying details of the government of La Rioja, himself retaining the real supremacy, which followed him to the Llanos. The breach between him and men like the Ocampos and Dávilas was too wide, and the change from their government to his, too sudden, to be effected at a blow; the spirit of the city was still too powerful for that of the country to control openly ; a Doctor of Laws was still thought to make a better government official than any laborer. But all this was afterwards changed.

Dávila undertook the government under Facundo, and for the time all occasion for trouble seemed over. The possessions and estates of the Dávilas were situated near Chilecito, and there, consequently, in the kinsmen and friends of the family, was concentrated the physical and moral force likely to sustain the new governor. As the population of Chilecito increased with the profitable working of the mines, and as large fortunes had been amassed there, the government established a provincial bank in this small town, to which it transferred its residence, either to carry out the undertaking or to withdraw itself from the Llanos and the disagreeable subjection in which Quiroga was disposed to keep that region. Before long, Dávila proceeded from these purely defensive measures to more decided action. Availing himself of Facundo's temporary absence at San Juan, he laid plans with Captain Araya to have him arrested on his return. Facundo learned what awaited him, and, secretly entering the Llanos, had Araya assassinated. The government whose authority had been thus contemptuously defied, summoned him to answer to the charge of assassination. Ridiculous parody! But there was no other means of appealing to arms and of kindling civil war between the government and Quiroga, between the city and the Llanos. Facundo, in his turn, sent commissioners to the Representative Assembly, to request the deposition of Dávila. The Assembly had urgently called upon the governor to invade the Llanos and with the support of all the citizens, to disarm Quiroga. The members had a local interest in the matter, which was the transfer of the bank to the city of La Rioja; but as Dávila persisted in residing at Chilecito, the Assembly yielded to Facundo's solicitations and declared Dávila deposed.

Governor Dávila had assembled many of Aldao's soldiers under the command of Don Miguel Dávila. He had a good supply of military equipments, many adherents desirous of preserving the province from the rule of the chieftain who was strengthening himself in the Llanos, and also several regular officers to lead his troops. Preparations for war were begun, then, with equal zeal, in Chilecito and in the Llanos. Rumors of these unhappy events reached San Juan and Mendoza, the government of which sent a commission to attempt to make an arrangement between the belligerents, who, by that time, were on the point of actual conflict. Corbalan, the same now serving in Rosas' ordnance corps, visited Quiroga's camp to attempt the mediation for which he had been sent, and which the chieftain accepted; he next went to the opposing camp, where he met the same cordial reception; and finally returned to the camp of Quiroga to arrange the exact terms of agreement, but Quiroga, leaving him there, marched hastily against his enemy, whose forces he easily routed and dispersed, owing to the negligence into which the deluded envoy's assurances had caused them to fall. Don Miguel Dávila, collecting some of his men, resolutely attacked Quiroga, and succeeded in wounding him in one thigh before being himself disabled by a shot in the wrist; he was afterwards surrounded and killed by Quiroga's soldiers. A fact very characteristic of the gaucho spirit is connected with this incident. A soldier takes pleasure in showing his wounds; the gaucho hides such as he has re-

ceived in close combat, and avoids having their existence known, because they attest a want of skill on his
part. Facundo, faithful to these notions of honor, never
mentioned the wound which Dávila had given him.

Here ends the history of the Ocampos and Dávilas,
and with it that of La Rioja. What follows is the history of Quiroga.

That day of evil omen corresponds to April of 1835
in the history of Buenos Ayres—when its country commandant, its desert hero, made himself master of the city.

I ought not to omit, since it is to Quiroga's honor, a
curious fact which (1823) occurred at this time. The
feeblest gleam of light is not to be disregarded in the
blackness of that night.

Facundo, upon his triumphant entry into La Rioja,
stopped the ringing of the bells, and after sending a message of condolence to the widow of the slain General,
directed his ashes to be honored with a stately funeral.
He appointed for governor one Blanco, a Spaniard of
low rank, and with him began the new order of affairs
which was to realize the best ideal of government, as
conceived by Facundo Quiroga; for, in his long career
among the various cities which he conquered, he never
took upon himself the charge of organizing governments; he always left that task to others.

The moment of the grasp of power over the destinies
of a commonwealth by a vigorous hand is ever an important one and deserves attention. Old institutions
are strengthened, or give place to others, newer and
more productive of good results, or better adapted to
prevailing ideas. From such a focus often diverge the
threads which, as time weaves them together, change
the web of history.

It is otherwise when the prevailing force is one foreign to civilization, — when an Attila obtains possession
of Rome, or a Tamerlane traverses the plains of Asia ;
old forms remain, but the hand of philosophy would
afterwards vainly remove them with the view of finding beneath them plants which had gained vigor from
the human blood given them for nourishment.   Facundo, a man imbued with the genius of barbarism,
gets control of his country ; the traditions of government disappear, established forms deteriorate, the law
is a plaything in vile hands; and nothing is maintained,
nothing established, amid the destruction thus accomplished by the trampling feet of horses.   Freedom
from restraint, occupation, and care, is the supreme
good of the gaucho.   If La Rioja had contained statues,
as it contained doctors, they would have had horses tied
to them, but they would have served no other purpose.

Facundo wanted to have means at his command, and,
as he was incapable of creating a revenue system, he resorted to the ordinary proceeding of dull or weak governments ; but in this case the monopoly bears the stamp
of South American pastoral life, spoliation, and violence.
The tithes of La Rioja were, at this time farmed out at
ten thousand piastres a year ; this was the average rate.
Facundo made his appearance at the board, and his presence overawed the shepherds.   " I offer two thousand
piastres a year," said he, " and one more than the best
bid."   The committee repeated the proposal three
times ; no one made a bid ; all present left, one by one,
reading in Quiroga's sinister glance that it was the last
one he would allow.   The next year he contented himself with sending to the board the following note : —

" I give two thousand dollars and one more than the best bid.
" FACUNDO QUIROGA."

The third year the ceremony of adjudication was omitted, and in 1831, Quiroga again sent to La Rioja the sum of two thousand dollars, his estimate for the tithes.

But to make his tithes bring in a hundred for one, another step was required, and, after the second year, Facundo refused to receive the tribute of animals otherwise than by giving his mark among the proprietors, so that they might brand with it the animals set apart for the tithe and keep them on the place until he called for them. The creatures multiplied, their number was constantly augmented by new tithes, and, after ten years, it might be reckoned that half the stock of a whole pastoral province belonged to the commanding general of the forces, and bore his mark.

It was the immemorial custom in La Rioja that the *estrays*, or the animals that were not marked at a certain age, should become the lawful property of the treasury, which sent its agents to collect these gleanings, and derived no contemptible revenue from them, but the annoyance to the proprietors was intolerable. Facundo demanded the adjudication to himself of these animals, to meet the expenses he had incurred for the invasion of the city ; expenses which were reducible to the summons of irregular forces, who assembled, mounted on horses of their own, and lived constantly on what came in their way. Already the proprietor of herds which brought him six thousand bullocks a year, he sent his agents to supply the city markets, and woe to any competitor who should appear ! This business of supplying meat for the markets was one which he carried on wherever he ruled, in San Juan, Mendoza, or Tucuman; and he was always careful to secure the monopoly of it by proclamation or simple notification. It is with shame and disgust that I mention these disgraceful transactions, but the truth must be told.

The general's first order, after a bloody battle which had laid a city open to him, was that no one should supply the markets with meat! In Tucuman he learned that a resident of the place was killing cattle in his house, in spite of this order. The general of the army of the Andes, the conqueror of the Citadel, thought the investigation of so dreadful a crime should be entrusted only to himself. He went in person, and knocked lustily at the door of the house, which refused to yield, and which the inmates, taken by surprise, did not open. A kick from the illustrious general broke it in, and exposed to his view a dead ox, whose hide was in process of removal by the master of the house, who also fell dead in his turn at the terrible sight of the offended general![1]

[1] In consequence of the present law, the government of the province has obtained the assent of His Excellency General Don Juan Facundo Quiroga, to the following stipulations, agreeably to his note of September 14, 1833.

1. That he will make good to the Most Excellent Government of Buenos Ayres the sum invested by it in the said property.

2. That he will supply the province without incumbrance to the revenue, with five thousand pesos, to meet the difficulty of filling its contingent; three thousand pesos in cash and the remainder in the produce of live stock: for the payment of which only the members of the trade of butchering shall be responsible.

3. That he is to have the exclusive right of supplying the markets, selling to the public at the rate of five reals the arroba of meat, which now

I do not intentionally dwell upon these things. How many I omit! How many misdeeds I pass over in silence which are fully proved and known to all! But I am writing the history of government by barbarians, and I am forced to state its methods.

Mehemet Ali, who became master of Egypt by means identical with those of Facundo, delivers himself up to a rapacity unexampled even in Turkey; he establishes monopolies in every occupation and turns them to his own profit; but Mehemet Ali, though he springs from a barbarous nation, rises above his condition so far as to wish to acquire European civilization for himself and for the people he oppresses. Facundo, on the contrary, not only rejects all recognized civilization, but destroys and disorganizes. Facundo, who does not govern, because any government implies labor for others' good, gives himself up to the instincts of an immoderate and unscrupulous avarice. Selfishness is the foundation of almost all the great characters of history; selfishness is the chief spring of all great deeds. Quiroga had this political gift in an eminent degree and made everything around him contribute to his advantage; wealth, power, authority, all centred in him; whatever he could not acquire, — polish, learning, true respectability, — he hated and persecuted in all those who possessed them.

costs six, and is of bad quality; and to the state at three reals without raising the current price of the article.

4. That his cattle are to be slaughtered gratis, from the 18th of the present month to the 10th of January inclusive, and to have pasture at the public expense for two reals a month for every head he shall provide from the 1st of October next.   RUIZ.—VICENTO ATIENZO.

Official Register of the Province of San Juan.

SAN JUAN, *September* 13, 1833.

His hostility to the respectable classes and to the refinement of the cities was every day more perceptible, and the governor of La Rioja, whom he had himself appointed, finally was forced, by daily annoyances, to resign his place. One day, Quiroga, feeling inclined to pleasantry, was amusing himself with a young man as a cat sports with a frightened mouse; he liked to play at killing; the terror of the victim was so ludicrous, that the executioner was highly diverted, and laughed immoderately, contrary to his habit. He must have sympathy in his mirth, and he at once ordered the *general*[1] to be beat throughout the city of Rioja, which called out the citizens under arms. Facundo, who had given the summons for diversion's sake, drew up the inhabitants in the principal square at eleven o'clock at night, dismissed the populace and retained only the well-to-do householders and the young men who still had some appearance of culture. All night he kept them marching and countermarching, halting, forming line, marching by front or by flank. It was like a drill-sergeant teaching recruits, and the sergeant's stick travelled over the heads of the stupid, and the chests of those who were out of line; "What would you have? this is the way to teach!" Morning came, and the pallor, weariness, and exhaustion of the recruits showed what a night they had passed. Their instructor finally sent them to rest, and extended his generosity to the purchase and distribution of pastry, each recipient made in haste to eat his share, for that was part of the sport.

Lessons of such a kind are not lost upon cities, and

---

[1] A certain call to arms.

the skillful politician who has raised similar proceedings to a system in Buenos Ayres, has refined upon them and made them wonderfully effective. For example : during the periods between 1835 and 1840 almost the whole population of Buenos Ayres has passed through the prisons. Sometimes a hundred and fifty citizens would be imprisoned for two or three months, to be then replaced by two hundred who would be kept, perhaps half the year. Wherefore ? What had they done ? What had they said ? Idiots ! Do you not see that this is good discipline for the city ? Do you not remember the saying of Rosas to Quiroga, that no republic could be established because the people were not prepared for it ! This is his way of teaching the city how to obey ; he will finish his work, and in 1844, he will be able to show the world a people with but one thought, one opinion, one voice, and that a boundless enthusiasm for the person and will of Rosas ! Then, indeed, they will be ready for a republic !

But we will return to La Rioja. A feverish excitement on the subject of investments in the mines of the new States of Spanish America had arisen in England ; powerful companies were proposing to draw profit from those of Mexico and Peru ; and Rivadavia, who was then residing in London, urged speculators to invest their capital in the Argentine Republic. The mines of Famatina offered an opening for a great enterprise. At the same time, speculators from Buenos Ayres obtained the exclusive right to work these mines, meaning to sell it for an enormous sum to the English companies. These two speculations, one started in England and the other in Buenos Ayres, conflicted with each other, and were irreconcilable. Finally, a bargain was made with another English house, which was to supply funds, and in fact, sent out English superintendents and miners. Later, a speculation was got up to establish a bank at La Rioja, which was to be sold at a high price to the national government when it should be organized. On being solicited, Facundo took a large number of shares, making payment with the Jesuits' College, which had been assigned to him, on his demand, in payment of his salary as general. A party of Buenos Ayres stockholders came to La Rioja to carry out the project, and soon asked to be presented to Quiroga, whose name had begun to exercise everywhere a mysterious and terrific power. Facundo received them in his lodgings, in very fine silk stockings, ill-made pantaloons, and a common linen poncho.

The grotesque appearance of this figure was not provocative of any smiles from the elegant citizens of Buenos Ayres. They were too sagacious not to read the riddle. The man before them meant to humiliate his polished guests, and show them what account he made of their European dresses.

The administrative system established in his province was finally completed by exorbitant duties on the exportation of cattle which did not belong to him. But in addition to these direct methods of acquiring wealth, he had one which embraced his whole public career, — gambling! He had a rage for play as some men have for strong drink, and others for tobacco. His mind, though a powerful one, had not the capacity of embracing a large sphere of ideas, and stood in need of this factitious occupation, in which a passion of the soul is

in constant exercise, as it is crossed, appeased, provoked, excited, and kept upon the rack. I have always
thought that the passion for gambling was some useful
faculty that organized society has perverted or left in
inaction. The will, self-control, and steadfastness which
it requires, are the same which advance the fortunes of
the enterprising merchant, the banker, and the conqueror who plays for empires with battles. Facundo
had habitually gambled since his childhood ; play had
been the only pleasure, the only relaxation of his life.
But what an agreeable partner he must be who controls the terrors and the lives of the whole party ! No
one can conceive such a state of things without having
had it before his eyes for twenty years. Facundo
played unfairly, say his enemies. I do not believe the
charge, for cheating at play was unnecessary in his
case, and he had been known to pursue to the death,
others who were guilty of it. But he played with unlimited means ; he never let any one carry from the
table the money he used for stakes ; the game could
not be stopped till he chose ; he would play forty hours
or more at a time ; he feared no one, and if his fellow
gamblers annoyed him, he could have them whipped
or shot at pleasure. This was the secret of his good
luck. Few men ever won much money from him, although, at some periods of the game, heaps of coin
lost by him lay upon the table ; the game would go on,
for the winner did not dare to rise, and in the end he
would have nothing but the glory of reckoning that his
winnings, afterwards lost, had once been so large.

Gambling, then, was to Quiroga a system of plunder
as well as a favorite amusement. No one in La Rioja

received money from him, no one possessed any, without being at once invited to a game, or, in other words, to leave his funds in the chieftain's hands. Most of the tradesmen of La Rioja failed and vanished, their money having taken up its quarters in the general's purse; and it was not for want of lessons in prudence from him. A young man had won four thousand dollars from Facundo, and Facundo declined to play longer. His opponent thought that a snare was in readiness for him, and that his life was in danger. Facundo repeated that he had finished playing; the stupid fellow insisted on another game, and Facundo, complying with the demand, won the four thousand dollars from the other, who then received two hundred lashes for his uncivil pertinacity.

I am weary of reading the accounts of infamous acts in which all the manuscripts I am consulting agree. I suppress them out of respect to my vanity as an author, and to the literary pretensions of my work. By saying more I should make my pictures appear too highly colored, coarse, and repulsive.

This terminates one period of the life of the country commandant after he had abolished and suppressed the city. Hitherto Facundo was what Rosas was in his own domain, although not so far degraded before reaching power, either by gambling or by the brutal gratification of various passions. But he is to enter upon a new sphere, and we are soon to follow him over the whole Republic and seek him on battle fields.

What consequences to La Rioja were occasioned by the destruction of all civil order? Reasonings and discussions are here out of place. A visit to the scene

of these occurrences will be sufficient to answer the
query.   The Llanos of La Rioja are now deserted;
their population has emigrated to San Juan; the cisterns are dry which once gave drink to thousands of
flocks.   Those Llanos which fed those flocks twenty
years ago, are now the home of the tiger who has re-
conquered his former empire, and of a few families of
beggars who live upon the fruit of the carob-tree. This
is the retribution the Llanos have suffered for the evils
which they let loose upon the Republic. " Woe to ye,
Bethsaida and Chorazin !   Verily I say unto you, that
the lot of Sodom and Gomorrah was more tolerable
than that which was reserved for you ! "

CHAPTER VII.

SOCIAL LIFE.

" Society in the Middle Ages was composed of the wrecks of a thousand other
societies. All the forms of liberty and servitude were found in it; the monarchical
liberty of the king, the individual liberty of the priest, the privileged liberty of kings,
the representative liberty of the nation, Roman slavery, barbarian serfage, and the
servitude of escheatage (aubane)." — *Chateaubriand.*

FACUNDO is now in possession of La Rioja, its um-
pire and absolute master; no other voice is heard
there, no other interest than his exists there. As there
is no literature, there are no opposing opinions. La
Rioja is a military machine which will move as it is
moved. Thus far, however, Facundo has done nothing new; Dr. Francia, Ibarra, Lopez, and Bustos, had
done the same; and Güemes and Araos had attempted
it in the North; that is, to destroy all existing rights
for the purpose of strengthening their own. But beyond La Rioja lay an agitated world of ideas and of
contradictory interests, whence came to Quiroga's residence in the Llanos the distant sounds of the contro-
versies of the press and of political parties. Again
his rise to power was necessarily attended by the spread
of the clamor resulting from his overthrow of the edifice of civilization, and by his becoming an object of
attention to the neighboring commonwealths. His
name had passed the frontiers of La Rioja; Rivadavia
was inviting him to assist in the organization of the
Republic; Bustos and Lopez wished him to oppose it;

the government of San Juan complacently reckoned him among its friends, and strangers came to the Llanos to pay him their respects and to ask support in behalf of one party or another.

At that time the Argentine Republic presented an animated and interesting picture. All interests, all ideas, all passions, met together to create agitation and tumult. Here, was a chief who would have nought to do with the rest of the Republic; there, a community whose only desire was to emerge from its isolation; yonder, a government engaged in bringing Europe over to America; elsewhere, another to which the very name of civilization was odious; the Holy Tribunal of the Inquisition was reviving in some places; in others, liberty of conscience was proclaimed the first of human rights; the cry of one party was for confederation; of others for a central government; while each different combination was backed by strong and unconquerable passions. I must clear up the chaos a little, to show the rôle which it fell to Quiroga to enact, and the great work he was to bring to pass. In order to depict the provincial commandant who took possession of the city and annulled its constitution, I have found it necessary to describe the face of nature in the Argentine Republic, with the habits induced and the forms of character developed by it. And to describe Quiroga extending his power beyond his own province and proclaiming a principle, an idea, and carrying it everywhere at the point of the bayonet, I must likewise sketch the geographical distributions of the ideas and interests which were agitated in the cities. With this object, it is requisite for me to examine two cities under the sway of opposite ideas. These cities are Cordova and Buenos Ayres, as they existed in 1825, and previously.

CORDOVA.

Cordova, though somewhat in the grave old Spanish style, is the most charming city in South America in its first aspect. It is situated in a hollow formed in an elevated region called the Altos. So closely are its symmetrical buildings crowded together for want of space, that it may be said to be folded back upon itself. The sky is remarkably clear, the winter season dry and bracing, the summers hot and stormy. Towards the east it has a promenade of singular beauty, the capricious outlines of which strike the eye with magical effect. It consists of a square pond surrounded by a very broad walk, shaded by ancient willow-trees of colossal size. Each side is of the length of a *cuadra*,[1] and the inclosure is of wrought iron grating, with enormous doors in the centre of each of the four sides, so that the promenade is an enchanted prison, within which its inmates circulate around a beautiful temple of Greek architecture. In the chief square stands the magnificent cathedral, of Gothic construction, with its immense dome carved in arabesques, the only model of mediæval architecture, so far as I know, existing in South America. Another square is occupied by the church and convent of the Society of Jesus, in the presbytery of which is a trap-door communicating with excavations which extend to some distance below the

[1] Eighty-five yards in Montevideo, one hundred and twenty-seven in Buenos Ayres.

city, which are at present but imperfectly explored ;
dungeons have also been discovered where the Society
buried its criminals alive. If any one wishes to become acquainted with monuments of the Middle Ages,
and to examine into the power and the constitution of
that celebrated religious order above referred to, Cordova is the place where one of its greatest central
establishments was situated.

In every square of that compact city stands a superb
convent, a monastery, or a house for unprofessional
nuns, or for the performance of specific religious exercises. In former times every family included a priest,
a monk, a nun, or a chorister ; the poorer classes con-
tenting themselves with having among them a hermit,
a lay brother, a sacristan, or an acolyte.

Each convent or monastery possessed a set of ad-
joining out-buildings, where lived and multiplied eight
hundred slaves of the Order, negroes, zamboes, mulattoes, and quadroons, with blue eyes, fair and waving
hair, limbs as polished as marble, genuine Circassians
adorned with every grace, but showing their African
origin by their teeth, serving for bait to the passions
of man, all for the greater honor and profit of the convent to which these houris belonged.[1]

Here is also the celebrated University of Cordova,
founded as long ago as the year 1613, and in whose
gloomy cloisters eight generations of medicine and
divinity, both branches of law, illustrious writers,
commentators, and scholars have passed their youth.
Let us hear the description given by the celebrated
Dean Funes of the course of instruction and the spirit

[1] A similar order of things exists to this day in the city of Havana.

of this famous university, which has for two centuries
provided a great part of South America with theologians
and doctors. " The course of theology lasted for five
years and a half. Theology had come to share in the
corruption of philosophy. The Aristotelian philosophy
applied to theology had resulted in a mixture of the
profane with the spiritual. Mere human reasonings,
deceptive subtleties and sophisms, frivolous and mis-
placed inquiries—such were the conditions under which
the ruling taste of these schools had been formed."
If you would look a little deeper into the spirit of liberty likely to be the result of such teaching, listen a
little longer to Dean Funes : " This university was
originated and established wholly by Jesuits, who
founded it in their college of the city of Cordova,
called Maximo." Very distinguished advocates have
proceeded from this institution, but no man of letters
who has not also been educated at Buenos Ayres with
modern books.

This learned city has never yet had a public theatre,
nor become acquainted with the opera. It is still without journals, and typography is a branch of industry
which has failed to take root in it. The spirit of Cordova up to 1829 was monastic and scholastic ; the conversation of its society always turned on processions,
the saints' days, university examinations, taking the
vail, and reception of the doctor's " tassels."

How far these circumstances tended to influence the
temper of a population occupied with such ideas for
two centuries, cannot be determined ; but some influence they must have had, as is plain at a glance. The
inhabitant of Cordova does not look beyond his own

horizon; that horizon is four blocks distant from his own. When he takes his afternoon stroll, instead of going and returning through a spacious avenue of poplars as long as the Paseo of Santiago, which expands and animates the mind, he follows an artificial lake of motionless and lifeless water, in the centre of which stands a structure of magnificent proportions, immovable and stationary. The city is a cloister surrounded by ravines; the promenade is a cloister with iron grates; every square of houses has a cloister of nuns or friars; the colleges are cloisters; the jurisprudence taught there, the theology, all the mediæval scholastic learning of the place, is a mental cloister within which the intellect is walled up and fortified against every departure from text and commentary. Cordova knows not that aught besides Cordova exists on earth; it has, indeed, heard that there is such a place as Buenos Ayres, but if it believes this, which it does not always, it asks: "Has it a university? but it must be an affair of yesterday. How many convents has it? Has it such a promenade as this? If not, it amounts to nothing."

"Whose work on jurisprudence do you study?" inquired the grave Doctor Gijena, of a young man from Buenos Ayres.

"Bentham's."

"Whose, sir, do you say? Little Bentham's?"[1] indicating with his finger the size of the duodecimo in which Bentham's work is published. . . . "That wretched little Bentham's! There is more sense in one of my writings than in all those wind-bags. What a university, and what contemptible doctors!"

[1] Benthancito, the termination expressing derision.

" And you," said the other, " whose book do you
study ? What ! "

" Cardinal Lucques."

" What say you, sir ? seventeen folio volumes ? "

It is a fact that as a traveller approaches Cordova,
he looks along the horizon without discovering the
sanctimonious and mysterious city, the city which
wears the doctor's cap and tassels. At last his guide
says, " Look there, it is down there among the bushes."
And in reality, as he fixes his gaze upon the ground
at a short distance in advance, there appear one, two,
three, ten crosses, followed by domes and towers, belonging to the many churches which adorn this Pompeii of mediæval Spain.

To conclude, the mechanics shared the spirit of the
upper classes : a master-shoemaker put on the airs of
a doctor in shoemaking, and would level a Latin apho-
rism at a man as he gravely took his measure ; the *ergo*
of the scholar might be heard in the kitchens, and
every dispute between a couple of porters took the
sound and shape of philosophical demonstrations. We
may add, that throughout the revolution, Cordova was
the asylum of all fugitive Spaniards. What impression
would the revolution of 1810 be likely to make upon a
population educated by Jesuits, and secluded thus by
nature, by teaching, and by art ?

Had revolutionary ideas, such as are found in Rousseau, Mably, and Voltaire, happened to spread over the
pampas and descend into this Spanish catacomb, — if
we may so speak, — what response would they have
been likely to find from those brains disciplined by the
Aristotelian system to reject all new ideas, those

intellects which, like their own promenade, had an immovable idea in their centre, unapproachable through a stagnant lake ?

Toward 1816 the illustrious and liberal Dean Funes succeeded in introducing into the ancient university of the city the studies previously so much contemned : mathematics, living languages, public law, physics, drawing, and music. From that time the youth of Cordova began to direct their ideas into new channels which, ere long, led them to consequences of which we will speak hereafter. At present, I am describing the old traditional spirit of the place, which was the dominant one.

The Revolution of 1810 found the ears of Cordova closed to it at the very time when all the provinces were at once responding to the cry of "To arms! Liberty!" It was in Cordova that Liniers began to raise armies to put down the revolution in Buenos Ayres. It was to Cordova that the Junta sent one of its members and its troops to decapitate Spain. It was Cordova, which, offended by this outrage, and looking for vengeance and reparation, wrote, with the learned hand of the University, and in the idiom of the breviary and the commentators, that celebrated acrostic [1] which pointed out to those who passed the spot the tomb of the first royalists who were sacrificed upon the altars of the state.

In 1820, a force stationed in Arequete revolted, and General Bustos, its leader, abandoning the banners of

[1] Concha. Liniers. Allende. Moreno. Orellana. Rodriguez.

his country, established himself quietly at Cordova, which congratulated itself for having thus robbed the nation of one of its armies. Bustos created an irresponsible colonial government, introduced court etiquette and the perennial torpor of Spain, and thus prepared, Cordova entered upon the year 1828, when the question before the country was the organization of the Republic and the establishment of the revolutionary system with all its consequences.[1]

[1] On going over the pages of this first historical essay, the author regrets certain defects which cannot be expunged without recasting the whole work, for it would thus be impossible to preserve the thread of the ideas. The heat of the early years of exile, the impossibility of verifying details in such circumstances, and the prejudices of party feeling, have left some indelible traces. The description of Cordova is stained with this capital vice, and the author would willingly expunge it, if it did not contain a certain malicious exaggeration which make striking the contrast of the modern spirit which characterized Buenos Ayres in 1825.

But the author owes to the friendly frankness of Dr. Alsina, corrections upon this and several other points, which as a point of honor as well as an excuse, he submits to the examination of the reader, thus making every possible reparation for error without destroying the spirit of the original text.

" I seem to see," he says in these notes, " a capital defect in this book, that of exaggeration, independent of a certain vivacity, if not in the ideas, in their allocution. If you do not propose to write a romance or an epic, but a veritable history, political, social, and military, your rule must be not to depart from rigid historical exactness, and exaggeration is inconsistent with this. You show a *penchant* for systems, and in social science, systems do not constitute the best means of arriving at the truth. When the mind is occupied with a previous idea, and proposes to make that triumph in its demonstration of it, it exposes itself to original errors without being aware of it. Then instead of proceeding analytically, instead of examining each fact in itself, to see what can be deduced from it, and from these collected deductions and observations, to bring out a general deduction or result, instead of proceeding thus, a writer uses synthesis, that is to say, he poses a certain leading idea, reviews whatever facts present themselves, not to examine them philosophically and in detail, but to make them prove his favorite idea, and to construct by their means the edifice of his system. The natural result of this is, that when he meets with a fact which supports his idea, he exaggerates and amplifies it, and when he finds another

BUENOS AYRES.

Let us now turn our attention to Buenos Ayres. Its first struggle was with the aborigines by whom it was

which does not square well with his system, or which contradicts it, he presents only one aspect of it, disfigures it, or interprets it in his own way; hence forced analogies and applications, inexact or partial judgments of men or events, and the generalizations with which a writer deduces a rule or a doctrine from an individual, and often accidental fact, perhaps insignificant in itself. All this is a necessity of systems. It is necessary to sacrifice a great deal to them. You propose to show the *active* struggle between civilization and barbarism, a struggle where germs began to move toward development long years ago, and which during years blindly excited the struggle between country and city, in which by a necessary law and almost by fatality, the latter triumphed, and ought to have triumphed. I think there may be truth at the bottom of this idea, although it has not any in my humble opinion.

" You treat with undeserved harshness that poor city of Cordova. You do not cite facts that justify your general assertion, made so strongly and severely. To recall the crime of Bustos in 1820 would be inopportune, that crime proves something else, but not that. That Leniers and other distinguished men, almost all Spaniards, acted like Spaniards in 1810, is not astonishing, and their rencontre at Cordova should not be imputed to a love of royalty in the people any more than the appearance of that kind of acrostic which you copy, and which might have been the work of an individual, should be imputed to the same thing. These proofs go out of the limits of the circumspection of history to justify an accusation so positive and so general. There were families of the Spanish party there as in all the provinces, without excluding that of Buenos Ayres, and this was natural. After it was delivered from Liniers and his associates, what fact reveals the opposition or dissent of Cordova to the revolution? What does Cordova do less than any other of the provinces where the Spanish armies did not go? What more have the others done than Cordova? It received with decision the first patriotic army, and contributed what it could to it. From 1810 it furnished many soldiers; from 1810 it furnished many men and young men who became excellent officers; it gave Valey, who died gloriously at Desaguadero; also Leevá, Bustos, Julian, and José Maria Paz, J. G. Echevarria, who died for liberty in 1831, as you say further on; it gave my client Colonel Rojas, who made his *debut* at Dehesa, and others whose names I do not now remember. Cordova sent its deputies to the first Junta, and has since sent them to all the national bodies. In what other way would you have a province take part in the revolution? In what manner *have* others taken part in it?

" ALSINA."

swept from the face of the earth. It recovered itself
more than once, until in 1620 it figured in the Spanish
dominions sufficiently to be erected into a district
governed by a Captain-general, and to be separated
from Paraguay, under whose government it had previously existed. In 1777, Buenos Ayres had already
become very conspicuous, so much so, indeed, that it
was necessary to remould the administrative geography of the colonies, and to make Buenos Ayres the
chief section. A viceroyal government was expressly created for it.

In 1806, the attention of English speculators was
turned to South America, and especially attracted to
Buenos Ayres by its river, and its probable future. In
1810, Buenos Ayres was filled with partisans of the
revolution, bitterly hostile to anything originating in
Spain or any part of Europe. A germ of progress, then,
was still alive west of the La Plata. The Spanish colonies cared nothing for commerce or navigation. The
Rio de la Plata was of small importance to them. The
Spanish disdained it and its banks. As time went on,
the river proved to have deposited its sediment of wealth
upon those banks, but very little of Spanish spirit or
Spanish modes of government. Commercial activity
had brought thither the spirit and the general ideas of
Europe ; the vessels which frequented the waters of the
port brought books from all quarters, and news of all
the political events of the world. It is to be observed
that Spain had no other commercial city upon the
Atlantic coast. The war with England hastened the
emancipation of men's minds and awakened among them
a sense of their own importance as a state. Buenos

Ayres was like a child, which, having conquered a giant, fondly deems itself a hero, and is ready to undertake greater adventures. The *Social Contract* flew from hand to hand. Mably and Raynal were the oracles of the press; Robespierre and the Convention the approved models. Buenos Ayres thought itself a continuation of Europe, and if it did not frankly confess that its spirit and tendencies were French and North American, it denied its Spanish origin on the ground that the Spanish Government had patronized it only after it was full grown. The revolution brought with it armies and glory, triumphs and reverses, revolts and seditions. But Buenos Ayres, amidst all these fluctuations, displayed the revolutionary energy with which it is endowed. Bolivar was everything; Venezuela was but the pedestal for that colossal figure. Buenos Ayres was a whole city of revolutionists — Belgrano, Rondeau, San Martin, Alvear; and the hundred generals in command of its armies were its instruments; its arms, not its head nor its trunk. It cannot be said in the Argentine Republic that such a general was the liberator of the country; but only that the Assembly, Directory, Congress, or government of such or such a period, sent a given general to do this thing or that. Communication with all the European nations was ever, even from the outset, more complete here than in any other part of Spanish America; and now, in ten years' time (but only, be it understood, in Buenos Ayres), there comes to pass a radical replacement of the Spanish by the European spirit. We have only to take a list of the residents in and about Buenos Ayres to see how many natives of the country bear English, French, German, or Italian

surnames. The organization of society, in accordance
with the new ideas with which it was impregnated,
began in 1820 ; and the movement continued until
Rivadavia was placed at the head of the government.
Hitherto Rodriguez and Las Heras had been laying
the usual foundations of free governments. Amnesty
laws, individual security, respect for property, the responsibility of civil authority, equilibrium of powers,
public education, everything, in fine, was in peaceful
course of establishment when Rivadavia came from
Europe, brought Europe as it were, but Europe was
yet undervalued. Buenos Ayres — and that means, of
course, the Argentine Republic — was to realize what
republican France could not realize, what the English
aristocracy did not even wish for, what despotic Europe
wanted still less. This was not an illusion of Rivadavia's ; it was the general thought of the city, its
spirit, and its tendency.

Parties were divided, not by ideas essentially opposed
to each other, but by the greater or less extent of their
aims. And how else could it have been with a people
which in only fourteen years had given England a
lesson, overrun half the continent, equipped ten armies,
fought a hundred pitched battles, been everywhere
victorious, taken part in all events, set at nought all
traditions, tested all theories, ventured upon everything
and succeeded in everything ; which was still vigorous,
growing rich, progressing in civilization ? What was
to ensue, when the basis of government, the political
creeds received from Europe, were vitiated by errors,
absurd and deceptive theories, and unsound principles ?
for the native politicians who were as yet without any

definite knowledge of political organization, could not be expected to know more than the great men of Europe. I desire to call attention to the significance of this fact. The study of constitutions, races, and creeds, in short, history, has now diffused a certain amount of practical knowledge which warns us against the glitter of theories based upon *a priori* conceptions ; but previous to 1820, nothing of that had transpired in the European world. France was roused into insurrection by the paradoxes of the Social Contract; Buenos Ayres was similarly roused ; Montesquieu designated three powers, and immediately we had three ; Benjamin Constant and Bentham annulled power ; here they declared it originally null; Say and Smith preached free-trade ; " commercial liberty," we repeated ; Buenos Ayres confessed and believed all that the learned world of Europe believed and confessed. Not till after the revolution of 1830 in France, and its incomplete results, did the Social Sciences take a new direction and illusions begin to be dispelled. From that time European books began to come to us, which demonstrated that Voltaire had not much reason, and that Rousseau was a sophist, and Mably and Raynal anarchists ; that there were no three powers, nor any Social Contract, etc. From that time we learned something of races, of tendencies, of national habits, of historical antecedents. Tocqueville revealed to us for the first time the secret of North America ; Sismondi laid bare the emptiness of constitutions; Thierry, Michelet, and Guizot, gave us the spirit of history; the revolution of 1830, all the hollowness of the constitutionalism of Benjamin Constant ; the Spanish revolution, all that

is incomplete and behindhand in our own race. Of
what then were Rivadavia and Buenos Ayres accused?
Of not knowing more than the European savans who
were their guides? On the other side, how was it
possible not to embrace with ardor the general ideas of
a people who had contributed so much and so well to
make the revolution general? How bridle the imaginations of the inhabitants of an illimitable plain bordered
by a river whose opposite bank could not be seen — a
step from Europe, not knowing even its own traditions,
indeed without having them in reality; a new, suddenly improvised people, which from the very cradle
had heard itself called great?

Thus elevated, and hitherto flattered by fortune,
Buenos Ayres set about making a constitution for
itself and the Republic, just as it had undertaken to
liberate itself and all South America: that is, eagerly,
uncompromisingly, and without regard to obstacles.
Rivadavia was the personification of this poetical, uto-
pian spirit which prevailed. He therefore continued
the work of Las Heras upon the large scale necessary
for a great American State — a republic. He brought
over from Europe men of learning for the press and for
the professor's chair, colonies for the deserts, ships for
the rivers, freedom for all creeds, credit and the national bank to encourage trade, and all the great social
theories of the day for the formation of his government.
In a word, he brought a second Europe, which was to
be established in America, and to accomplish in ten
years what elsewhere had required centuries. Nor was
this project altogether chimerical; all his administrative
creations still exist, except those which the barbarism of

Rosas found in its way. Freedom of conscience, advocated by the chief clergy of Buenos Ayres, has not been repressed; the European population is scattered on farms throughout the country, and takes arms of its own accord to resist the only obstacle in the way of the wealth offered by the soil. The rivers only need to be freed from governmental restrictions to become navigable, and the national bank, then firmly established, has saved the people from the poverty to which the tyrant would have brought them. And, above all, however fanciful and impracticable that great system of government may have been, it was at least easy and endurable for the people; and, notwithstanding the assertions of misinformed men, Rivadavia never shed a drop of blood, nor destroyed the property of any one; but voluntarily descended from the Presidency to poverty and exile. Rosas, by whom he was so calumniated, might easily have been drowned in the blood of his own victims; and the forty millions of dollars from the national treasury, with the fifty millions from private fortunes which were consumed in ten years of the long war provoked by his brutalities, would have been employed by the "*fool* — the *dreamer* — Rivadavia," in building canals, cities, and useful public buildings. Then let this man, who died for his country, have the glory of representing the highest aspirations of European civilization, and leave to his adversaries that of displaying South American barbarism in its most odious light. For Rosas and Rivadavia are the two extremes of the Argentine Republic, connecting it with savages through the pampas, and with Europe through the River La Plata.

I am not making the eulogy, but the apotheosis of
Rivadavia and his party, which has ceased to exist as
a political element of the Argentine Republic, though
Rosas persists in calling his present enemies " *Unitarios*." The old union party, like that of the Giron-
dists, disbanded many years ago ; but with all its im-
possibilities and fanciful illusions it had much that was
noble and great to which the succeeding generation
should do justice. Many of those men are still among
us, though no longer as an organized party ; they are
the remains of the Argentine Republic, as noble and
as venerable as those of Napoleon's empire. These
Unitarios of the year 1825 form a distinct class of
men, recognized by their manners, tone of voice, and
opinions. A Unitario would be known among a thousand by his stately bearing, his somewhat haughty
manner of speaking, and his positive gestures ; on the
eve of a battle he will pause to discuss a question logi-
cally, or to establish some new legal formality ; for
legal formulas are the outward worship which he offers
to his idols — the Constitution and individual rights.
His religion is the future of the Republic, whose image,
sublime and colossal, is ever before him, covered with
the mantle of its past glory. Never was there a generation so enterprising, so gifted with reasoning and de-
ductive powers, and so wanting in practical common
sense. A Unitario will not believe in the evident
success of his enemies. He has such faith in the greatness of his cause, that neither exile, nor poverty, nor
lapse of years can weaken his enthusiasm ; and in
calmness of mind and in energy of soul he is infinitely
superior to the present generation. These men also

excel us in ceremonious politeness and refinement of manner; for conventionalities are more and more disregarded among us as democracy progresses, and it is now difficult to realize the culture and refinement of society in Buenos Ayres before 1828. Europeans who went there found themselves, as it were, still in Europe, in the saloons of Paris; nothing was wanting, not even the insolence of the Parisian *élegant*, which was well imitated by the same class of young men in Buenos Ayres.

I have been particular in mentioning these little things in order to give an idea of the period when the Republic was in the process of formation, and of its different elements struggling for precedence. On one side Cordova, Spanish in education, in literature, and in religion, conservative and strongly opposed to all innovations; and on the other, Buenos Ayres, revolutionary by nature, ready for any change and progress.

These were the types of the two parties that divided every city; and I doubt if there is another such phenomenon in America; that is, two parties, conservative and revolutionary, retrograde and progressive, each represented by a city having its own peculiar form of civilization, and receiving opinions from entirely different sources: Cordova, from Spain, the Councils, the Commentators, the Digest; Buenos Ayres, from Bentham, Rousseau, Montesquieu, and French literature in general.

To these elements of antagonism must be added another not less important, namely, the want of any national bond after the provinces became independent of Spain. When government authority is removed from one centre to another, time is necessary for its firm establishment.

The " Republican " recently declared that " government is no more than a compact between the governors and the governed." Evidently there are still many Unitarios among us ! *Government is in reality founded upon the unpremeditated consent which a nation gives to a permanent fact.* Where there is deliberation, there is no authority. This transition state is called a confederation. Out of each revolution and consequent change of government, different nations derive their ideas and modes of confederation.

I will explain myself. When Ferdinand VII. was driven from Spain, government — *that permanent fact* — ceased to exist ; and Spain was formed into provincial assemblies which denied the authority of those who governed in the name of the king. This was the *Spanish Confederation.* When the news reached America, the South American provinces revolted from Spain, and being divided into sections, formed the *South American Confederation.* From Buenos Ayres came at the end of the contest, four states, — Bolivia, Paraguay, Banda Oriental, and the Argentine Republic ; these formed the *Confederation of the Viceroyalty.* Finally, the Argentine Republic was divided, not as formerly into districts, but according to its cities, and so became a *confederation of cities.*

It is not that the word confederation signifies separation, but that when separation has already taken place, it expresses the union of the different parts. The Argentine Republic was at this crisis social, and many persons of note in the cities believed that, for mere convenience, or whenever an individual or a community felt no respect for the nominal government, a new confederation might be formed. Here then was another apple of discord in the Republic, and the two parties, after having been called " Royalists " and " Patriots," " Congresistas " and " Executivistas," " Conservatives," and " Liberals," now bore the names of " Federales " and " Unitarios." [1] Perhaps, to finish the list, I should give the name bestowed upon the latter party by Don Juan Manuel Rosas, that is, " *salvajes inmundos Unitarios.*"

But the Argentine Republic is so situated geographically, that it is destined to a consolidation, whatever Rosas may say to the contrary. Its continuous plain, its rivers confined to one outlet, and therefore to one port, force it inevitably to be " *one and indivisible.*" Rivadavia, who well understood the necessities of the country, advised the provinces to unite under a common constitution, and to make a national port of Buenos Ayres. Aguero, his supporter in Congress, said to the citizens of Buenos Ayres, " Let us voluntarily give to the provinces what, sooner or later, they will claim by force." The prophecy failed in one respect; the provinces did not claim the port of Buenos Ayres by force of arms, but by force of the barbarism which they sent upon her in Facundo and Rosas. Buenos Ayres feels all the effects of the barbarism, while the port has been of no use to the provinces.

I have been obliged to explain all these antecedents

---

[1] *Federales*, those who held to a confederation of the old provinces, or a union of states. *Unitarios*, those who advocated a consolidated central government.

in order to continue the life of Juan Facundo Quiroga ; for, though it seems ridiculous to say it, Facundo was the rival of Rivadavia. Everything disconnected with these men was of little importance, and left no impression. There were in the Republic two parties : one in Buenos Ayres, supported by the Liberals in the provinces ; the other originating in the provinces and supported by the provincial commanders who had obtained possession of cities. One of these powers was civilized, constitutional, European ; the other barbarous, arbitrary, South American.

These two parties had reached their full development, and only needed a word to begin the contest ; one, as the revolutionary party, was already called " Unitario," the opposite party assumed the name of " Federal," without well understanding it.

But that barbarian party or power was scattered throughout the Republic, in the provinces, and in the Indian territories, and a strong arm was needed to establish it firmly in a compact form, and Quiroga offered his for the work.

Though the Argentine gaucho has some qualities common to all shepherds, he has strong local attachments. Whether he belongs in Buenos Ayres, Santa Fé, Cordova, or the Llanos, all his aspirations are confined to his own province ; and he is an enemy or a stranger to all the others. These provinces are like different tribes ready to make war upon one another. Lopez, as governor of Santa Fé, cared nothing for what was passing around him, except occasionally when obliged to drive out troublesome intruders from his territory. But as these provinces had points of contact, nothing could prevent them from finally joining in a common interest, thus bringing about that consolidation which they had so struggled against.

As I have already said, Quiroga's wandering life in youth gave rise to his future ambition ; for, though a gaucho, he was troubled with no local attachment. He was born in Rioja, but educated in San Juan, and lived afterwards both in Mendoza and Buenos Ayres. He was acquainted with the whole Republic, and his ambition had no narrow limits. Master of Rioja, he delighted to present himself clothed with authority in that town, where he had learned to read ; in another city, which was the scene of his boyish *escapadas ;* and in another still, where he had distinguished himself by his prison exploit. If it was for his interest to leave a province, he was not detained by his affections ; and, unlike Lopez or Ibarra, who only cared to defend their own possessions, he was fond of attacking his neighbor's territory and taking it into his own hands.

CHAPTER VIII.

EXPERIMENTS.

How long are the days now ? for to-morrow I wish to gallop ten leagues over a
field sown with corpses. — *Skakespeare.*

THE political condition of the Republic was such as
we have described in 1825, when the governor of Buenos Ayres[1] invited the provinces to unite in a congress
and assume the form of a general government. This
idea was everywhere favorably received, either because
every military commander expected to be made governor of his own province, or because the glory of Buenos Ayres dazzled all eyes. The governor of Buenos
Ayres has been blamed for proposing this question, the
solution of which was to be so unfortunate for himself
and for the civilization of the country.

Facundo, in behalf of La Rioja, eagerly accepted
the invitation, perhaps on account of the sympathy
which all highly gifted minds have for good plans !

In 1825 the Republic prepared for the Brazilian
war by calling upon each province to raise a regiment
for the army. Colonel Madrid went to Tucuman for
this purpose, and impatient to obtain the reluctant
recruits and other necessaries for his company, did not
hesitate to set aside the slow authorities and to take
things into his own hands in order to expedite the

[1] Rivadavia.

necessary decrees. This act of subversion placed the governor of Buenos Ayres in a very delicate position ; for there was already some distrust among the governments, arising from provincial jealousies, and the coming of Colonel Madrid from Buenos Ayres, and his interference with provincial authorities, were regarded as acts instigated by the governor himself.

To remove this suspicion, Facundo was sent to Tucuman for the purpose of reëstablishing the local authorities. Madrid explained to the governor the real motive — certainly a very insufficient one — which had actuated him, and professed sincere devotion to the cause. But it was too late, Facundo was already on his way, and he could only prepare to resist him. Madrid had at his disposal a company which was passing through Salta ; but not wishing to aggravate the charges already made against him, contented himself with fifty guns and as many swords ; enough, as he thought, to meet the invading force.

This Colonel Madrid belonged to a class of men essentially Argentine by birth and spirit. At the age of fourteen he began to fight the Spaniards, and the stories of his romantic valor are numerous and often incredible. He was said to have been in a hundred and fifty encounters, his sword always bearing marks of much service ; the very smell of powder and neighing of the horses so excited him, that cavalry, artillery, infantry, everything that came in his way, fell before his mad energy. Besides his love of fighting, he had the gift of the Argentine *cantor*, and animated his soldiers with war-songs, such as have already been described. Unfortunately, he was not a well-balanced general, such as Napoleon liked ; his bravery predominated over the other qualities desirable in a general in the proportion of a hundred to one, — a fact well proved by the event at Tucuman. Though able to call in a sufficient force, he persisted in giving battle with only a handful of men, accompanied by Colonel Diasvelez, who was not less brave than himself. Facundo had with him two hundred of infantry and his own Red Cavalry ; Madrid had fifty-foot soldiers and a few squadrons of militia. At the beginning of the contest, Facundo and his cavalry were routed, and he himself did not return to the field of battle until all was over. Meanwhile the body of infantry stood firm ; Madrid ordered his men to charge upon them, but not being obeyed, he actually rushed upon them alone. He was thrown from his horse, but, recovering himself, charged about him, slaying on the right, on the left, and before him, until horse and horseman fell pierced with balls and bayonets, and victory was decided in favor of the infantry.

Facundo now came back to recover his black flag which had been lost, and found his victory gained, and Madrid dead, actually dead. His equipments were there, — sword, horse, and all, — but his body could not be recognized among the stripped and mutilated corpses that lay upon the field. Colonel Diasvelez, who was a prisoner, said that his ally had a bayonet wound in his leg, and no body was found with such a wound.

Madrid had dragged himself under some bushes where his aid found him raving deliriously about the battle ; and at the sound of approaching footsteps, he cried, "I do not surrender!" Never until then had Colonel Madrid surrendered.

This was the famous fight at Tala, the first exploit of Quiroga beyond the limits of his province. He had conquered "the bravest of the brave," and kept his sword as a trophy of the victory. Will he stop there? But let us see the force which sustained itself against the colonel of the 13th regiment, who overthrew a government to equip his company. Facundo raised at Tala a flag which was not Argentine, but of his own invention; namely, a black ground with a skull and cross-bones in the centre. This was the flag which he had lost early in the engagement, and which he intended to recover, as he said to his routed soldiers, even at the mouth of hell. Terror, death, hell, were represented on the banner and in the proclamations of this general of the Llanos.

And there was still another revelation of the Arab-Tartar spirit of that power which was to destroy the cities. The Argentine colors are blue and white; the clear sky of a fair day, and the bright light of the disk of the sun: "peace and justice for all." In our hatred of tyranny and violence, we reject on our national flag warlike devices. Two hands, as a sign of union, support the Phrygian cap of Liberty. "The United Cities" says this symbol, "will sustain their acquired liberty." The sun begins to illumine the background of this device, while the darkness of night is disappearing. The armies of the Republic, which were to spread over the whole country to enforce the coming of that promised light, wear a uniform of dark blue. But now, in the very heart of the Republic, the color red appears on the national banners, in the dress of the soldiers, and in the cockade which every native Argentine must wear under pain of death.   Let us look up the significance of the color red.   I have before me a picture of all the national flags of the world.   In civilized Europe there is but one in which this color prevails, notwithstanding the barbaric origin of its banners.   The *red* ones are : Algiers, a *red* flag with skull and cross-bones ; Tunis, a *red* flag ; Mongolia, the same ; Turkey, a *red* flag with a crescent ; Morocco ; Japan, *red* with the exterminating knife ; Siam has the same.

I remember that travellers in the interior of Africa provide themselves with *red* cloth for the negro princes. " The king of Elve," say the brothers Lander, " wore a Spanish coat of *red* cloth and pantaloons of the same color."

I remember that the presents sent by the government of Chili to the caciques of Aranco, were *red* cloaks and coats, because savages liked this color especially.

The royal robes of the barbarian kings of Europe were always *red*.   The royal edict of Genoa declared that the senators must wear a red toga, and especially in pronouncing judgment on criminals, that they might inspire the prisoners with terror.

Until within the last century it was the custom in all the countries of Europe for the executioner to be dressed in *red*.   The armies of Rosas wore a red uniform ; his likeness is stamped on a red ribbon.

What remarkable connection is there between these facts ? Is it chance that Algiers, Tunis, Japan, Turkey,

Siam, the Africans, the savages, the Roman Neros, the barbarian kings, the hangmen, and Rosas, should be clothed in a color now proscribed by Christian and civilized communities? No, it is because red is the symbol of violence, blood, and barbarism. If not, why this antagonism?

The Argentine revolution of independence was symbolized by two blue stripes and one white one; signifying, *justice, peace, justice.*

The amendment made by Facundo and approved by Rosas, was a red band, signifying *terror, blood, barbarism.*

In all ages this significance has been given to the color purple or red; study the history of those nations who have hoisted this color, and you will always find a Rosas and a Facundo — terror, barbarism, and blood always prevailing. In Morocco, the emperor has the singular prerogative of killing criminals with his own hand. Each phase of civilization is expressed in its garments, and every style of apparel is indicative of an entire system of ideas. Why do we wear beards at the present day? Because of the researches recently made in mediæval history; the direction given to romantic literature is reflected in the fashions of the day. And why are these constantly changing? Because of the freedom of thought in Europe; let thought be stationary, enslaved, and the costume will remain unchanged. Thus in Asia, where men live under such governments as that of Rosas, the same style of dress has been worn since the time of Abraham.

And still further; every form of civilization has had

its style of apparel, and every revolution of institutions has produced a change of costume. The Roman civilization had one style of dress; the Middle Ages another; the frock-coat was not worn in Europe until after the revival of letters. It is ever the most civilized nation that imposes its fashions on the rest of the world. All Christian nations now wear the coat, and when the Sultan of Turkey, Abdul-Medjid, desired to introduce European civilization into his dominions, he laid aside the turban and caftan for the frock-coat, pantaloons, and cravat.

The Argentine people know the violent opposition to civilized costume made by both Rosas and Facundo. One night, in the year 1840, a couple of *mazorqueros* [1] were dodging around the streets of Buenos Ayres in pursuit of a man who wore a coat, and at last he was seized by the throat, when he exclaimed, " I am Simon Pereira ! " " Pardon, sir," said the men, " but you expose yourself by wearing this coat." " That is just why I wear it; who else wears a coat ? I do it to be known at a distance."

This Simon was the purveyor and agent of Rosas. But to finish the illustration of the spirit of the civil war by its symbols, I must refer to the history of the " *red ribbon* " of quite extensive notoriety.

In 1820, Rosas appeared in Buenos Ayres with his *Colorados de las Conchas*.[2] Twenty years afterwards, he colored the whole city with red; houses, doors, paper-hangings, tapestry, etc. ; but finally he consecrated the color to official purposes, and made it a test of loyalty to the state.

---

[1] *Mazorqueros*, agents of Rosas, employed in cases of secret vengeance.
[2] A company of provincial militia, dressed in red.

The history of the red ribbon is rather singular. At first it was adopted only by party enthusiasts ; then it was ordered that every one should wear it as a *proof of unanimity of opinion.* If there was no intentional disobedience, but in changing the dress the badge was forgotten, the police came to the assistance of memory. *Mazorqueros* were stationed in all the streets, and particularly at the doors of the churches, and when the ladies came out, slashes with a cowhide were distributed without mercy. There were yet stricter regulations. If the ribbon was carelessly tied: " Stripes! the fellow must be a Unitario." If the ribbon was too short: "Stripes for the Unitario!" And if a man did not wear it at all, he was put to death for contempt of the laws. The care of the governor for the public education did not stop here. It was not enough to be a Federal and to wear the red ribbon; the likeness of the illustrious Restaurador must be stamped upon it, with the motto, " Death to the dirty savages, Unitarios," and it must be worn near the heart in token of deep love. It might be thought that the work of debasing a cultivated people and destroying all personal dignity, was now ended. But they were not yet sufficiently disciplined. One morning a ridiculous figure painted on paper, with a streamer of red ribbon half a yard long, appeared at the corner of a street in Buenos Ayres. The first person who saw it rushed back, terrified, and gave the alarm. Immediately every one hurried to the shops and soon appeared wearing half a yard of ribbon. A few days after, a slight alteration in the ribbon or the painted figure was followed by the same result. If any ladies happened to forget the red knots prescribed for them instead of the ribbon, the police would most likely furnish them one gratis — of melted tar ! Thus was uniformity of opinion secured, and not a person was to be found who was not a Federal, or did not imagine himself one. It frequently happened that some one coming out of his house found the end of the street swept, and in less than a half hour the whole street was swept, the impression having become general that there was a police order to that effect.

One day a grocer put out a small flag to attract customers ; the example was followed from house to house, from street to street, until banners floated over the whole city ; and the officials thought that some great news had come, unknown to them. And this was the people who once forced eleven thousand English to surrender in the streets, and who afterward sent five armies against the Spaniards !

The fact is, that terror is a mental disease which attacks a people like cholera, small-pox, or scarlet fever. Every one is liable to the contagion, and when the inoculation has been going on for ten years, it is doubtful if even the vaccinated escape. Do not laugh then at the sight of so much degradation. Remember that you are Spaniards, and that the Inquisition educated Spain ! We bear this disease in our blood.

Let us now resume the thread of our history. Facundo entered Tucuman in triumph, where he passed several days without committing any remarkable acts of violence, and without imposing taxes ; for the constitutional course of Rivadavia had given the people an amount of knowledge which could not at once be ignored. Facundo then returned to Rioja, inimical to the Presidency, though not knowing what motive to give for this opposition, for he could not have explained it to himself.

"I am not a Federal," he always said, "I am not such a fool." "Do you know," he said once, to Don Dalmacio Velez, "why I went to war? For this," showing, as he spoke, an ounce of gold. This was not true.

At other times he said, "Carril, governor of San Juan, treated me very badly in paying no attention to my recommendation of Carita, and for this I put myself in opposition to the Congress." This also was false. His enemies said, that he owned many shares in the bank, and proposed to sell them to the national government for three hundred thousand dollars. Rivadavia rejected this proposition as a scandalous theft, and from that time Facundo enlisted among his enemies. This was true as a fact, but it was not his motive. It was believed that he yielded to the suggestions of Bustos and Ibarra in joining the opposition party; but there is a document which proves the contrary. In a letter which he wrote in 1832 to General Madrid, he said, "When I was invited by those two low fellows, Bustos and Ibarra, I did not consider them capable of making a successful opposition to that despot, President Don Bernadino Rivadavia, and refused to join them; but having been informed by Colonel Manuel del Castillo, aide-de-camp of Bustos, that you were engaged in this affair, and much interested in it, I did not hesitate a moment in deciding to join unconditionally; counting upon your sword alone for success. . . . . What was my misfortune," etc.

So he considered it a fool's part to be a Federal! Was it necessary then to be as ignorant as a country commandant to know what form of government was most suitable for the Republic? Was the least educated man most capable of judging of difficult political questions? Were such thinkers as Lopez, Ibarra, and Facundo, with their great historical, social, geographical, philosophical, and legal information to solve the problem of the proper organization for a state? Ah! let us lay aside the vain words that have deceived so many. Facundo turned against the government by which he was sent to Tucuman, for the same reason that he turned against Aldao who sent him to Rioja. He found himself with the power and the will for action ; and, impelled by a blind, vague instinct, he obeyed it. He was commander of a company, *a gaucho-outlaw*, an enemy of civil justice, of civil order, of educated men, of savans, of the frock-coat, in a word, of the city. He was ordained for the destruction of these by Providence, and must needs fulfill his mission.

At this time a singular question arose to complicate affairs. In Buenos Ayres, the seaport and residence of sixteen thousand foreigners, the governor granted these foreigners liberty of conscience ; and the higher clergy approved of and sustained this law. Convents of different orders had been already suppressed, and the priests provided for. In Buenos Ayres this matter gave no trouble, for all were agreed upon necessity of toleration. The question of liberty of conscience is in South America a question of political economy, for it implies European emigration and population. This was so fully recognized in Buenos Ayres that even

Rosas did not dare to revoke the law of freedom; and that thing must be impossible, indeed, which Rosas would not attempt.

In the provinces, however, this was a question of religion, of salvation, and of eternal damnation. Imagine how it would be considered in Cordova! In Cordova, an inquisition was established. In San Juan, there was a *Catholic* insurrection, so called to distinguish its party from the Liberalistas, their enemies. This revolution having been suppressed in San Juan, they found one day that Facundo was at the gates of the city with a black flag, bearing a red cross, and the device " RELIGION OR DEATH ! "

As the reader will remember, I have quoted from a manuscript that Facundo never went to confession, nor heard mass, nor prayed, and that he himself said he believed in nothing. And yet party spirit led a celebrated preacher to call him *one sent by God*, to induce many to follow his banner. When the eyes of this same priest were opened, and he withdrew from the wicked crusade which he had preached, Facundo said he was only sorry that he did not have him at hand to give him six hundred lashes.

On his arrival at San Juan, the chief men of the city, the magistrates who had not fled, and the priests grateful for this divine aid, went out to meet him, forming two long files in the streets. Facundo passed through without looking at them. They followed at a distance, mortified, and exchanging glances in their common humiliation, until they reached a clover pasture, which this shepherd-general, this modern *hicso*, chose for his quarters, and preferred to the fine edifices of the city. A negress, who had nursed him in his infancy, came to see her boy Facundo. He seated her by his side and conversed affectionately with her, while the priests and dignitaries of the city stood unaccosted, the chief not even deigning to dismiss them.

The Catholics must have been somewhat doubtful of the importance and divinity of the aid which came to them in such an unexpected form. A few days after, learning that the Curé of the Conception was in favor of free worship, Facundo caused him to be arrested, thrown into prison, and sentenced to death. My Chilian readers must know that there were in San Juan at this time, priests, curés, and monks, who believed in freedom of conscience, and belonged to the party of the President. Among others the presbyter Centeno, well-known in Santiago, together with six others, was very zealous in the ecclesiastical reform. But something must be done in the cause of religion, to justify the device of the flag. With this laudable aim, Facundo wrote to a priest of his party, asking his advice about the resolution he had formed to shoot all the city authorities for not having decreed the restitution of the secular revenues of the clergy.

The good priest, who had not foreseen the consequences of arming crime in the name of God, felt some scruple about such a mode of reparation, and advised that the officials should be commanded to make the necessary decrees.

Was there any real question of religion in the Argentine Republic? I should deny it utterly if I did not know that the more barbarous and irreligious a people is, the more liable it is to prejudice and fanaticism.

But the masses did not move of their own accord, and it is plain that those who adopted this device, Facundo, Lopez, Bustos, etc., were completely indifferent. The religious wars of the fifteenth century in Europe were maintained on both sides by sincere believers, fanatical and devoted even to martyrdom, without political aims, and without ambition. The Puritans read the Bible at the moment of going into battle, prayed, and observed fasts and penances. The spirit of a party is evidently sincere, when after triumph it accomplishes all and even more than it promised before the contest. When this result is wanting, there is a deception in terms. When the so-called Catholic party had triumphed in the Argentine Republic, what did it do for religion or the interests of the priesthood?

As far as I know, it only drove out the Jesuits, beheaded four respectable priests in Santos Lugares, after having flayed their heads and hands, and carried in procession the host and the portrait of Rosas side by side, under a canopy. Did the Liberal party ever commit such horrible profanations?

But enough of this. While at San Juan, Facundo occupied his time in gambling; leaving to the authorities the care of providing him with the sums necessary to defray the expenses incurred in the defense of religion. All the time that he remained there he lived in a tent on the clover field, ostentatiously dressed in the *chiripà*, an intentional insult to a city where most of the inhabitants used English saddles, and where the barbarous dress and habits of the gauchos were especially disliked, San Juan being an exclusively agricultural province.

One more campaign against General Madrid at Tucuman, completed the *début* of this new emir of shepherds. General Madrid had resumed the government of Tucuman, sustained by the whole province, and Facundo thought it his duty to dislodge him. There was a new expedition, a new battle, and a new victory. I omit the details with the exception of one characteristic anecdote. Madrid had in the battle of Rincon one hundred and ten infantry; and when the combat ended, there were sixty dead, while of the remaining fifty all except one were wounded. On the following day Madrid declared himself again ready for battle, but Quiroga sent one of his aides to say that the action would begin by shooting the fifty prisoners already kneeling to receive their fate. Madrid abandoned all further attempt at resistance.

In these three expeditions, in which Facundo tested his power, there was no unusual effusion of blood and but few outrages. It is true that in Tucuman he seized upon some flocks and hides, and imposed heavy taxes upon them, but as yet there was no cowhiding of the citizens, no outrages upon the women; there were the evils of conquest, but none of its horrors. The pastoral system had not yet developed that brutality and entire absence of restraint which afterwards characterized it.

What part had the legitimate governor of Rioja in these expeditions? The government only existed nominally; all the real power was in the hands of the "Provincial Commander." Blanco resigned the office, overwhelmed with humiliations; and Aguero assumed the government. One day, however, Quiroga rode up to his door and said to him, "Sir, I came to inform you that I have encamped with my escort two miles from here." It is hardly necessary to say that Aguero resigned. A new governor was now to be chosen, and at the petition of the people, Quiroga condescended to nominate Galvan, who accepted the office, but was assaulted the same night by a troop of soldiers, and fled. Quiroga enjoyed the adventure excessively. It is well to mention that the assembly of representatives was composed of men who did not know how to read.

Facundo needed money for his first expedition to Tucuman, and demanded of the treasurer of the bank eight thousand dollars on account of his shares for which he had never paid. In Tucuman, he demanded twenty-five thousand dollars to pay his soldiers, who received none of it ; and some time after sent a bill of eighteen thousand dollars to Dorrego to pay the cost of the expedition made by order of the governor of Buenos Ayres. Dorrego did not hesitate to satisfy so just a demand. This sum was shared with Moral, the governor of Rioja, who had suggested the idea. Six years after, in Mendoza, he gave this same Moral seven hundred lashes for his ingratitude. While Blanco was governor, there was a dispute about a game of cards, and Facundo, seizing his opposer by the hair, shook him until his neck was broken. The body was buried, and the man declared to have died a *natural death*.

When about to leave Tucuman, he sent a party of soldiers to the house of one Sarate, who was shot at his own door and left for his widow to bury ; the victim was a man of property and a peaceable citizen, but well known for his bravery and contempt of Quiroga. On his return from the expedition, Facundo happened to meet with Gutierrez, ex-governor of Catamarca, whom he persuaded to go and live at Rioja. There they were quite intimate for some time, but seeing Gutierrez surrounded one day by some gaucho friends, Facundo had him arrested and sentenced to death, to the terror of all Rioja, for Gutierrez was much respected, and had gained the affections of every one. The presbyter, Dr. Colina, and several other clergymen of high standing, petitioned that the miserable man might at least have time to arrange his affairs and confess his sins. "I see," answered Facundo, "that he has many partisans here. Ho! there! Take these men to prison and let them be shot instead of Gutierrez." They attempted to flee, and two escaped; one lost his life, and the others were imprisoned; but Facundo laughed loudly when he heard the adventure, and ordered them to be set at liberty. Such scenes as this were frequent between the priests and their aid " *sent by God.*"

In San Juan he had a negro dressed up as a priest, and made him walk through the streets. In Cordova, he refused to receive any one except Dr. Castro Barros, with whom he had an account to arrange. In Mendoza, he walked to the place of execution by the side of a priest whom he had condemned to death; he did the same with the curé of Alguia and the prior of Tucuman. It is true that in these cases he did not go so far as to have the sentence actually executed, but it was a great terror and humiliation to the clergymen; yet in spite of all this, the old people and bigots still offered prayers to heaven for the success of his arms.

But the story of Gutierrez is not quite ended yet. Fifteen days later he received a sentence of exile, and an escort was to conduct him beyond the boundaries. The party having encamped for the night, a fire was made to cook supper, and while Gutierrez was stooping to blow the scarcely lighted sticks, the chief official struck him on the head with a staff, and blows from others followed, until his brains were literally knocked out.

These were some of the events which took place in Facundo's first attempt at union in the Republic, for these were but attempts; the time had not yet come for the alliance of the pastoral powers by which the Republic was to be reorganized. Rosas was already famous in the province of Buenos Ayres, though he bore no titles as yet; nevertheless he was busy in his own cause. The constitution proposed by Congress was rejected wherever the provincial commanders had any influence. When the government deputy presented himself in Santiago del Estero, in his official dress, Ibarra received him in shirt-sleeves and *chiripá*. Rivadavia resigned the presidency because the provinces were opposed to him, — " but barbarism will soon be down upon us," he added, after his farewell. He did well to resign. Rivadavia's mission was to present before us the constitutionalism of Benjamin Constant with all its empty words, its deceptions, and absurdities. Rivadavia did not know that when the civilization and liberty of a people are in question, a ruler has great responsibilities both to God and future generations ; and that there is neither charity nor compassion in abandoning a nation for thirty years to the devastation of the first ruthless sword that offers. Communities in their infancy are like children who foresee nothing and understand nothing, and need men of knowledge and foresight to guide them.

CHAPTER XI.

CIVIL WAR. — TABLADA, A CITY.

There is a fourth element coming ; they are the barbarians, new hordes who come to throw themselves upon the old society with complete freshness of manners, soul and spirit, and who have as yet done nothing, but are ready to receive everything with the aptitude of the most suave and naïve ignorance. — *Cherminier.*

THE presidency had fallen amid the hissings and rejoicings of its enemies. Dorrego, the able leader of the opposition in Buenos Ayres, was the friend of the governors of the interior, who were his abettors and supporters in the Provincial Congress in which he was triumphant. Victory was no longer with the Republic in its foreign wars ; and, though its arms had met with no disasters in Brazil, the necessity for peace was everywhere felt. The opposition of the provincial leaders had weakened the army by destroying regiments, or refusing to furnish recruits. An apparent tranquillity reigned in the interior, but the earth trembled ; strange rumors were afloat. The newspapers of Buenos Ayres were filled with gloomy prophecies. Threats came alike from the government and the opposition. The administration of Dorrego began to show a want of strength, because the party of the *city*, called Federal, which had established it, had not the power to sustain itself with honor after the fall of the presidency. The new administration, far from resolving any of the questions which divided the Republic, showed, on the contrary, all the weakness of Federalism. Dorrego was essentially Buenos Ayrean in his sympathies, and had little regard for the fate of the provinces. He had promised the provincial leaders and communities to do all he could to favor the interests of the former and to insure the rights of the latter; but, having once obtained the government, he said to his immediate friends, " What is it to us if the petty tyrants carry things with a high hand? What are the four thousand dollars' salary to Lopez, or the eighteen thousand to Quiroga, to us who control the seaport, and a custom-house that brings us in a million and a half, which that stupid Rivadavia wished to convert into national revenue?" Let us not forget that the motto of egotism is always " Each for himself." Dorrego and his party did not foresee that the provinces would come some day to punish Buenos Ayres for having refused them its civilizing influence; and that, because of the indifference to their ignorance and barbarism, this very ignorance and barbarism would penetrate into the streets of Buenos Ayres and take up its quarters even in the fort.

But Dorrego might have seen it, if he or his party had had better eyes. Here were the provinces at the gates of the city, only waiting an occasion to invade it. From the time of the fall of the presidency the decrees of the civil authorities could not be enforced beyond the suburbs of the city. Dorrego had employed, as an instrument of opposition, this outside resistance; and, when his party triumphed, he bestowed upon his ally beyond the walls the title of commander-in-chief of the provinces. What logic of the sword is it that makes the rank of commander-in-chief of the provinces a necessary step in the elevation of a military leader? Where this rank does not exist, as was then the case in Buenos Ayres, it is created expressly; as if, before letting the wolf into the fold, it was necessary to expose him to general observation.

Dorrego afterward found that the provincial commander, who had caused the presidency to totter, and had contributed so powerfully to overthrow it, was a lever perpetually applied to the government; and that when Rivadavia had fallen, and Dorrego was in his place, the lever still continued its action. Dorrego and Rosas were face to face, each watching and threatening the other. Dorrego's friends recall his favorite phrase, — "The gaucho-rogue! Let him be as troublesome as he pleases; and when he is least expecting it, I will shoot him." This was just what the Ocampos said when they first felt Quiroga's heavy arm upon them.

Indifferent to the people of the interior, not in high favor with the Federal party of the city, and already in antagonism with the provincial power which he had called to his aid, Dorrego, who had obtained the government through parliamentary opposition, now tried to win the Unitarios, whom he had conquered; but parties have neither charity nor foresight. The Unitarios laughed in their sleeves, and said among themselves, "He totters, let him fall." The Unitarios did not understand that with Dorrego would fall those who might have interposed between them and the provinces; or that the monster whom they feared was not seeking Dorrego, but the *city*, the civil institutions, of which they themselves were the exponents.

Things were in this condition when peace was concluded with Brazil, and the first division of the army, commanded by Lavalle, was disbanded. Dorrego knew well the spirit of these veterans of the War of Independence, who, covered with wounds, and grown gray in the service, had obtained only the rank of colonels, majors, or captains; two or three, perhaps, becoming generals; while in the interior of the Republic, without ever having passed the frontiers, were dozens of leaders, who, in four years, had been raised from the rank of gaucho-outlaws to that of commanders; from commanders to generals, and from generals to absolute masters of provinces. Need we look for any other motive for the implacable hatred of the veterans for these men? What had they to anticipate, now that the new order of things had taken from them the hope of entering the capital of Brazil as conquerors?

On the 1st of December, two companies of regulars were drawn up in Victoria Square. Governor Dorrego had fled to the country, and the Unitarios filled the air with shouts of triumph. A few days afterward, seven hundred cuirassiers, commanded by general officers, went out through Peru Street toward the pampas to meet several thousand gauchos and Indians, together with a few soldiers, commanded by Dorrego. For a moment the field of Navarro was covered with the dead, and the following day an officer, now in the service of Chili, brought in Dorrego as prisoner. An hour later, the body of Dorrego lay pierced with balls. The officer who had ordered his execution announced it to the city in the following terms : —

" I have the honor of informing the deputy-governor that Colonel Manuel Dorrego has just been shot by my order, in front of the regiments which compose this division. History will judge impartially whether Señor Dorrego should have lived or died ; or whether in sacrificing him for the peace of a city, brought to grief by him, I could have had any other motive than that of the public good. Let the people of Buenos Ayres be persuaded that the death of Colonel Dorrego is the greatest sacrifice that I could make for them.

" I salute, Señor, the minister with all due consideration.

" JUAN LAVALLE."

Was Lavalle wrong? It is needless to add another affirmative in support of those who, after seeing the consequences, assumed the easy task of criticizing his motives. If an evil exists, it is in things not in persons. When Cæsar was assassinated, he re-lived more terrible than ever in Octavius. Lavalle did not then know that in killing the body he could not kill the spirit ; and that political personages take their character and existence from the ideas, interests, and ends of the party they represent. If Lavalle had shot Rosas instead of Dorrego, perhaps he would have saved the world from a great scandal, humanity from a great opprobrium, and the Republic from much blood and many tears ; but, even if Rosas had been shot, the provinces would still have had representatives ; and there would have been only the change of one historical picture for another. But what people pretend to ignore to-day, is, that—notwithstanding the purely personal responsibility of the deed, as far as Lavalle is concerned — the death of Dorrego was a necessary consequence of the prevailing ideas of the time ; and that by this act the soldier who was brave enough to defy history, only accomplished

the avowed wish of the citizens. What had interfered
with the proclamation of the Constitution of 1826 but
the hostility of Ibarra, Lopez, Bustos, Quiroga, Ortiz,
and the Aldaos, each of whom ruled a province, and
some of whom influenced the others? Now, what
would appear so reasonable at that time, and to those
men who reasoned *à priori*, as to get rid of what they
considered the only obstacle to the desired organization
of the Republic?

These political errors which belonged to the time
rather than to the men, are yet worthy of consideration, for upon them depend the explanation of many
social phenomena. Lavalle in shooting Dorrego, just
as he would have shot Bustos, Lopez, Facundo, and
others of that class, only fulfilled the requirements of
his time and party. Even in 1834 there were still
men in France who believed that if they could get rid
of Louis Philippe, the French Republic would revive
in all the greatness and glory of the past! Perhaps
also the death of Dorrego was one of those fated events
which form the nucleus of history, without which it
would be incomplete and unmeaning. Civil war had
been long threatening the Republic. Rivadavia had
foreseen it with all its horrors; Facundo had unconsciously kept his hordes on the slopes of the Andes in
waiting for this event; and Rosas' private life had
been a ten years' preparation towards the same end.
Dorrego was in the way of all parties: of the Unitarios,
for they despised him; of the provincial leaders, for he
had proved useless to them; and in that of Rosas, because he was impatient of keeping under the shadow of
the city parties, and eager to obtain the government,

or in other words, to become what he was not, and could never be, that is, a Federal, in the strict sense of the term. He represented the third social element, which from Artigas to Facundo had been eager to show itself without disguise, and to measure its strength with that of European civilization. If Dorrego had not died, it does not follow that the craving thirst of Facundo would have been quieted, or that Rosas would have failed to represent the provinces in the struggle which had begun long before 1820. No, Lavalle only lighted the match which was to fire the mine long ago prepared by both Unitarios and Federals.

From this moment there was nothing for the timid but to stop their ears and shut their eyes. All others everywhere rushed to arms; the tread of horsemen was heard over the pampas, and the cannon's black mouth was seen at the gates of the cities.

We must now leave Buenos Ayres to see what is passing in the other provinces. It must be mentioned, by the way, that Lopez, having been beaten in several encounters, sued in vain for reasonable terms of peace; and that Rosas had serious thoughts of going over to the side of Brazil. Lavalle refused to share in any of the transactions, and was soon put down; here was the true Unitario disdain of the gaucho, and faith in the final triumph of the " city." If Lavalle had adopted another line of conduct and kept the seaport in the hands of the citizens, might not the cruel Pampas Government have been prevented?

Facundo was in his element. A campaign was about to begin; expresses rushed to and fro; the feudal system of independence was to become a confederation of war.

Everything was put in requisition for the coming campaign, and it was found unnecessary to go to the banks of the La Plata for a good battle-field.   General Paz, with eight hundred veterans, had gone to Cordova, fought and conquered Bustos, and taken possession of the city, which was but a step from the Llanos, and within reach of the cries from the " montoneras " of the Sierra Cordova.

Facundo hastened his preparations ; he longed for a personal encounter with a one-armed general who could not manage a lance or flourish a sword.   What could Paz hope for in an encounter with the conqueror of Colonel Madrid ?   Facundo was to be joined by Don Felix Aldao, a friar general from Mendoza, with a regiment of trained auxiliaries equipped entirely in red ; and without waiting for a force of seven hundred regulars from San Juan, he set out for Cordova with four thousand men, eager to measure arms with the cuirassiers of the second division and their officers.

The battle of Tablada is so well known that details are unnecessary.   It has been brilliantly described in the " Revue des deux Mondes ; " but there is one fact worth remembering.   Facundo attacked the city with all his army, and was repulsed for a day and night by one hundred young clerks, thirty mechanics, and seven sick soldiers, from behind slight breastworks defended by only four pieces of artillery.   And it was only when he announced his intention of burning the beautiful city, that they consented to surrender the place.   Knowing that Paz was approaching, he left his infantry as useless, and went out to meet him with a cavalry force at least three times as large as the army of his opponent; then came hard fighting, and the cavalry charged again and again, but in vain. That mass of horsemen, though surrounding the eight hundred veterans, were driven back every moment, and compelled to return to the charge. The lance of Quiroga forcing back his own retreating men, caused as much terror in the rear of his army as the guns and swords of the enemy in front. But all was in vain; it was like the raging billows of the sea beating against a rough, motionless rock; sometimes, indeed, it is engulfed by the angry waves, but its black summit presently reappears firm and unshaken. Of the eight hundred auxiliaries only sixty survived, and of the six hundred red cavalry, not a third were living; the numerous other companies lost all discipline, and fled in every direction. Facundo retreated to the city, and the next day lay with his guns and infantry like a tiger in ambush : but all was soon over, and fifteen hundred dead bodies proved how obstinate the contest had been on both sides.

The battles of Tablada and Cordova were trials of strength between the provincial and city forces under their great leaders, Facundo and Paz, worthy representatives of the two powers which were struggling for dominion in the Republic. Facundo, ignorant, barbarous, for the greater part of his life an outlaw, and famous only for his acts of desperation; brave to rashness, endowed with herculean strength, always upon his horse, which he managed skillfully through terror and violence, knowing no other power than that of brute force, had no faith but in his horse, and depended for success upon bravery, the lance, and the terrible charges of his cavalry. In all the Argentine Republic there was not a more perfect specimen of the " *gaucho malo*."

Paz, on the contrary, was a true son of the city, and representative of the power of civilization. Lavalle, Madrid, and others like them, were native Argentines; cavalry officers, as brilliant as Murat, perhaps, but the cuirass and epaulets could not hide the gaucho nature. But Paz was a European soldier, and only believed in bravery as subordinate to tactics, strategy, and discipline. He hardly knew how to ride, and having only one hand, could not use a lance. A very large army was unwieldy and troublesome to him; what he liked, was a small number of soldiers thoroughly disciplined. A regiment of his training was sure to be perfect of its kind, and could he have selected his own battle-fields, the fate of the Republic would have been secure. He was in spirit a European soldier, even to the arms he used; he was an artillery officer, and therefore mathematical and scientific. A battle was a problem which he could solve by equations, and foretell the unknown quantity — that is, the victory. General Paz was not a genius, but an able officer, who employed science where others made use of brute force; in a word, he was the representative of European civilization, which was in a fair way to die out in our country. Unfortunate General Paz! Honor be to thee in thy repeated disasters! With thee are the household gods of the Republic! Destiny has not yet decided between thee and Rosas, between the cities and the pampas, between the blue stripe and the red ribbon! Thou hast the only quality of mind that in the end conquers brute force, — the quality in which lay the power of the old martyrs! Thou hast faith. Faith has saved thee, and in thee is the only hope of the Republic.

There is certainly a destiny about this man. He alone, in the ill-advised revolution of the first of December, was able to justify it by victory. Taken at last from the head of his army by the irresistible power of the gaucho, he was kept ten years in prison, Rosas, even, not daring to kill him, as if a guardian angel watched over his life. He escaped almost miraculously one stormy night, and through the rough waters of the La Plata, reached the eastern bank. Repulsed at one place, and disappointed at another, he at last obtained command of the few remaining forces of a province which had seen three armies successively destroyed. From such remnants he again gathered with much care and patience means of resistance, and when the armies of Rosas had triumphed everywhere, and carried terror throughout the Republic, the one-armed general called aloud from the marshes of Caguazu, "The Republic still lives!" Afterwards, despoiled of his laurels by those he had served, and ignominiously taken from the head of his army, he sought refuge among his enemies in Entre Rios, where the very elements seemed to protect him, and even the gauchos of the forest Montiel did not have it in their hearts to kill the one-armed man who harmed no one. At last he reached Montevideo, and learned that Ribera had been defeated, probably because he was not there to take the enemy in his own snares. The whole city was in consternation, and hurried to the poor lodging of the fugitive to beg for advice and comfort. "If I can only have twenty days, they will not take

164 LIFE IN THE ARGENTINE REPUBLIC.

the city," was the only answer, given, not with enthusiasm, but with mathematical certainty. Oribe gave Paz all he asked for, and three years have passed since that day of terror at Montevideo. When he had secured the place well, and accustomed the garrison to fight daily as a matter of course, he went to Brazil and remained longer than was agreeable to his friends, and when Rosas was hoping to hear of him in the hands of the imperial police, he learned that he was at Corrientes training six thousand men ; that he had formed an alliance with Paraguay, and also that Brazil had invited France and England to take part in the contest ; so that the question between the provinces and the cities had now become a struggle between the one-armed, scientific Paz and the gaucho barbarian Rosas ; between the Pampas on one side and Paraguay, Uruguay, Brazil, England, and France on the other.

It was especially to the honor of General Paz that even the enemies he had fought with neither hated nor feared him personally. The " Gaceta " of Rosas, so prodigal of its calumniations, never succeeded in abusing him thoroughly, a proof that he inspired his very detractors with respect. Many of the followers of Rosas in their hearts admired Paz, and the old Federals never forgot that he had always protected them from the fury of the old Unitarios. Who knows if Providence, which holds in its hand the fate of nations, has not preserved this man through many dangers to aid in the reconstruction of the Republic under laws which permit liberty without license, and do not need to be enforced by violence. Paz is a provincial by birth, a guarantee

that he would never sacrifice the provinces to Buenos
Ayres and the port, as Rosas has done to obtain millions while he impoverishes the people of the interior ;
just what the Federals had accused the Congress of 1826
of wishing to do.

The conquest of Tablada was the beginning of a
new era for the city of Cordova, which, until then,
according to the message of General Paz to the provincial representatives, " had occupied the lowest place
among the Argentine cities, constantly opposing effort
towards the construction of a constitution for the
nation, or for its own province, either under the rule
of Federals or Unitarios."

However, Cordova, like all the Argentine cities, contained its liberal element, but kept under until then by
an absolute and conservative government like that of
Bustos. From the moment that Paz entered the city,
this element appeared openly, and showed how much it
had strengthened during nine years of that Spanish
government.

I have before described Cordova as antagonistic in
spirit to Buenos Ayres ; there is one circumstance in
favor of its future development. The inhabitants have
the greatest possible respect for learning, an effect produced by the university of two centuries standing.
The love of learning presupposes a certain degree of
civilization, so that notwithstanding the conservative
nature and direction of the studie's, there must be in
Cordova a large number in favor of progressive culture and intelligence. This respect for learning ex-
tends even to the lower classes of society, and this
explains why the masses embraced the revolution with

an ardor which ten years have not abated, and which has furnished many victims for the vengeance of the Mazorqueros.

Paz brought with him an interpreter who should explain his ideas and objects to the common people — Barcala, the negro colonel, who had so gloriously distinguished himself in Brazil, and was on an equality with the chief officers of the army: Barcala the freedman, who had devoted himself to the task of interesting the working classes in a revolution which regarded neither color nor class in rewarding true merit. This Barcala was, as far as possible, to make the change of ideas and aims popular among the citizens; and he succeeded beyond the most sanguine expectations. The middle classes of Cordova were from that time in favor of civil order and progressive civilization.

The young men of Cordova were distinguished in the war for their disinterested devotion to the cause; many fell on the field of battle, or under the knife of the assassin, and still more were condemned to the pains of exile. In the battles of San Juan, the bodies of Cordovian "doctors" lay piled in the streets, obstructing the artillery that they were carrying against the enemy.

On the other hand, the clergy, who had encouraged the opposition to Congress and the constitution, had had time to measure the abyss to which civilization would be brought by such defenders of the faith as Facundo, Lopez, etc., and did not hesitate to declare in favor of General Paz.

Thus the "doctors" and young men, the clergy as well as the masses, were now of one opinion, and ready to uphold the principles implied in the new order of things ; and Paz could at once begin to reorganize the province and to establish friendly relations with others. A treaty was confirmed with Lopez of Santa Fé, who was induced, by Don Domingo de Oro [1] to join Paz. [2] Salta and Tucuman had already submitted, and only the western provinces remained hostile.

[1] Domingo de Oro was a noble patriot, who opposed Rosas at the cost of everything that makes life dear.

[2] General Paz, late Vice-President of the Argentine Republic, died of cholera within this year.

CHAPTER X.

CIVIL WAR.

WHAT has become of Facundo in the mean time? At Tablada he had lost everything, — arms, officers, men, reputation; everything except rage and valor. Moral, governor of Rioja, taken aback by the news of this unlooked-for disaster, availed himself of a slight excuse for leaving the city, and from Sañogasta sent Quiroga a despatch offering him what assistance the province could afford. Before the expedition the friendship between this nominal governor and the all-powerful commander had somewhat cooled. Quiroga thought he had not had the full number of armed men that he considered due him from the result of the census, in addition to the troops already in the province, and which had come from Tucuman, San Juan, Catamarca, etc. And another circumstance strengthened the suspicions with which Quiroga regarded the governor. Sañogasta was the manorial residence of the Dorias Davilas, the enemies of the commander; and the governor, foreseeing what the suspicions of Facundo would deduce from the date of the despatch, dated it from Uanchin, a place about four leagues distant. But Quiroga knew that Moral was in Sañogasta, and all his doubts were confirmed. Fontanel and Barcena, two of Facundo's odious instruments, were sent out with a party to scour the country for the purpose of impressing as many men as they could find, but the inhabitants took care to escape, so that they were not very successful in their day's hunt, and returned with only eleven persons who were shot upon the spot. Don Inocencio Moral, an uncle of the governor, with his two sons, one only fourteen years of age, were among the victims of that day. There was also among them a Don Mariano Pasos, who had once before incurred the anger of Quiroga. When he was starting on one of his previous expeditions, this man, seeing the disorderly troops, had said to a fellow-merchant, "What men for fighting!" Quiroga hearing it, had the two criticizers brought before him; one was tied to a post and received two hundred lashes, while the other stood by awaiting his share. The latter, however, was spared when his turn came, and afterwards became the governor of Rioja and a great friend of Quiroga.

Meanwhile, Governor Moral, knowing what he might expect, fled from the province, but he was eventually caught, and received seven hundred lashes for his ingratitude, for it was he who had shared the eighteen thousand dollars extorted from Dorrego.

That Barcena before mentioned was ordered to assassinate the commissioner of the English mining company; and I heard from himself the details of this atrocious murder, which he committed in his own house, desiring his wife and children to stand out of the way of the balls and sword-cuts.

Barcena accompanied Oribe in his expedition to Cordova; and during a ball given in honor of the triumph

over Lavalle, threw the bloody heads of three young
men into the hall where their families were dancing.
This Barcena was the leader of the band of Mazorqueros which went with the army sent to Cordova in persecution of Lavalle, a regularly organized band, each
Mazorquero wearing at his side a knife with a blade
curved like a small cimeter, which was invented by
Rosas himself for the purpose of beheading men dex-
terously.

What motive could Quiroga have had for these atrocities? He is said to have told Oro at Mendoza that his
only object was to inspire terror. And again, during
the continual assassinations of wretched peasants, on
his way to the head-quarters at Atiles, one of the Vil-
lafañes said to him in a tone of fear and compassion,
"Is it not enough, General?"   "Don't be a fool,"
Quiroga answered; "how else can I establish my
power!" This was his one method, — terror with the
citizen, that he might fly and leave his fortune; terror
with the gaucho, to make him support a cause in which
he had no personal interest. With him terror took the
place of administrative power, enthusiasm, tactics,
everything. And it cannot be denied that terror, as a
means of government, produces much larger results
than patriotism or liberty. Russia has made use of it
from the time of Ivan, and has conquered the most
barbarous nations; the bandits of the forest obey the
chief, wielding this power which controls the fiercest
natures. It is true that it degrades men, impoverishes
them, and takes from them all elasticity of mind, but
it extorts more from a state in one day than it would
have given in ten years; and what does the rest matter

to the Czar of Russia, the bandit chief, or the Argentine commander?

Facundo ordered all the inhabitants of Rioja to emigrate to the Llanos under pain of death, and the order was literally obeyed. It is hard to find a motive for this useless emigration. Quiroga was not apt to fear, yet he might have feared at the moment; for the Unitarios were raising an army in Mendoza to take possession of the government; Tucuman and Salta were on the north; and on the east, Cordova, Tablada, and General Paz; he was, therefore, pretty well surrounded, and a general hunt might very well have brought the Tiger of the Llanos at bay. These terrorists do have their moments of fear: Rosas cried like a child when he heard of the rebellion at Chascomus, and eleven huge trunks were packed with his effects ready to fly an hour before news came of the victory of Alvarez. But woe to the people when such moments have passed! Then follow *September massacres*, and pyramids of human heads arise in the squares!

Notwithstanding the order of Facundo, two persons remained in Rioja — a young girl and a priest. The story of Severa Villafañe is a pitiful romance; a fairy tale in which the loveliest princess is a wandering fugitive, sometimes disguised as a shepherdess, sometimes begging a morsel of bread, or for protection from a frightful giant, — a cruel Bluebeard. Severa had the misfortune to excite the lust of the tyrant, and made superhuman efforts to escape his persecution. It was not only virtue resisting seduction, but the unconquerable repugnance of a delicate woman who detests those coarse types of brute force. A beautiful woman will

sometimes barter something of her honor for something
of the glory which surrounds a celebrated man ; not
for the glory which depends on the debasement of
others for its brilliancy, but the glory which was the
cause of Madame de Maintenon's frailty, or the literary
glory to which Madame Roland and other such women
are said to have sacrificed their reputations.   For
whole years Severa resisted.   At one time she came
near being poisoned by her tiger ; at another, Quiroga,
in a fit of desperation, tried to poison himself with
opium.   Once she escaped with difficulty from the
hands of some of his creatures, and again she was surprised by Quiroga in her own court-yard, where he
seized her by the arm, beat her with his fist until she
was covered with blood, then threw her upon the
ground and kicked in her skull with the heel of his
boot.   And was there no one to protect this poor girl,
no relatives, no friends !   One might well think so ;
yet she belonged to the first families of Rioja ; General Villafañe was her uncle, she had brothers who
witnessed the outrages ; and there was a curé who
shut the doors against her when she sought a refuge in
the sanctuary.   Finally, Severa fled to Catamarca and
went into a convent ; two years afterwards, when
Facundo was passing through that place, he forced his
way into the convent, and ordered the nuns into his
presence ; at the sight of him one nun uttered a cry
and fell senseless upon the floor — it was Severa.

But we must return to the encampment at Atiles,
where an army was preparing for the purpose of recovering the reputation lost at Tablada.   Two Unitarios
of San Juan had fallen into the hands of the tyrant :

a young Chilian by the name of Castro y Calvo, and
Alexandro Carril. Quiroga asked the latter how
much he would give for his life.

"Twenty-five thousand dollars," he answered, trembling.

"And you, sir," asked Quiroga, of the other, "how
much will you give?"

"I can only give four thousand," said Castro. "I
am only a merchant and have no property."

They sent to San Juan for the money, and behold
thirty thousand dollars collected for the war at a very
small cost. While waiting for the money, Facundo
lodged them under a carob-tree, and employed them
in making cartridges, paying them two reals a day for
their work.

The governor of San Juan, hearing of the efforts
made by the family of Carril to collect this ransom,
took advantage of the knowledge. As governor of the
city he could not exactly shoot his own citizens, though
an independent Federal, and neither did he have the
power to extort money from the Unitarios. But he
ordered all the political prisoners in the gaols to be
sent to the camp at Atiles to join the army. The
mothers and wives understood what fate they were to
expect, and first one, and then another and another,
succeeded in scraping together the sums necessary to
keep back their sons and husbands from the den of the
Tiger. Thus Quiroga governed in San Juan merely
by the terror of his name.

When the brothers Aldao were all powerful in Mendoza, and had not left in Rioja one man, old or young,
married or single, who was able to carry arms, Facundo

transported his head-quarters to San Juan, where there
were still many wealthy Unitarios. There he soon
ordered six hundred lashes to a citizen noted for his
influence, talent, and wealth, and walked himself by
the side of the cart which carried his expiring victim
through the streets ; for Facundo was very careful
about this part of his administration ; and not at all
like Rosas, who, from his private room where he was
taking his *maté*, sent Mazorqueros to execute the atrocities afterward charged upon the *federal enthusiasm* of
the people.   Not thinking this example sufficient, Facundo seized upon an old man, whom he accused — or
scarcely troubled himself to accuse — of having served
as a guide to some fugitives, and had him shot without
permitting him to speak a word ; for this heaven-sent
defender of the faith cared very little whether his victims confessed or not.

Public opinion being thus prepared, there were no
sacrifices the city of San Juan was not ready to make
for the defense of the Confederation ; contributions
were given in without remonstrance, and arms appeared as if by magic.   The Aldaos triumphed in the
incapacity of the Unitarios to violate the treaty of Pilar,
and then Quiroga left for Mendoza.   There no additional terror was needed, for the daily executions
ordered by the monk Aldao had paralyzed the city ; but
Facundo thought it necessary to justify the terror carried everywhere by his name.   Some young men of
San Juan had been made prisoners, and these, at least,
belonged to him.   He asked one of them how many
guns he could furnish by the end of four days ; the
young man answered that if he might have time to

send to Chili for them, he would do all he could.
Quiroga repeated, " How many can you furnish now ? "

" None," was the answer ; and the next moment his
body was taken away to be buried, six others soon following. The same question was put orally or in
writing to the prisoners from Mendoza, and the answers
were more or less satisfactory. Among these was a
General Alvarado, who was brought before Facundo.

" Sit down, General," he said. " How soon can you
deliver six thousand dollars for your ransom ? "

" Sir, I cannot bring it at all ; I have no money."

" But you have friends who would not let you be
shot," said Quiroga.

" No, sir ; I have none. I was only passing through
the province when I was induced by the public wish to
take charge of the government."

" Where would you like to go ? " continued Quiroga, after a moment of silence.

" Wherever you may order, sir."

" What do you think of San Juan ? "

" Just as you please, sir."

" How much money do you need ? "

" None, I thank you, sir."

Facundo went to a desk and opening a bag of gold,
said, " Take what you need, General."

" Thanks, sir, nothing."

An hour later the carriage of General Alvarado was
at his door with his baggage in it, and also General
Villafañe, who conducted him to San Juan, and on his
arrival there, gave him a hundred ounces of gold from
General Quiroga, begging him not to refuse it.

This would seem to prove that Quiroga's heart was

not entirely dead to noble impressions.   Alvarado was
an old soldier, a grave and prudent general, who had
given him no trouble.   He afterward said of him, —
" That Alvarado is a good soldier, but he doesn't understand our warfare."

At San Juan they brought before him a Frenchman
named Barreau, who had written about him as only a
Frenchman can write.   Facundo asked him if he was
the author of the abusive articles, and was answered in
the affirmative.

" Then what do you expect ? "

" Death, sir; " said the man; but Quiroga threw him
a purse, saying, " There, take that, and go somewhere
else to be hung."

At Tucuman, Quiroga one day lay stretched on a
bench, when an Andalusian came up and asked for the
General.

" He is in there," said Quiroga; " what do you
want with him ? "

"I have come to pay the four hundred dollars' contribution he has charged upon me, — the fellow gets
his living easy."

" Do you know the General, friend ? "

" No, and I don't want to know him, the rogue ! "

" Come in and take a drink," said Quiroga, but at
that moment an aide came up, and began: " General ——."

" General ! " cried the man, opening his eyes, " so
you are the General ! Ah, General," he continued, falling on his knees, " I am a poor devil, — you
wouldn't be the ruin of me, — the money is all ready,
General, — come, don't be angry, now ! "

Facundo burst into a loud laugh, told the man to make himself easy, and giving him back the contribution, only took two hundred of it as a loan, which he afterwards faithfully repaid. Two years after this, a paralyzed beggar called out to him in the streets of Buenos Ayres, —

" Good-bye, General, I am the Andalusian of Tucuman, and I'm paralyzed." Facundo gave him six dollars.

These things prove the theory, which the modern drama has exhibited with so much brilliancy, namely, that in the darkest characters of history there will always be found a ray of light, however totally it seems sometimes to vanish.

But let us resume the course of public events. After the solemn inauguration of terror in Mendoza, Facundo retired to Retamo, whither the Aldao brothers had carried a contribution of a hundred thousand dollars extorted from the Unitarios. There they gambled day and night, playing for enormous stakes, until Facundo had won the hundred thousand dollars.

A year passed in preparations for the war, and at the end of 1830 a new and formidable army, composed of divisions recruited in Rioja, San Juan, Mendoza, and San Luis, marched against Cordova. General Paz, desirous of avoiding bloodshed, though sure of winning new laurels should an engagement take place, sent Major Pawnero, an officer of prudence, energy, and sagacity, to meet Quiroga with proposals of peace, and even of alliance. It might be thought that Quiroga would be disposed to accept any reasonable opportunity for adjustment ; but the intervention of the Buenos Ayres commission, which had no other object than to prevent any adjustment, and his own pride and presumption on finding himself at the head of a more powerful and better disciplined army than the first, made him reject the peace proposals of the more modest General Paz. Facundo had this time arranged something like a plan for the campaign. Communications established in the Sierra de Cordova had excited the pastoral population to rebellion ; General Villafañe approached on the north with the division from Catamarca, while Facundo came up from the south. It was not very difficult for General Paz to see through the designs of Quiroga, and to disappoint them. One night the army disappeared from the immediate neighborhood of Cordova, no one knew where ; it had been seen by many persons, but in different places at the same time. If there has ever been in America anything like the complicated strategy of Bonaparte's campaigns in Italy, it was when Paz made forty companies cross the Sierra de Cordova and take a position where they would inevitably intercept all fugitives from a regular battle. The Montonera, paralyzed, surrounded on all sides, fell into the net which had been spread for it. It is not necessary to give the particulars of that memorable battle. General Paz, in his despatch, gave the number of his loss as seventy, for appearance sake, but in fact, he had only lost twelve men in a contest with eight thousand men, and twenty pieces of artillery. A simple maneuvre had defeated the valiant Quiroga ; and the army which had cost so many tears and horrors of all kinds, only served to show Facundo's bad management, and to give to Paz several thousand useless prisoners.

CHAPTER XI.

SOCIAL WAR.

" A horse, a horse ! my kingdom for a horse." — *Shakespeare.*

CHACON.

FACUNDO, the gaucho outlaw of the Llanos, did not return to the country this time, but went directly to Buenos Ayres, and it was this unexpected step that prevented him from falling into the hands of his pursuers. He saw that he could do nothing more in the provinces, and for this once he could not even stop to harass the peasantry on his way, for his conquerors were ready to come to their defense from all directions.

Important advantages were secured by this battle of Oncativo or Laguna Larga. Cordova, Mendoza, San Juan, San Luis, La Rioja, Catamarca, Tucuman, Salta, and Jujui, were now free from the rule of the country commandants. The unity of the Republic, which Rivadavia had hoped to bring about through parliamentary means, seemed now about to be effected by means of arms, at least in this portion of it; and General Paz called a congress of deputies from these provinces to consider what form of constitution would be desirable. Lavalle had been less fortunate in Buenos Ayres, and Rosas, who was destined to play such a terrible part in Argentine history, had already begun to influence public affairs, and to rule the city. The Republic was now, therefore, divided into two parts : one in the interior, which desired Buenos Ayres for the capital of the union ; the other in Buenos Ayres, which made a pretense of not wishing this city to be the capital, that it might separate itself from European civilization and civil order.

Another fact had been disclosed by this battle, namely, that the Montonera had lost its primitive strength, and that civilized armies could compete with it successfully. It is a significant fact in Argentine history, that, as time passes, the pastoral bands lose their early vigor. Facundo was already obliged to spur them on with terror, and they were but a dull, disorderly set, opposed to troops disciplined and guided by rules of strategy and art. In Buenos Ayres, however, the result was different. Lavalle, notwithstanding his bravery, which had been sufficiently proved at Puente Marquez, and his large number of regular troops, yielded at the end of the campaign, shut up as he was in the city by thousands of gauchos collected by Rosas and Lopez. By a treaty which was to all purpose a capitulation, he gave up his authority, and Rosas entered Buenos Ayres. I believe that only through an unfortunate mistake of his, Lavalle lost the victory. He had been famous for the success of his cavalry charges ; at the defeat of Toreta or Moquegua, I do not remember which, Lavalle made forty charges during the day to protect the retreating army, and I doubt if the cavalry of Murat ever did as much. But unfortunately, Lavalle, remembering in 1839 that the Montonera had conquered him in 1830, abandoned his military education and adopted the Montonera system.

He equipped four thousand horse, and went into the streets of Buenos Ayres at the same time that Rosas who had conquered him in 1830, gave up his cavalry, in spite of native instincts, and finished the campaign with infantry and artillery. They exchanged parts : the gaucho assumed the military uniform, and the soldier the poncho ; the former triumphed, the latter died pierced by a ball from the Montonera. A hard lesson ! If Lavalle had made the campaign of 1840 according to military rules, we should now, on the banks of the Plata, be preparing for steam navigation on the rivers, and distributing farms to European emigrants. Paz was the first citizen general who triumphed over the pastoral or provincial element ; because he brought to bear against it all the resources of European military art, directed by a mathematical head.

The labors of Paz in Cordova had been to such purpose that after two years Facundo found it impossible to reëstablish his influence in the provinces ; it was only the civilized, the refined city of Buenos Ayres that offered an asylum for his barbarism.

The journals of Cordova at that time gave the European news, the sessions of the French assembly ; the likenesses of Casimir Perier, Lamartine, Chateaubriand, served as models in the school of design. Such was the interest of Cordova in European affairs. And at this very time the " Mercantile Gazette " was assuming the semi-barbarous tone that henceforth characterized the Argentine press.

Facundo fled to Buenos Ayres, not without shooting two of his own officers for trying to maintain order among his followers. He never belied his theory of terror, — it was his talisman, his palladium. He would sacrifice everything rather than this weapon.

On arriving at the city, he presented himself at the court of Rosas ; there he happened to meet General Guido, the most courteous and ceremonious of the generals who have made their way in the world by compliments in the antechamber ; he offered one of his very best to Quiroga, who replied surlily, " Am I a dog, for you to laugh at ? You people here sent a nice set of doctors (Cavia and Cernadas) to get me into trouble with General Paz. Paz beat me according to rule." He often regretted not having listened to the proposals of Major Pawnero.

Facundo soon merged in the crowd of the great city, and was only occasionally heard of at the gaming-table. General Mancilla once threatened to throw a candlestick at his head, saying, " Do you think you are still in the provinces ? " His gaucho dress at first attracted much attention — the poncho, and the long beard which he had sworn never to cut until he had wiped out the disgrace of the defeat at Tablada ; but after a little while he was scarcely noticed.

A great expedition against Cordova was then in preparation, and six thousand men from Buenos Ayres and Santa Fé had enlisted for the enterprise. Lopez was the commander-in-chief, with Balcarce, Enrique Martinez, and other officers under him. Facundo undertook a desperate attack upon Rioja or Mendoza. He received for the purpose two hundred criminals from the prisons, collecting in addition sixty men in the city, and with this company began his march.

At Pavon, Rosas was collecting his red cavalry ;

Lopez of Santa Fé was also there, and Facundo stopped to wait for the other leaders. Here, therefore, were the three famous provincial leaders met together on the pampas : Lopez, the pupil and successor of Artigas ; Facundo, the barbarian of the interior ; and Rosas, the bloodhound, who had been in training, but was now about to begin the hunt on his own account. The old classics would have compared them to the triumvirate Lepidus, Mark Anthony, and Octavius, who divided the empire among themselves, a comparison quite perfect even in respect to the baseness and cruelty of the Argentine Octavius. The three leaders were now in their element, and refreshed themselves with a bit of true gaucho life ; scouring the pampas daily, and making trials of skill in racing, lassoing horses, and fighting ; in all of which Rosas was usually victorious. He one day invited Lopez to have a bout, but Lopez said, " No, comrade, you are too rough for me." And in fact he had left them pretty well covered with cuts and bruises.

Quiroga crossed the pampas by the same road by which, twenty years before, he had fled as an outlaw from Buenos Ayres. At the city of Rio Quarto he met with an obstinate resistance, was delayed three days by the marshes which served as a defense to the garrison, and was about to retreat when a traitor came to him with the information that they had no more cartridges. Thanks to this timely revelation, Facundo took the place without difficulty.

At Rio Quinto he had to contend with the brave Pringles, the veteran of the war of independence, who on one occasion, when he was met by the Spaniards in a narrow pass, spurred his horse into the sea, with the cry, "Viva la Patria!" This same Pringles, whom the viceroy Pezuela had loaded with presents, and for whom San Martin had struck off the singular medal, " *Honor to the vanquished of Chancai*," was now to die by the hands of Quiroga's convicts.

Excited by this unhoped-for triumph, Facundo advanced upon San Luis, where little resistance was offered. Beyond this the road branched off into three, and Quiroga considered which to take. The one to the right led to the Llanos, the theatre of his early deeds, the cradle of his power; in this direction there were no forces superior to his own, but neither had he any resources there to fall back upon. The middle road led to San Juan, where there were a thousand men in arms, but unable to resist a charge of cavalry with Quiroga's terrible lance at its head. Finally, the road to the left led to Mendoza, where the real forces were under command of General Videla Castillo. There was a battalion of eight hundred trained men, commanded by Colonel Barcala; a squadron of cuirassiers, under command of Lieutenant-Colonel Chenaut, and also some militia-men, and pickets of cuirassiers of the Guard. Facundo had with him only three hundred undisciplined men, and was not in very good health himself. Which road should he take? He chose the road to Mendoza, — came, saw, and conquered. But how was this possible; was there cowardice or treachery? Neither. An unwise imitation of European strategy; an error in tactics in part, and in part an Argentine prejudice, caused the shameful loss of this battle. Videla Castillo knew that

Quiroga was approaching, but did not believe, as no other general would have believed, that he would attack Mendoza; he therefore sent to the Lakes his veteran troops, who, with some other detachments from San Juan under the command of Major Castro, formed a force strong enough to resist an attack, and to force Quiroga to take the road to the Llanos. So far it was all right. But Quiroga did march upon Mendoza, and the whole army went out to meet him. In the place called Chacon there is an open field in which the army left its rear guard; but soon after, hearing the firing of a company in retreat, General Castillo ordered the army to fall back hastily, in order to occupy the level field of Chacon. This was a double error; in the first place, because a retreat at the approach of a formidable enemy paralyzes inexperienced soldiers, who do not understand the cause of the movement; and secondly, because the rougher and more broken the ground, the better it would have been for fighting Quiroga, who only had with him a small body of infantry. What could he have done in such a field against six hundred infantry with a formidable battery of artillery in front? But unfortunately the officers were all native Argentines, who were devoted to horses; for them there would be no glory except in a victory won by the sword, and therefore they thought an open field for cavalry charges was absolutely necessary; this is the mistake in Argentine strategy.

The battle began, and a squadron of militia was ordered to charge, — another Argentine mistake is this of beginning the fight with a charge of cavalry, a mistake which has lost to the Republic a hundred battles.

And in addition to this error there was a misapplication of the European art of warfare. In Europe, where the masses of the troops are in column, and where the battle-field includes several towns or hamlets, the picked troops are kept in reserve until needed. In South America, a pitched battle generally takes place in an open field, the troops are not numerous, and the heat of the contest lasts but a short time, so that it is always desirable to rush in at once with the best men. In the present case, a cavalry charge was the worst possible beginning, but if it must needs be, it should at least have been made by the best troops, in order to rout at once the three hundred men who made up both army and reserve of the enemy. Instead of this, the old routine was followed : ordering to the front a large number of awkward militia, each man afraid of wounding himself with his own lance, and when the order to charge was given, they stood stock still, then fell back, and being charged upon by the enemy, gave way and embarrassed the best troops behind. In a moment all was confusion, and the battle lost ; and Facundo passed on in triumph to Mendoza, without caring for the generals, infantry, and guns, which he left to his rear guard. This was the result of the battle of Chacon, which left exposed the flank of the army of Cordova at the moment it was about to march upon Buenos Ayres. Quiroga's inconceivable audacity was crowned with the most complete success. It was useless to try to drive him from Mendoza ; terror and the prestige of victory gave him means of resistance, while defeat had left his enemies discouraged. He would only have hastened to San Juan, where arms and money were to be had, and commenced a useless and interminable war. The generals, therefore, went to Cordova, and the infantry and officers of Mendoza came to terms the next day. The Unitarios of San Juan emigrated to Coquimbo, to the number of two hundred, and Quiroga remained in peaceful possession of Cuyo and Rioja. These two cities had never suffered from all the evils Quiroga had hitherto brought upon them, as they did now from the interruption of business caused by such a large emigration of the wealthiest inhabitants.

But I must especially remark upon the still greater harm done to the spirit of civilization. Considering the inland situation of Mendoza, it had been a highly civilized city, with a spirit of enterprise and progress greater than any city of the Republic; it was the Barcelona of the interior. The spirit of progress had attained its height under the administration of Videla Castillo. Two forts had been built towards the south with the double advantage of extending the boundaries of the province, and of securing it permanently from the savages. The swamps had been drained, the city ornamented, societies of agriculture, industry, mines, and of public education had been formed, and directed by intelligent, enthusiastic, and enterprising men; a manufactory of woollen and flax had been established which furnished clothing for the troops, and an armory for the making of swords, cuirasses, lances, and bayonets, with none of the work imported except some parts of the cannon. A French chemist, by the name of Charron, had put up a machine for moulding bullets, and types for the printing-press, and investigated the metals of the province. It is impossible to conceive of a more rapid development. These things would not have attracted so much attention in Chili or Buenos Ayres, but in an inland province with only the aid of native workmen, the progress was prodigious, and in ten years it might have been one of the most remarkable places in the country ; but Facundo's army crushed this promising civilization, and the monk Aldao passed his plough over it and watered the earth with blood for ten years. What could remain ?

But the progress of ideas was not entirely stopped with the occupation of Quiroga ; the members of the mining society, who emigrated to Chili, there gave themselves up to the study of chemistry, mineralogy, and metallurgy. Godoi Cruz, Correa, Villanueva, Doncel, and many others, looked up all books treating of the subject, and made a large collection of different metals from all parts of South America ; they also examined the Chilian archives for information about the mines of Uspallata, and with much labor succeeded in establishing modes of operation by which these mines have become profitable, notwithstanding the scarcity of metal. From that time dates the new and profitable working of the mines of Mendoza. The Argentine miners, not satisfied with these results, scattered themselves throughout Chili, which afforded a rich field for the experiments of their science, and they have accomplished much at Copiapo and other places by the introduction of new machinery and tools.

Godoi Cruz had another object in his researches : he endeavored, by introducing the cultivation of the white mulberry, to solve the problem of the possible future of San Juan and Mendoza, which depends upon the discovery of some production of great value, yet of small compass. Silk answers this condition, imposed upon these inland cities by their great distance from the seaports, and the high price of transportation. Godoi, not satisfied with publishing at Santiago a long and complete treatise on the cultivation of the mulberry, and the care of the silkworm and cochineal, had it distributed through the provinces free of cost, kept the question of the mulberry constantly before the public for ten years, urging its cultivation, and setting forth its advantages, while he carried on a correspondence with Europe, learning the current prices, and sending over specimens of the silk he had himself obtained, thus discovering the failings or excellences in quality, and also the best methods of spinning. The results of this great, patriotic labor, were all that he could hope for ; now there are already some thousands of mulberry-trees, and the silk gathered by the quintal was spun, twisted, dyed, and sold in Buenos Ayres and Santiago, for the European market, at the rate of six or seven dollars a pound ; for the silk of Mendoza was as glossy as that of the best quality in Spain or Italy.

The old man finally returned to his native place to rejoice in the sight of a whole city succeeding in a profitable change of employment, hoping that he might live to see a caravan depart for Buenos Ayres, bearing the valuable production which made the wealth of China for so many years, and for precedence in which the manufactories of Lyons, Barcelona, Paris, and all

Italy still dispute.[1] Mendoza preceded all Spanish America in developing this useful branch of industry.

Have Facundo or Rosas ever done the least thing for the public good, or been interested in any useful object? No. From them come nothing but blood and crimes. I have given these details at length, because in the midst of horrors such as I am obliged to describe, it is comforting to pause on the few progressive impulses which revive again and again after being apparently crushed by savage barbarians. Civilization will, however feeble its present resistance, one day resume its place. There is a new world about to unfold itself, and it only awaits some fortunate general to put aside the iron heel which has so long crushed it. Besides, history should not be considered merely a tissue of crimes, and for this reason it is desirable to bring before the mind of a subjugated people a remembrance of past epochs. If they desire for their posterity a better record than they themselves have, let them not hope for it because the cannibal of Buenos Ayres is just now tired of shedding blood, and permits exiles to return to their homes. This fact is of no import in the progress of a people. The great evil to be dreaded is a government which fears the influence of thoughtful and enlightened men, and must either exile or kill them. This evil results from a system which gives one man such absolute power that there can be no liberty of thought or action, no public spirit — the desire of self-preservation outweighing all interest for others.

---

[1] The final result did not justify these flattering expectations. The cultivation of silk died out in Mendoza for want of encouragement.

Every one for himself, and the executioner for all without discrimination, this is the *résumé* of the life and government of an enslaved people.

Facundo, once more master of Mendoza, adopted his old methods of raising money and soldiers. One evening his agents were all over the city arresting the officers who had capitulated at Chacon; for what purpose it was not known, but the officers felt no great fear, confiding as they did in the good faith of the treaty. Nevertheless, a number of priests were also brought in and ordered to hear the confessions of the officers, who were then placed in a line and shot, one after another, under the direction of Facundo; the execution lasting about an hour. He afterwards gave as an excuse for this horrible violation of faith, that the Unitarios had killed General Villafañe. There was some foundation for the charge, but the revenge was monstrous. At another time he said, " Paz shot nine of my officers, but I have shot ninety-six of his." Paz, however, was not responsible for that deed, which he deeply lamented, and which was also an act of retaliation.

But the system of giving no quarter, so tenaciously followed by Rosas, and the constant violation of all customary forms, treaties, capitulations, etc., are the result of causes not depending on the personal character of the provincial leaders. Acknowledgment of individual rights which lessens the horrors of war, is the result of centuries of civilization, and was not to be expected among the semi-barbarians of the pampas. The savage kills his prisoner, and respects no compact when he has occasion to violate it.

The death of Villafañe had happened in Chili, and had already been avenged "eye for eye, tooth for tooth," in accordance with the *lex talionis*. The perpetrator of this deed was a remarkable specimen of the class of men I have been endeavoring to describe, and is therefore worthy of mention. Among the San Juan emigrants who went to Coquimbo, there was a Major Navarro, from the army of General Paz. This man, who came of a distinguished family of San Juan, was small in size, with a thin, flexible body, and celebrated in the army for a rash courage. At the age of eighteen he mounted guard as lieutenant of militia on the night when (in 1820) the battalions of the first division of the army of the Andes revolted, and, forming in four companies before the guard-house, ordered the city militia to surrender. Navarro alone remained in the guard-house, and defended the entrance; and then, holding one hand over three wounds in his thigh, covering with the other arm five wounds in his breast, and blinded by the blood streaming from his head, made his way home, where he was six months recovering his strength; a cure altogether unhoped for and well-nigh miraculous. Thrown out of his place by the disbanding of the militia, he devoted himself to trade, but a trade accompanied with dangers and adventures. At first he was engaged in introducing contraband goods into Cordova; afterwards he carried on a trade with the Indians, and finally married the daughter of a cacique, lived with her faithfully, took part in the wars of the savages, and accustomed himself to eat raw meat, until, in the course of three years, he became a thorough savage. While there he heard that the war with Brazil was about to commence, and leaving his beloved savages, entered the army with his old rank of lieutenant, where his bravery was so conspicuous that he soon became a captain and brevet major, and one of Lavalle's chosen men. At Marquez the whole army was astonished at his daring. After these expeditions he remained at Buenos Ayres with Lavalle's other officers, Arbolito, Pancho el ñate, and other chiefs, who displayed their bravery in coffee-houses and hotels. The animosity against the officers of the army became greater every day, and on one occasion they were drinking to the death of Lavalle, when Navarro heard them, and stepping up, poured out a glass and drank, saying in a loud voice, " To the *health* of Lavalle." A duel followed on the spot, and Navarro, who killed his man, fled from the city, and overtook the army before it reached Cordova. Before reëntering the service, he went in the interior to see his family, and learned with regret the death of his wife. Taking leave of his friends, he went back to the army accompanied by two young men — his cousin and nephew.

In the battle of Chacon he got a shot in his breast which burned off his beard, and blackened his face with powder; and in this condition he emigrated to Coquimbo, still accompanied by his young relatives; but every day he felt a strong desire to go back, and could hardly be prevented from doing so. " I am a true son of the army," he would say, " and war is my element; the first drop of blood shed in the civil war was from my veins; and from them should come the last." At other times he said, " I cannot go a step farther; I am getting farther and farther from the epaulets of a general. What would my friends say if they knew that Major Navarro was treading a foreign soil without a squad behind him ? "

The day they crossed the boundary ridge, there was quite a pathetic scene. They were obliged to give up their arms, and the Indians could not conceive of a country where one was not permitted to go about lance in hand. Navarro explained in their own language, while two great tears rolled down his cheeks ; they then laid their arms upon the ground, with much emotion, and even after starting on, went back and rode slowly around them as if bidding them farewell.

It was in this state of mind that Major Navarro passed into Chili, and took up his lodging at Guanda, a place situated at the beginning of the road which leads to the cordillera. There he learned that General Villafañe was going back to join Facundo, and openly announced his intention of killing him. The emigrants, who knew what these words meant coming from Navarro, left the neighborhood, after trying in vain to dissuade him from his purpose. Villafañe was warned beforehand, and asked protection from the public authorities, who gave him some militia, by whom he was abandoned as soon as they learned what was the trouble. But Villafañe was well armed, and accompanied by six natives of Rioja. Just as he was passing through Guanda, Navarro appeared before him, with only a brook between them, gravely declared his intention, and then returned quietly into the house where he was breakfasting. That night Villafañe was so imprudent as to lodge at Tilo, a place only about four leagues off. In the night Navarro armed himself and took with him a company of nine men, whom he left at a convenient place near Tilo. He then approached by moonlight, entered the court-yard, and called out to Villafañe, who was sleeping with his men in the corridor, " Villafañe, arise ! those who have enemies should not sleep." Villafañe seized his lance, but Navarro attacking him with his sword, ran him through the body. He then fired off a pistol, the signal agreed upon with his companions, who came up and falling upon Villafañe's men, killed or dispersed them. They then took horses and equipments and set out for the Argentine Republic to join the army. Mistaking the road, they found themselves after a while at Rio Quarto, where they encountered Colonel Echevarria, who was pursued by enemies. Navarro hastened to his aid, and the horse of his friend falling at that moment, begged him to get up behind himself; but Echevarria would not consent, and Navarro, determined not to fly without him, dismounted, shot his own horse, and both men soon shared the same fate. It was three years before his family knew what had become of him, the story being told by the men who had killed him, and who, by way of proof, dug up the skeletons of the two friends.

During Major Navarro's short absence, events had taken place which entirely changed the condition of public affairs. The famous capture of General Paz, who was caught at the head of his army by a lasso, decided the fate of the Republic. It may be said that the constitution failed to be established at that time through a singular accident; for Paz with an army of four thousand trained men, and a wisely arranged plan of operations, was sure of conquering the army of Bue-

nos Ayres.   Those who have since seen him triumphing in every direction, can judge if he was very pre-
suming to take this conquest for granted.   We might
chime in with the moralists who so often attribute the
fall of empires to the merest accidents ; but if it was
an accident to catch a great general with a lasso, it
was not accidental that the men who did it should have
used such means, being as they were of true gaucho
nature, though converted into a political element.

Facundo, having so cruelly revenged the death of
General Villafañe, marched upon San Juan to prepare
an expedition against Tucuman, where the army had
retired after the loss of its general had destroyed all
hope of accomplishing anything.   On his arrival, all
the Federal citizens went out to receive him as they
had done in 1827 ; but Facundo was not fond of repe-
titions.   He therefore sent one company in advance of
the assembled citizens, and another behind them; then
entered the city himself by a different route, leaving
his officious hosts prisoners in the street, where they
passed the whole day and night, lying down among
the horses' feet if overpowered with sleep.

When he reached the public square, he stopped his
carriage, put an end to the noise of the bells, and ordered all the furniture of the house provided for him
by the city, to be thrown into the street, carpets, cur-
tains, chairs, tables, mirrors, — all heaped in confusion
in the middle of the square ; nor would he go in until
sure that nothing remained but the bare walls, a little
table, a single chair, and a bed.   While this was going
on, he called a child who was passing by his carriage,
and asked him what his name was, and when he an-

swered "Roza," said, "Your father, Don Ignacio Roza, was a great man; give my compliments to your mother."

The next day a bench was prepared for the shooting of his usual victims. Who were they to be this time? The Unitarios had fled in great numbers, and many timid people not Unitarios. But Facundo began to impose contributions upon the women whose husbands, fathers, or brothers were absent, and the results were quite satisfactory, and accompanied by the usual circumstances, — sobs and cries of women threatened with the lash, some actually whipped, two or three men shot, one lady compelled to cook for the soldiers, and other nameless outrages. There was one especial day of horror to be remembered; it was when Facundo was about to depart for Tucuman; the divisions were filing off one after another, and the muleteers were taking care of the baggage, when a mule broke loose, and in trying to get away ran into the church of Santa Anna. Facundo ordered them to catch it; the muleteer went in for this purpose, and at the same moment an officer, by command of Quiroga, entered on horseback, tied both man and mule, and brought them bound together, the unfortunate muleteer suffering from the kicks of the animal. Just then it appeared that something was not quite ready for the departure, and Facundo ordered the negligent authorities before him. His Excellency the Governor and Captain General of the Province received a buffet, the chief of police narrowly escaped a bullet as he ran, and all reached their offices as quickly as possible to give the neglected orders.

A little later, Facundo, seeing an officer strike two soldiers who were fighting, with the flat of his sword, called him up and attacked him with his lance; the officer used his own for the defense of his life, and presently disarmed Quiroga, whose lance he then picked up and returned respectfully. Quiroga again attacked him; there was another encounter, and he was again disarmed. He then called six men, had the officer seized, and stretched across the window-frame with his hands and feet tied fast, and ran him through with a lance again and again, until life was entirely extinct. His rage was without bounds; General Huidobro, his second, was also threatened with his lance, and prepared to defend his life.

And yet Facundo was not cruel or blood-thirsty in comparison with other barbarians; he was only a barbarian, who did not know how to restrain his passions, and these once aroused were without limit, without restraint; he was a terrorist who, on entering a city, shoots one, and perhaps lashes another, but for a reason. The person shot is blind, or paralyzed; the unhappy victim of the lash is a respectable citizen, a young man of one of the first families. His brutalities to women come from a want of delicacy; the humiliations imposed upon the citizens from the coarse desire to ill-treat and to mortify the self-respect of those by whom he feels himself to be despised. It is the same motive which makes terror a means of government. What would Rosas have done without it in a society like that of Buenos Ayres? How else could he have commanded from an intelligent people that respect which they never willingly show for persons who are

in themselves low and contemptible ? It is incredible
what an accumulation of atrocities is necessary to per-
vert a people, and nobody knows the amount of close
observation and sagacity employed by Don Manuel
Rosas in order to subject the city to that magical influence which destroyed in six years all knowledge of the
just and the good ; which broke the bravest spirits and
put them under the yoke.

Terror in France in 1793 was an effect and not a
means. Robespierre did not guillotine nobles and
priests to create a reputation, nor to elevate himself
upon the heaps of the slain. He was a stern man, who
believed that he must remove from France all her
aristocratic members to insure the object of the rebellion. " Our names," said Danton, " will be execrated
by posterity, but we shall have saved the Republic."
With us, terror is a method of government invented to
crush out knowledge, and force men to recognize as a
thinking head, the feet which are upon their necks ; it
is the compensation an ignorant man in power takes
for the contempt which he knows his insignificance
inspires in a people infinitely superior to him. This is
why we have in our times a repetition of the extrava-
gances of Caligula, who caused himself to be worshipped as a god, and associated his horse with him in
the government. Caligula knew that he was the very
lowest of those Romans whom he nevertheless held
under his foot. Rosas caused his sacred likeness to be
placed in the churches, and borne through the streets
on a car, to which were harnessed officers and even
ladies, for the purpose of giving celebrity to his name.
But Facundo was only cruel when in a passion. His

deliberate acts were limited to shooting or lashing a man. Rosas, on the contrary, was never in a passion. He made his plans in his closet, and gave his orders to his emissaries.

CHAPTER XII.

SOCIAL WAR.

"Les habitants de Tucuman finissent leurs journées par réunions champêtres, ou, à l'ombre de beaux arbres, ils improvisent, au son d'une guitare rustique, des chants alternatifs dans le genre de ceux que Théocrite et Virgile ont embellis. Tout, jusqu' aux prénoms grecs, rappelle au voyageur étonné l'antique Arcadie." — *Malté-Brun.*

CIUDADELA.

THE expedition departed, and the people of San Juan breathed once more as if awakening from a horrible nightmare. Facundo displayed in this campaign a spirit of order and a rapidity of march which showed how much he had learned from past disasters. In twenty-four days he passed over with his army about three hundred leagues ; so that he came near surprising some squadrons of the enemy which only became aware of his approach when he took up his quarters at Ciudadela, an old encampment of the patriot armies under Belgrano. It would be inconceivable how such an army as that commanded by Madrid, at Tucuman, with brave officers and experienced soldiers, could be conquered, if moral causes and prejudices against strategy did not solve the enigma.

General Madrid, commander-in-chief, had under him Colonel Lopez, a provincial leader from Tucuman, who was personally opposed to him ; and, besides that, a retreat demoralizes troops. General Madrid was not the man to govern inferior officers. The army went into battle half-federal and half-montonero in spirit, while that of Facundo had the unity produced by terror and obedience to a leader who is not a cause but a person, and who on this account overcomes free-will and destroys individuality. Rosas triumphed over his enemies by that power, which made all his satellites passive instruments and blind executors of his supreme will.

The evening before the battle, Colonel Balmaceda asked of the general-in-chief permission to make the first charge. If it had been allowable for a battle to begin with a cavalry charge, or for an inferior officer to take the liberty of suggesting it, the battle would have been gained; for nothing in Brazil or the Argentine Republic had ever been able to withstand the charges of the second regiment of cuirassiers. The General acceded to the demand of the commander of the second; but Colonel Lopez declared that this would take away some of his best men; for to him the select troops had been given in charge, which, according to rule, form the reserve; therefore the general-in-chief, not having sufficient authority to stop these disputes, sent back to the reserve the invincible battalion, and the brave officer commanding it.

Facundo deployed his men at such a distance as to shelter them from the infantry commanded by Barcala, and to weaken the effect of eight pieces of artillery directed by the intelligent Arengreen. Could Quiroga have foreseen what his enemies were first doing? In a previous battle he had shot his own victorious officer for not pursuing with an inferior force the defeated enemy.

From one end to the other of Quiroga's line the

soldiers trembled with terror, not of the enemy, but of their chief, who walked up and down behind the line, brandishing his lance. They could only hope to escape from this oppressive terror by throwing themselves upon the enemy. They rushed forward, broke the line of bayonets merely to put something between them and the image of Facundo, which pursued them like a phantom. Thus on one side reigned terror, and on the other anarchy. At the first attempt to charge, the cavalry of Madrid gave way, the reserve followed, and there only remained five officers, with the artillery, whose discharges became fainter and fainter, and the infantry, which rushed to a hand-in-hand fight with the enemy. But why say more? The victor should give the details of a battle.

Consternation reigned in Tucuman; immense numbers emigrated, for this was Facundo's third visit. The following day a contribution was levied. Quiroga, knowing that there were valuables hidden in a church, questioned the sacristan, who, being a silly fellow, answered with a laugh, for which he was shot on the spot. The chests of the general were soon filled with gold; therefore it is not strange that the guardian of San Francisco and the priest Colombres, were the next victims of the lash. Facundo then visited the prisoners, counted out the officers, and retired to rest after his fatigue, leaving orders for them to be shot.

Tucuman is a tropical country, where Nature has displayed its greatest pomp; it is the Eden of America, and without a rival on the surface of the earth. Imagine the Andes covered with a most luxuriant vegetation, from which escape twelve rivers at equal distances, flowing parallel to each other, until they converge and form a navigable stream, which reaches to the heart of South America. The country watered by these branches comprises more than fifty leagues. Primeval forests cover the surface, and unite the gorgeousness of India with the beauties of Greece.

The walnut interlaces its long branches with the mahogany and ebony; the cedar and the classic laurel grow side by side, and beneath these the myrtle consecrated to Venus; still leaving space for the fragrant spikenard and the white lily.

A belt of odoriferous cedar allows a passage through the forest, which is everywhere else impassable because of the thick and thorny rose-bushes. The old trunks are covered with various species of flowering mosses, and the bindweed and other vines festoon and entwine all these different trees.

Over all this vegetation, which defies the brush of fancy in combination and richness of coloring, fly myriads of golden butterflies, brilliant humming-birds, green parrots, blue magpies, and orange-colored toucans. The sound of these noisy birds greets one all day long like the roar of a cataract.

Major Andrews, an English traveller, who has devoted many pages to the description of these beauties, relates that he used to go out every morning to enjoy the sight of this magnificent vegetation, and that he often penetrated far into the thick, aromatic forests, so enraptured 'hat only after his return home did he know that his clothes were torn, and his face scratched and bleeding. The city is surrounded for many leagues by a forest of orange-trees, rounded to about the same

height, so as to form a vast canopy supported by millions
of smooth columns. The rays of the torrid sun have
never shone upon the scenes which are enacted under
this immense roof. The young girls of Tucuman pass
the Sundays there, each group choosing a convenient
place. According to the season, they gather fruit or
scatter blossoms under the feet of the dancers, who are
intoxicated with the rich perfume and the melodious
sounds of the guitar. Perhaps one might believe this
description to be taken from the " Thousand and One
Nights," or other Eastern fairy tale; but I cannot half
describe the voluptuous beauty of these damsels, daughters of the tropics, as they recline for their siesta beneath
the shade of the myrtles and laurels, enjoying such
odors as would bring asphyxia upon one unaccustomed
to the atmosphere.

Facundo went into one of these recesses formed by
shady branches, perhaps to consider what he should do
to the poor city fallen into his hands, like a squirrel
into the paw of a lion. Presently a deputation of
young girls, radiant with youth and beauty, approached
the place where Facundo was lying upon his poncho.
The bravest and most eager led the way, hesitating
from time to time. Those who followed urged her
forward; then all paused, seized with fear. They
glanced at one another for encouragement; then, advancing timidly, stood before him. Facundo received
them kindly, made them sit down around him, and
asked the object of their visit. They came to beg for
the lives of the officers who were to be shot. Sobs,
smiles, all the little fascinations of women were put
in requisition to obtain their charitable end. Facundo

seemed deeply interested, and smiled benignantly ; he wished to hear from each one, of their families, their homes, a thousand details which seemed to please him ; and thus passed an hour of expectation and hope. At last he said to them, with the greatest complacency, " Do you hear those guns ? It is too late : they are shot." A cry of horror arose, like that which escapes from a flock of doves pursued by a falcon. They had indeed been shot — and how ? Thirty-three officers, from the rank of colonel upwards, received the fatal balls entirely naked. Two brothers, sons of one of the first families of Buenos Ayers, embraced each other at the last moment, so that the body of one prevented the ball from reaching the other. The latter cried, " I am saved." A mistake, unfortunate one ! How much he would have given to live. While confessing, he had taken a ring from his mouth, where it was concealed, and had charged the priest to give it to his betrothed ; who, on receiving it, lost her reason, and never again recovered it.

The cavalry took charge of the corpses, and dragged them to the cemetery ; so that bits of brain, arms, and legs remained on the square of Tucuman, and served as food for the dogs. How many victories are thus tarnished !

Don Juan Manuel Rosas had killed in the same manner and almost at the same time, at St. Nicholas de los Arroyos, twenty-eight officers, not to speak of more than a hundred assassinations. If anything can add to these horrors, it is the fate of Colonel Arraya, the father of eight children, and a prisoner, with three lance wounds in his shoulder. He was forced to enter

Tucuman on foot, naked, bleeding, and loaded with eight guns. Exhausted with fatigue, a bed was allowed him in a private house. At the hour appointed for his execution, which was to take place on the public square, some musketeers forced their way into the house and pierced him with balls in his bed; leaving him to die in the flames of the burning sheets.

Colonel Barcala, the celebrated negro, was the only chief saved from this butchery. He was the ruling spirit of Cordova and Mendoza, and the civic guard idolized him. He was an instrument that they might preserve for the future.

On the following day a process was commenced throughout the city, called sequestration. It consisted in placing sentinels at the doors of all the shops, warehouses, leather and tobacco stores, tanneries, indeed everywhere, for there were no Federals. Federalism is a plant which grew there only after the soil was three times watered with blood by Quiroga, and once more by Oribe. Now it is said there are some Federals, as is proved by their ribbon, upon which is written, "Death to the savage Unitarios."

All movable property, and the flocks and herds, were claimed by Facundo. Two hundred and fifty carts, each loaded with sixteen beeves, were sent to Buenos Ayres. The European goods were gathered to be sold at auction by the commanders. Everything was offered for a low price. Facundo himself sold shirts, women's skirts, and children's clothes, unfolding and showing them to the crowd; any bid was received; the sale was soon finished; the affair was a success, — the crowd was dense.

After a few days, however, purchasers were scarce, and embroidered handkerchiefs were offered in vain for four reales — there was nobody to buy. What had happened? Did the people repent? Not at all; but there was no longer any money in circulation. The contributions on one hand, sequestration on the other, the auction finally, had taken the last medio in the province. If indeed a few still remained in the hands of the officials, the gaming-table emptied their purses. Leather bags filled with money were piled in front of the general's house, and remained there all night unguarded; for the passers-by did not even dare to look at them.

And yet the city had not been abandoned to pillage, nor had the soldiers had that immense booty. Quiroga used to say to his friends in Buenos Ayres that he never permitted his men to pillage, because of the immorality of the thing. A farmer once complained to him that some soldiers had stolen his fruit, and ordering the regiment before him, he discovered the guilty ones, who each received six hundred lashes; the terrified old man begged that the victims might be spared, and was threatened with a share of the punishment. This is the gaucho nature: he kills because his leader commands him to kill, and does not steal because he is not commanded to steal. It might seem strange that these men should not rebel and throw off the dominion of one who gave them nothing in exchange for their valor or their lives, did we not know from Don Juan Manuel Rosas how much terror can do, not only with the poor gaucho, but with the illustrious general and the proud, wealthy citizen. As I have already said, terror produces greater results than patriotism.

A colonel of the army of Chili, Don Manuel Gregorio Quiroga, Federal ex-governor of San Juan, and, at that time, a major-general in Quiroga's army, perceived that this booty of half a million was destined for the general alone, who would not hesitate to box the ears of an officer for keeping a few reales from the sale of a handkerchief. He therefore conceived the idea of obtaining his pay by abstracting several valuable rings from the general stock. But Facundo found out the theft, and had him tied to a post to be publicly humiliated ; and when the army returned to San Juan, the major-general went on foot over almost impassable ground yoked with a bull. The companion of the bull expired at Catamarca without attracting any notice. At another time Facundo, having found out that a young man by the name of Rodriguez, of high standing in Tucuman, had received letters from the exiles, had him arrested, conducted him to the square himself, tied him up, and ordered him to receive six hundred lashes. But the soldiers did not administer the punishment skillfully enough, and Quiroga took the leather straps used for the purpose, and swinging them through the air with his mighty arm, gave fifty lashes by way of example. At the end of the performance he himself poured salt water over the back, and picked off the bits of skin from the wounds. This done, he went home and read the intercepted letters, in which were messages from husbands to wives, charges not to be uneasy about them, together with receipted bills for merchants, etc., but not a word of politics. Quiroga then asked for Rodriguez, but hearing that he was dying, sat down to cards, and won immense sums. Don

Francisco Reto, and Don N. Lugones, were heard murmuring at the horrors they witnessed, and each received three hundred lashes, with an order to walk home through the streets naked, their hands over their heads, and their backs dripping blood; armed soldiers following at a little distance to see the sentence duly executed. To what a degree of indifference men may be brought by an infamous tyrant against whom there is no appeal, was shown by Don Lugones, who, turning to his companion in punishment, said, " Hand over a cigar, and let's have a smoke."

Dysentery prevailed at that time in Tucuman, and the physicians said there was no remedy for it, that it came from mental causes, from terror, a disease for which no remedy has yet been found in Buenos Ayres. One day Facundo presented himself before the house of a young widow who had taken his fancy, and asked some children who were playing at the door, where the lady was; one of the boys answered that she was not in. "Go tell her I am here," said Quiroga. "What is your name?" asked the boy, who, when the other replied, " I am Facundo Quiroga," fell down senseless, and has only recently recovered his reason.

A young girl having excited his admiration, he proposed to take her to San Juan. It can be imagined how the poor girl received this proposition from a tiger. Stammeringly she said that she could not; that her father ——. Facundo went to the father, and the miserable man, trying to conceal his horror, took courage to say that perhaps he would abandon his daughter, and she would be unprotected. Facundo declared that he should have no cause for that objection; and the

unhappy father, still hoping to put him off or to gain
time, proposed that a paper should be drawn up and
signed; but Facundo immediately wrote and signed
the required document, and passed it to the other for
his signature. At the last moment the father asserted
himself in the man, and he cried, "Kill me! but I will
not sign." "Ah, old rascal!" cried Facundo, leaving
the house in a rage.

Quiroga, the champion of the provinces, as he called
himself, was barbarous, avaricious, lustful, and gave
himself up to his passions without restraint; his successor did not rob cities, nor outrage women; he had
only one passion, — the thirst for human blood and despotism. Instead, he knew how to use words and forms
which satisfy the indifferent, such as: *the savages, the
bloodthirsty creatures; perfidious, wretched Unitarios;
the perfidious minister of Brazil; the dirty money of
France; the iniquitous claims of England;* — words
thus sufficing to cover the longest and most frightful
series of crimes that the nineteenth century has witnessed. Rosas! Rosas! I bow before thy mighty wisdom. Thou art as great as the Plata, as the Andes!
Thou alone hast discovered how contemptible are the
liberties, the knowledge, and the pride of mankind.
Trample upon them all; let all the governments of the
civilized world honor thee, the more insolent thou art.
Abuse them! thou wilt always find dogs to snatch up
the spoils thrown to them!

In Tucuman, Salta, and Jujui, a great, progressive,
industrial movement was interrupted by the invasion
of Quiroga. Dr. Colombres, whom Facundo loaded
with manacles, had introduced and encouraged the

cultivation of sugar-cane, for which the climate is so well adapted. He had bought plants from Havana, sent agents to the mills of Brazil to study the processes and apparatus; succeeded in distilling the molasses; and did not rest until ten mills were established and in successful operation. But this was scarcely accomplished when Facundo turned his horses into the fields of cane, and destroyed the mills.

An agricultural society was already publishing its proceedings, and preparing to attempt the cultivation of indigo and cochineal. At Salta, looms and workmen had been brought from Europe for weaving woolen goods, cloth, carpets, etc., all of which had turned out profitably. But what particularly occupied the attention of those cities was the navigation of the Bermejo, the great stream which flows between the two provinces, unites with the Parana, and thus provides an outlet for the valuable productions of that tropical country. The future prosperity of those beautiful provinces depended upon turning their streams to the uses of commerce; from poor inland cities, with small populations, their capitals might in ten years be converted into great centres of civilization and wealth, if, under the protection of an able government, their inhabitants could devote themselves to removing the slight obstacles in the way of their progress. Nor are these chimerical dreams of a possible but distant future.

In North America, not only hundreds of large, populous cities, but even whole States have sprung up throughout the region watered by the Mississippi and its branches, in less than ten years. And the Mississippi is not more available for commerce, than the

Parana ; nor do the Ohio, Illinois, or Arkansas water a larger or richer territory than the Pilcomayo, Bermejo, Paraguay, and so many other great rivers which designate the path to be taken by the people who shall hereafter inhabit the Argentine Republic. Rivadavia considered the navigation of the inland rivers of the greatest importance ; an association was formed at Salta and Buenos Ayres with a capital of half a million dollars for this purpose, and Sala had made his voyage and published a map of the river. How much time has since been lost from 1825 to 1845! And how long will it still be before God shall destroy the monster of the pampas?

For Rosas, in so obstinately opposing the free navigation of rivers, in pretending to fear European intrusion, in keeping up the hostility of the inland cities and leaving them to their own resources, does not simply obey the instinctive prejudice against foreigners, nor even the impulse of the ignorant native of the port who, possessing the seaport and the general custom-house of the Republic, does not care for the development of civilization and wealth of the whole nation, or see that this would fill the harbor with ships bearing the products of the interior, and the custom-house with merchandise. He follows, rather, the natural instinct of the gaucho of the pampas, who has a horror of water, a contempt for ships, and knows no greater delight than riding a good horse. What does he care for mulberry-trees, sugar, indigo, the navigation of rivers, European immigration, or anything beyond the narrow circle of ideas in which he has lived? What does he care for the progress of the interior when he himself is in the midst of wealth, possessing a custom-house which brings in two millions a year without any trouble on his part?

Salta, Jujui, Tucuman, Santa Fé, Corrientes, and Entre Rios, would now rival Buenos Ayres if the industrial movement so eagerly begun, could have continued. As it is, some of its results remain : Tucuman now has large sugar-presses, and distilleries, which would bring great wealth if the products could be carried with less expense to the coast and exchanged in Buenos Ayres for merchandise. But no evils are eternal, and a day must come when the eyes of this people will be opened, who are now denied all liberty of progress, and are deprived of all capable and intelligent men, who could carry on the great work, and bring about in a few years the prosperity for which Nature has destined this now stationary, impoverished, devastated country. Why are such men persecuted? Brave, enterprising men, who employed their lives in various social improvements, encouraging public education, introducing the cultivation of the mulberry and the sugar-cane, exploring the water-courses, with only the national interest at heart, and desiring no other reward than the satisfaction of serving their fellow-citizens! Why do we not see again arising the spirit of European civilization which, however feeble, did once exist in the Argentine Republic? Why has the present government — more truly Unitarios in spirit than ever Rivadavia intended — never given a thought to the investigation of the inexhaustible and yet untouched resources of a favored soil? Why has not even a twentieth part of the millions employed in a fratricidal war been used to educate the people or to facilitate trade? What has been given to this people in exchange for its sacrifices and sufferings? A red rag! This is the extent of the government's care of them for fifteen years; this is the only measure of the national administration; the only relation between master and slave, the mark upon the cattle!

CHAPTER XIII.

BARRANCA. — YACO !!!

"The fire which burnt Albania so long was at last extinguished. All the red blood has flowed, and the tears of our children have been wiped away. Now we hold the cord of federation and friendship." — *Colden's History of the Six Nations.*

THE conqueror of Ciudedala had driven the last supporters of the Unitario system beyond the confines of the Republic. The guns were hushed, and the tramp of cavalry was no longer heard on the pampas. Facundo returned to San Juan, and disbanded his army; but he restored the nominal value of what money he had taken from San Juan by the spoils of Tucuman. What more was there to do? Peace was then the normal condition of the Republic, as war had been before.

The conquests of Quiroga had destroyed all feeling of independence in the provinces, all regularity of administration. Liberty had ceased, and Quiroga's name took the place of law. In this portion of the Republic all leaders were united in one, and Jujui, Salta, Catamarca, Tucuman, Rioja, San Juan, and Mendoza, remained under the sole influence of Quiroga. In a word, the Federals had disappeared as well as the Unitarios, and the most complete unity existed in the person of the conqueror. Thus the undivided organization of the Republic which Rivadavia had attempted, and which had occasioned the contest, was realized in the interior at least, unless we can admit the existence of a *confederation* of cities which have lost all free will, and are at the mercy of a single leader. But in spite of the misapplication of common terms, the facts are too plain to be doubted. Facundo even spoke contemptuously of the much talked-of Confederation; proposed to his friends that they should choose a provincial for President of the Republic, and suggested Dr. José Santos Ortez, ex-governor of San Luis, his own friend and secretary. "He is not a rough gaucho like myself," he said, "but a scholar and an honest man ; the man who knows how to do justice to his enemies, is worthy of confidence."

Thus it appears that Quiroga, after routing the Unitarios, went back to the old idea he entertained before the struggle — the advocacy of a presidency and the necessity of putting in order the affairs of the Republic. Yet some doubts troubled him. "Now, general," some one said to him, "the nation will be governed by Federal principles." "Hum," he answered, shaking his head, "there are still some obstacles in the way," and he added, with a significant look, "our friends below (Buenos Ayres) do not wish for a constitution."

When communications from Buenos Ayres came, and journals which gave the promotions of various officers who had commanded in the useless army of Cordova, Quiroga said to General Huidobro, "You see they have no titles to bestow upon my officers after all we have done here ; we should belong to the port, to get anything." Knowing that Lopez was in possession of his Arabian horse, and did not send it to him, he was very angry, and exclaimed, " Ah, gaucho-stealer of cows, you will pay dearly for the pleasure of being well mounted ! " And he continued his threats and abuse until his friends were alarmed at his indiscretion.

What did Quiroga intend to do now ? He was governor of no province, and had no army under his command ; nothing remained to him but his arms and the terror of his name. On his way to Rioja he had left hidden in the woods all the guns, swords, and lances which he had collected in the eight cities he had overrun, numbering more than twelve thousand. He deposited in the city twenty-six pieces of artillery, with plenty of baggage and ammunition, and moreover he had sixteen hundred fine horses at pasture in the ravines of Cuyo. Rioja was the cradle of his power, the very centre of his influence in the provinces ; at a signal its arsenal would equip twelve thousand men for war. Some may incline to doubt these facts, but even as late as 1841 arms were dug up that had been concealed at that time. In 1830 General Madrid took possession of a treasure of thirty thousand dollars belonging to Quiroga, and soon after it was said that fifteen more had been found. Quiroga wrote to him charging him with having taken thirty-nine thousand dollars ; and doubtless much more had been buried before the battle at Oncativo, during the time when so many cities were despoiled. As to the real amount concealed in those two parcels, Madrid afterwards thought that Quiroga gave it rightly, for the discoverer of the last parcel, having been taken prisoner, offered ten thousand dollars for his life, and when this was not accepted, committed suicide by cutting his throat.

Thus the interior had now a chief; he who had been conquered at Oncativo, and who had in Buenos Ayres only been entrusted with a few hundred convicts, was now the second, if not the first in power. To make the division of the Republic into two parts more decided, the provinces bordering on the Plata had made a league or confederation by which their liberties and independence were mutually assured; though a certain kind of feudalism still existed in the persons of Lopez of Santa Fé, Ferré, and Rosas, — leaders sprung from the people whom they governed. Rosas had already begun to influence public affairs very decidedly. After the victory over Lavalle, he was made governor of Buenos Ayres, and until 1832 filled the office as well as any other would have done. I must not omit a significant fact. From the first, Rosas demanded to be invested with absolute power, but was strongly opposed by his partisans in the city. By persuasions and deceptions he succeeded in obtaining it during the war of Cordova, and when that was ended, he was eagerly desired to give up this unlimited power. The city of Buenos Ayres did not then imagine that it could exist as an absolute government, whatever the principles of its political parties might be. Rosas, however, resisted, gently but ably. "It is not that I wish to make use of such power," he said, "but, as my secretary, Garcia Zuñiga, says, the schoolmaster must hold his whip in hand that his authority may be respected." He considered this comparison entirely appropriate, and repeated it frequently, — the citizens were the children, the governor, man and master.

Rosas was obliged to yield; but the ex-governor had

no intention of becoming a mere citizen ; the labor and patience of many years were about to bring their reward.   During his legal term of service he learned all the entrances to the citadel, and all the ill-fortified points ; and if he then left the government, it was only to take it by assault from the outside, without any constitutional restrictions, without being fettered by responsibility to any one.   He laid down the truncheon to take up first the sword, and afterward the battle-axe. Not long before he resigned the government, a great expedition, led by himself, was prepared to extend and protect the southern boundaries of the province which were exposed to frequent invasions of the savages. Everything was arranged on a large scale : an army composed of three divisions was to form a line of four hundred leagues, from Buenos Ayres to Mendoza. Quiroga was to command the forces of the interior, while Rosas, with his division, followed the Atlantic coast.   The magnificence and utility of the enterprise concealed from the eyes of the people the political manœuvre hidden under this plausible pretext.   For what could be more desirable than to secure the southern frontier by making a large river the boundary between it and the Indians, and protecting it with a line of forts ; a very practicable design, which had already been clearly marked out in the voyage of Cruz from the city of Conception, in Chili.

But Rosas had no idea of engaging in any enterprise which tended only toward the good of the Republic. His troops marched as far as Rio Colorado, moving slowly, and making observations on the soil, climate, and other circumstances of the country through which

they passed. They destroyed some Indian huts, and
took a few poor prisoners; and this was all that was
effected by the great expedition, which left the frontier
as defenseless as it had been before, and is still. The
divisions of Mendoza and San Luis returned equally
unsuccessful from the deserts of the south. Rosas
then raised for the first time his red flag, like that of
Algiers, and assumed the title of *Hero of the Desert*, in
addition to that already acquired, of Restorer of the
Laws — those same laws which he was now about to
destroy.

Facundo, too keen to be deceived as to the object of
the expedition, remained at San Juan until the divisions of the interior returned. The division commanded
by Huidobro, which had been in the desert opposite
San Luis, marched towards Cordova, and its approach
put a stop to a rebellion headed by the Castillos, the
object of which was to take the government from the
Reinafes who were under the influence of Lopez. This
rebellion was evidently gotten up at the instigation of
Facundo; its leaders were from San Juan, the residence
of Quiroga, and their supporters were his well-known
partisans. The journals of the time, however, say
nothing about Facundo's connection with that movement; and when Huidobro retired to his provincial
home, and Arridondo, with other leaders of the rebellion, was shot, there was nothing more to be said or
done; for the war about to begin between the two
parties of the Republic, between the two leaders who
were contending for supremacy, was to be a war of
ambuscades, snares, and treachery. It was a silent
combat; not a trial of strength between armies, but

between audacity on one side, and skill and cunning on the other. This struggle between Quiroga and Rosas is but little understood, though it lasted five years. Each hated and despised the other, and neither lost sight of the other for a moment, for each felt that his life and success depended on the result of this terrible game.

Perhaps it will be well to make a political chart of the Republic from 1822, that the reader may better comprehend the following operations.

ARGENTINE REPUBLIC.

Region of the Andes.		*Borders of the Plata.*
UNITY — UNDER THE INFLUENCE OF QUIROGA.		CONFEDERATION UNDER THE LEAGUE OE THE PLATA.
		Corrientes, — *Ferré.*
Jujui,	Rioja,	Entre Rios, ⎫
Salta,	San Juan,	Santa Fé, ⎬ *Lopez.*
Tucuman,	Mendoza,	Cordova, ⎭
Catamarca,	San Luis.	Buenos Ayres, — *Rosas.*

FEUDAL FACTION.
Santiago del Estero, — *Ibarra.*

Lopez, of Santa Fé, extended his influence by means of Echague, a creature of his, and over Cordova through the Reinafés. Ferré, a man of independent spirit, kept Corrientes out of the struggle until 1839. Under the rule of Beron de Astrada, that province turned against Rosas, who, with his increase of power, had regarded the League as of no effect. This same Ferré was led by his narrow provincial spirit to denounce Lavalle as a deserter in 1840, for having crossed the Paraná with the army of Corrientes; and after the battle of Chaaguazu he took the victorious army from General Paz, thus losing the important advantages which might have been secured by that victory. Ferré in these proceedings and others, was actuated by the spirit of provincial independence which had grown up during the war with Spain. Thus the same feeling which had thrown Corrientes into opposition to the Unitario constitution in 1826, made it in 1838 oppose Rosas, who was attempting a centralization of power. Thence came Ferré's mistakes, and the misfortunes which followed the battle of Chaaguazu, making it of no use to the Republic, the general, or the province itself; for if the rest of the Republic should be consolidated under Rosas, Corrientes could not maintain its feudal and federal independence.

The southern expedition being ended, or rather stopped, for it had neither plan nor end, Facundo marched to Buenos Ayres with Barcala and his chosen band, and entered the city without taking the trouble to announce his arrival. Such neglect of ordinary forms might be commented upon were it not entirely characteristic. What brought Quiroga to Buenos Ayres at this time? Was it another invasion like that of Mendoza in the very stronghold of his rival? Or did this barbarian at last desire to live amidst the luxuries of civilization? It is probable that all these causes urged Facundo to his ill-advised journey to Buenos Ayres. Power instructs, and Quiroga had all the high qualities of mind which enable a man to adapt himself to any new position, whatever it may be. He established himself in Buenos Ayres, and was soon surrounded by the principal men of the place; he bought shares in the public funds to the amount of six hundred thousand dollars ; played for various stakes ; spoke contemptuously of Rosas ; declared himself a Unitario among Unitarios, and talked continually about the constitution. His past life, his barbarous deeds, little known at Buenos Ayres, were explained and excused by the desire of conquest, and the necessity of self-preservation. His present conduct was temperate, his manner dignified and imposing, though he still wore the *chaqueta*, the striped poncho, and long hair and beard.

During his residence at Buenos Ayres, Quiroga made some trials of his personal strength. As he was walking, wrapped up as usual in his poncho, he [saw a man with his knife drawn, refusing to yield to a policeman ; and seizing the fellow, disarmed him, and carried him to the station ; he had not given the policeman his name, but was recognized at the station by an officer, and next day the papers all related the story. He heard one day that an apothecary had spoken contemptuously of his barbarity in the provinces, and went to his office to inquire about it, but this time was not very successful ; the physician, nothing daunted, told him that he would not be able to ill-treat people in Buenos Ayres as he had done in the provinces, and the story was circulated with great satisfaction in the city. Yet this Buenos Ayres, so proud of its institutions, was, before the end of a year, to be treated with greater barbarity than the interior had ever received at the hands of Quiroga. The police once went to Quiroga's house in search of him, and he overcame his first impulse to defend himself, feeling that there was a greater power than his, and that he might at any time be imprisoned should he take his defense into his own hands. Quiroga's sons were in the best schools, and he made them wear the European dress; and when one of them insisted on leaving his studies for the army, he was placed by his father in one of the regiments as drummer, until he should repent of his folly.

Quiroga used to declare that the only writers good for anything were the Varelas, who had abused him so much, and that the only honest men in the Republic were Rivadavia and Paz. To the Unitarios he said that he only wanted a secretary like Dr. Ocampo, — a politician who could write out a constitution, and he would march with it to San Luis, and thence show it to the whole Republic at the point of a lance. Quiroga represented himself as the leader of a new attempt to organize the Republic, and he might be said to have conspired openly had he done more than talk. His natural habit of idleness, and of expecting everything from terror, and perhaps the novelty of surrounding circumstances, prevented him from acting with energy, and at last put him in the power of his rival. There is no proof that Quiroga proposed any immediate action, unless it be found in his understanding with the governors of the interior, and his indiscreet words, repeated by both parties, though the Unitarios did not dare to trust their cause to such hands, and the Federals looked upon him as a deserter from their ranks.

While he thus gave himself up to dangerous indolence, the serpent which was to crush him in its folds, drew nearer and nearer. In the year 1833, Rosas, while nominally occupied with the great expedition, kept his army in the south, and narrowly watched

Buenos Ayres and the progress of Balcarce's government. The province of Buenos Ayres soon presented a most singular spectacle. Imagine what would happen if a large comet should approach the earth : first a general disturbance, then deep, far-off rumblings, then oscillations of the earth attracted from its orbit, then a mighty convulsion followed by the upheaval of mountains, and finally the deluge and chaos that have preceded the successive creations on our globe. Such was the influence exerted by Rosas in 1834. The government of Buenos Ayres became more and more restricted, more embarrassed in its movement, more dependent on the "hero of the desert." Every communication from him was a reproach to the governor, exorbitant requisitions for the army or some unprecedented demand. Soon the civil authorities lost all influence over the country population, and complaint was made to Rosas, who was supposed to control the peasantry ; but in a short time the same disregard of authority spread rapidly over the city itself, until it became no uncommon thing for armed men to ride through the streets, now and then firing upon the citizens. This disorganization of society increased daily, and it was not difficult to trace an influence from the camp of Rosas to the country districts, —from these to the suburbs of the city, and thence to a certain class of men within the city. The government of Balcarce succumbed to this power from without, and the partisans of Rosas worked hard to open the way for him, but the Federal party of the city made constant opposition. The chamber of representatives assembled in the midst of the confusion caused by the resignation of Balcarce, and chose General Viamont governor, who readily accepted the office.

For a short time order seemed to be reëstablished, and the city once more breathed freely, but soon the same confusion began again, and the same outrages were committed in the streets. It is impossible to describe the state of constant alarm in which the people lived during two years of this strange and systematic persecution. Frequently, without any apparent cause, people were seen running through the streets, the noise of closing doors was heard from house to house; some whisper had passed around — some one had observed a suspicious looking group of men, or the clatter of hoofs had been heard.

On one of these occasions Quiroga was passing by a street, and seeing well-dressed men running without knowing for what, he looked contemptuously at a group of armed ruffians, and said, " It would not have been so, had I been here."

" And what would you have done, general ? " asked his companion, " you have no influence over these people."

Quiroga raised his head, and with flashing eyes, answered, " Look you, if I should go into the street, and say to the first man I met, ' Follow me,' would he not follow ? "

There was such an overpowering energy in Quiroga's words, and his figure was so imposing, that they rarely failed to impress strongly.

General Viamont resigned at last, because he saw that he could not govern ; that there was a powerful hand holding the reins of the administration ; and no one could be found to succeed him, none dared accept the office. After awhile, however, Dr. Maza was placed at the head of the government, and as he was the old master and friend of Rosas, it was hoped that a remedy had been found for the evil. A vain hope, for the distress increased rather than diminished. Anchorena petitioned the governor to repress the social disorders, knowing that this was not in his power, that the police force would not obey ; that the real power came from without.

General Guido and Dr. Alcorta, in the chamber of representatives, earnestly protested against the violent commotion in which the city was kept, but the evil still increased, and to aggravate it, Rosas, from his camp, reproached the governor with the disorders which he himself had fomented. Finally a committee of representatives went to offer him the government, saying that he alone could put an end to the suffering which they had endured for two years. But Rosas refused, and then there were new commissions, and new persuasions, until Rosas consented to do the people the favor of governing them, on condition that the legal term of three years should be extended to five years, and that the "highest public power" should be given him ; an expression invented by himself, he alone understanding its meaning.

In the midst of these arrangements between Rosas and the city of Buenos Ayres, news came of a difficulty between the governors of Salta, Tucuman, and Santiago del Estero, which might result in war. Five years had passed since the Unitarios disappeared from the political world, and two since the city Federals had lost their influence in the government, but had courage to exact conditions which made capitulation tolerable. While the "*city*" surrendered at discretion, with its institutions, its liberties, etc., Rosas was carrying on complicated machinations outside. He was evidently in communication with Lopez of Santa Fé, and there was even a conference between the two leaders. The government of Cordova was under the influence of Lopez, who had placed the Reinafés at its head. Facundo was now invited to go and use his influence to settle the difficulties which had arisen in the northern part of the Republic, no one else being chosen to aid him in this mission of peace. He refused at first, then hesitated, and finally accepted.

It was on the 18th of December, in 1835, that Facundo took leave of the city, saying to his friends, " If I succeed, you will see me again, if not, farewell forever." At the last moment this intrepid man was assailed by dark presentiments ; it will be remembered that something similar happened to Napoleon when he was leaving the Tuilleries for Waterloo.

He had scarcely made half a day's journey when a muddy brook stopped his carriage. The travelling attendant came up and tried to get it over ; new horses were put in, and every effort made to move the carriage, but in vain, and Quiroga falling into a rage, ordered the man himself to be harnessed to the vehicle. His brutality and terrorism appeared again as soon as he found himself without the city. This first obstacle being overcome, he went on across the pampas, always travelling until two o'clock in the night, and starting again at four. He was accompanied by Dr.

Ortez, his secretary, and a well-known young man, who had been prevented from continuing the journey in his own carriage by the loss of a wheel soon after starting.

At every post Facundo eagerly asked how long it was since a courier from Buenos Ayres had passed ; the usual answer was, "about an hour," after which he called hurriedly for horses, and drove on rapidly. Their comfort was not increased by the rain, which fell in torrents two or three days. On entering the province of Santa Fé, Quiroga's anxiety increased, and it became absolute agony when, on reaching the post at Pavon, he found that the post-master was absent, and that there were no horses to be had immediately. His companions saw no cause for this mood, and were astonished to find this man who was a terror to the whole Republic, a prey to what seemed groundless fears.

When the carriage once more started, he muttered in a low tone to himself, " If I only get beyond the boundaries of Santa Fé, it is enough."

At last they arrived at Cordova, at half-past nine at night, just an hour after the courier from Buenos Ayres, who had preceded them all the way. One of the Reinafés hastened to the post-station where Facundo still sat in his carriage calling for horses, and greeting him respectfully, invited him to pass the night in the city where the governor had already prepared for his reception. But to each renewed offer of hospitality, Quiroga only answered by a call for horses, until Reinafé retired mortified, and Facundo set out again at twelve o'clock at night.

Meanwhile the city of Cordova was filled with mysterious rumors; the friends of the young man who had by chance come with Quiroga, and who stopped at Cordova, his native place, went to see him in crowds, seeming to be much astonished at finding him alive. They informed him that he had a narrow escape; that Quiroga was to have been assassinated at a certain place; that the assassins were engaged and the pistols purchased; but he had escaped them by his haste, for the courier had scarcely arrived and announced his coming, when he appeared himself, frustrating all their plans. Never was such a thing undertaken with so little secrecy; the whole city knew all the particulars of the crime intended by the government, and Quiroga's assassination was the only subject of conversation.

Quiroga arrived at his destination, settled the difficulties between the hostile governors, and started back to Cordova, in spite of the reiterated entreaties of the governors of Santiago and Tucuman, who offered him a large escort, and advised him to return by way of Cuyo. It would seem that some avenging spirit made him obstinately persist in defying his enemies, without escort, and without any means of defense, when he might have gone by the Cuyo road, disinterred his immense deposit of arms at Rioja, and armed the eight provinces which were under his influence. He knew all; had received repeated intimations in Santiago del Estero; he knew the danger he had escaped by his rapid progress; knew the greater one which awaited him, for his enemies had not given up their design. " To Cordova! " he cried to the postilion, as if Cordova was to be the end of his journey.

Before they reached the post-station of Ojo del Agua, a young man came out of the woods into the road, and asked at the carriage for Dr. Ortez, who got out and heard from the young man, that Santos Perez with a military company was stationed near a place called Barranca-Yaceo ; that as the carriage passed they were to fire into it from both sides, and afterwards kill the postilions ; no one was to escape ; the orders were positive. The young man, who had formerly been befriended by Ortez, now came to save him, and had a horse ready at a little distance for him to ride. The secretary, astounded by this news, told Quiroga what he had heard and urged him to save himself. Facundo questioned the young man again, and thanked him for the information, but told him he might make himself easy, adding in a loud voice, " The man is not born who will kill Quiroga ; at a word from me to-morrow, that whole company will put itself under my command, and escort me to Cordova."

These words of Quiroga, which I have but recently learned, explain why he so strangely persisted in defying death. Pride and faith in the terror of his name, urged him on to the fatal catastrophe. I had already so accounted for it in my own mind, before I had the confirmation of his words.

The night which the travellers passed at the post-station of Ojo del Agua, was one of great agony to the unhappy secretary, who was going to a certain death without the half-savage valor and rashness which inspired Quiroga ; death never seems more terrible than when imposed by the senseless bravado of a friend, and when there would be no dishonor in avoiding it. Dr.

Ortez took the post-master aside and asked him about the report he had heard, promising not to abuse his confidence ; he was told that Santos Perez had been there with his company of thirty men not an hour before, and they were then stationed at the appointed place, fully armed ; that all who accompanied Quiroga were to be killed, as Perez himself had said. This corroboration of the information before received did not alter the determination of Quiroga, who, after taking a cup of chocolate, as usual, slept profoundly ; unlike Ortez who lay awake thinking of his wife and children whom he would see no more, and only because he could not incur the charge of disloyalty to his friend, — a friend more to be feared than many enemies. At midnight, his agony becoming insupportable, he got up with a faint hope of receiving some comfort from the post-master. But the man could only repeat what he had already told, and showed unfeigned anxiety himself, for, as he said, the two postilions he was obliged to provide would have to share the same fate. Ortez then aroused Quiroga, and made one more attempt to dissuade him from his purpose, saying that he could not accompany him if he persisted. Quiroga laughed at his fears, and gave him to understand that his own anger would be more dangerous than anything he could meet at Barranca-Yacco ; so that the unfortunate man could only submit. Quiroga then called his strong negro servant and sét him to cleaning some arms ; this was all he could be induced to do in the way of precaution.

Daylight came at last, and the carriage started, accompanied by two postillions, one of whom was a mere lad and nephew of one of the company which lay in wait for them ; two couriers who accidentally joined the party, and the negro who went on horseback. They soon reached the fatal spot, two discharges were fired into the carriages from each side of the road, but without wounding any one ; then the soldiers rushing up sword in hand, disabled the horses in a moment, and cut to pieces the driver and couriers. Quiroga meanwhile put his head out of the window and said to the commander of the company, " What is all this ? " His only answer was a ball through his head. Santos Perez then passed his sword several times through the body, and when the butchery was completed, had the carriage filled with dead bodies, and dragged into the woods, with the murdered postilion still on his seat. The young lad alone was alive, and Perez seeing him, asked who he was. His sergeant replied, that the boy was a nephew of his, and that he would answer for him with his life. Without a word, Perez walked up to the sergeant, shot him through the heart, and then seizing the boy by the arm, threw him on the ground and cut his throat in spite of his childish cries for mercy. Yet in after life the death cries of this lad became a pursuing torment to him, and sounded in his ears, sleeping or waking, wherever he might be. Facundo had said of all the deeds he had committed, but one remorse troubled him, which was for the death of the twenty-six officers shot at Mendoza.

This Santos Perez was a gaucho-outlaw, celebrated in all the Sierra and city of Cordova for the many murders he had committed, for his bold audacity and extraordinary adventures. While General Paz was at Cordova this man had gathered about him a large band of the most lawless men, and occupied one of the wild mountain districts. With higher ideas, he would have been equal to Quiroga, as it was, he was only his assassin. He was very tall, had a pale, handsome face, with a curly black beard.

Perez was long pursued as a criminal by the government, and more than four hundred men were sent out to look for him. Once he narrowly escaped being poisoned by Reinafé; at another time a party sent to take him was commanded by an old friend of his, who sent for him under pretense of having something to say to him. Perez went down to him, saying, "Here I am, what is wanted?" and when the captain hesitated a moment with embarrassment, he turned on his heel, saying contemptuously, "I knew you wanted to betray me, and only came to make sure of it;" and before they could seize him, he had disappeared. After numerous escapes of this kind, he was at last delivered up to justice through a woman's revenge. He had beaten his mistress one night, and when he had fallen asleep, she went out and told some policemen where he was, having first removed his pistols from beside his pillow. Being suddenly awakened, and seeing himself surrounded by armed men, he reached out his arm, and then said, quietly, "I surrender, they have taken my pistols."

An immense crowd assembled in the streets when he was carried into Buenos Ayres, and showered upon him every kind of abusive epithet, but he only held his head the higher, and murmured disdainfully, "If I but had my knife." He was followed with execrations as he walked to the scaffold, and his gigantic form, like that of Danton, towered above the crowd around him.

The government of Buenos Ayres gave great solemnity to the execution of Quiroga's assassins ; the blood-stained, ball-pierced carriage was long exposed to public view, and lithographs of Quiroga, and of those executed on the scaffold, were distributed among the people. But the impartial historian will one day expose the real instigator of the assassination.

CHAPTER XIV.

On the 4th of February, 1817, the following incident happened in a deep, narrow valley of the Andes,
through which the river Aconcagua rushes from rock
to rock in its sudden descent. It was near sunset as
the vanguard of the division, commanded by Colonel
Las Heras, marched silently down the mountain towards Chili, by the rough, rocky road leading through
Uspallata. The fort, known by the name of "La
Guardia Vieja," was visible far down in the valley, and
had the appearance of being entirely unoccupied, but
a detachment of Spanish soldiers was concealed within,
watching the approach of the insurgents, and prepared
for a combat. Presently two discharges were fired
from the fortifications ; a company of the eleventh
rebel regiment immediately advanced, firing, from the
bank of the river to within twelve paces of the fort,
while another defiled along the mountain side to prevent all possibility of the escape of the Spaniards. A
moment afterwards they carried the walls at the point
of the bayonet, and wherever the contest was most
desperate, were seen flashing the swords of thirty
grenadiers, under Lieutenant José Aldao. Among
these was a strange figure dressed in white, like some

phantom, and dealing blow after blow with wild ferocity. This was the chaplain of the division, who, carried away by excitement, had obeyed the order to charge, which, when given to the conquerors of San Lorenzo, was sure to be followed by a battle in which no quarter was given.

When the victorious vanguard returned to the fortified encampment occupied by Las Heras and the rest of the division, the commander saw by the blood-stains on the scapulary of the chaplain, that he had been increasing the number of the dead instead of comforting the dying, and signified to him that he would do better to keep to his breviary and leave the sword to warriors. The hot-tempered chaplain could ill-brook this reproof, and turned hastily away with flashing eyes and compressed lips. On dismounting at his lodgings, he grasped the sword still hanging at his side, saying to himself, " We shall see." Thus was formed an irrevocable resolution. That evening's combat had revealed his natural instincts in all their strength, proving how little fitted he was for a profession requiring mildness and brotherly love ; he had felt the pleasure in shedding blood which is natural to those who have the organ of destructiveness strongly developed ; war attracted him irresistibly ; he wished to rid himself of the troublesome gown he wore, and to win the laurels of the soldier in place of the symbol of humiliation and penitence ; he therefore determined that he would be no longer a priest, but a soldier, as were José and Francisco, his brothers. The fear of scandal would not deter him, for he could cite many examples in his favor ; the celebrated engineer Beltran, who had lighted

with resinous torches the dangerous passes of the
and who afterwards prepared at Santiago c
rockets to be thrown into the forts of Callao, was
a priest who had laid aside the gown, finding that he
was able to serve his country more effectually than the
church.   In all parts of America, especially in Mexico,
priests and monks had led the insurgents, taking advantage of the influence which their priestly office
gave them over the common people.   However, the
chaplain Aldao was not troubled with a scrupulous
conscience, and would not have been deterred from
his resolution even without the excuse of such examples.   He belonged to a poor, but honorable family of
Mendoza, and had shown from his infancy such willful-
ness and disregard of authority, that his parents educated him for the priesthood, in the hope that its
solemn duties would reform his evil tendencies; a fatal
mistake, for his novitiate was, like his childhood, a
continued course of violence and immorality.   Notwithstanding this, he received sacred orders in Chili,
in 1806, under the episcopacy of Meran, and the pat-
ronage of the reverend father Velasquez, who assisted
him at his first mass at Santiago, and who was greatly
scandalized at seeing the newly made priest after the
battle of Chacabuco in military costume, and with the
martial bearing of a soldier.   " Thou wilt repent of
this," cried the good priest, in his horror at this profanation ; but unfortunately for the Argentine people
the prophecy was not fulfilled, for the apostate, though
unmourned, died a natural death, and with the honors
of a victorious general.

Colonel Las Heras, in his official report of the battle of La Guardia Vieja, made favorable mention of the priest, for capturing two officers, which, according to military rule, gives a claim to promotion; and consequently, the priest who had made his first experiment in fighting at Guardia Vieja, appeared at the battle of Chacabuco in the uniform of a lieutenant of grenadiers, and won a soldier's laurels. Though he could never rid himself of his priestly title, he soon proved in his new career that he did not wear the sword in vain, and became renowned as a formidable warrior and an implacable enemy; known to the army and the public generally, as " El fraile," or the monk.

I will mention one of the many remarkable deeds performed by him at that time. In the pursuit after the battle of Maipu, a Spanish grenadier of gigantic stature was cutting his way through the surrounding enemies, and with each blow of his mighty sword stretching a lifeless body on the ground; the brave Lavalle attempted to approach him, but felt his eager valor cool whenever the confusion of the struggle brought them together. Aldao, seeing this, made his way up to the giant, and, instead of falling with the many other victims, beat aside the terrible sword and passed his own again and again through the body of the huge Spaniard, amidst the loud acclamations of his party.

But whatever honorable deeds in arms the recreant priest may have accomplished, his conduct would at any other time, or in any other circumstances, have covered him with opprobrium. Freed from the restraint hitherto imposed upon his inclinations by the priestly office, eager for pleasure, and perhaps impelled to excesses by the necessity for excitement in which men often seek to drown any possible remorse for a wrong step in life, the monk henceforth became famous for his disorderly habits ; his private life being devoted to intoxication, cards, and women. But perhaps even these vices would have been forgiven, had they not outlasted the first excitement of unrestrained youth, and followed him to the end of his life. He abused even the large indulgence with which his companions in arms regarded his conduct, and though his commanders were very willing to make use of his courage, they took care to send him to a distance whenever it was possible to do so with advantage. Whatever differences of opinion there may be among men, all feel a repugnance at seeing a priest stained with blood, and given over to intoxication and vice.

Aldao had the rank of captain in the army which left Valparaiso under command of San Martin, to deliver Peru from the Spanish dominion. In that country, where the main body of Spanish forces was stationed, the insurgent army needed auxiliaries to harass the enemy on all sides, and act as reserve forces. For this purpose bands of guerrillas were organized in the mountains, which kept the royalists in continual alarm. These bands required bold, fearless commanders, who would risk everything to attain their ends, and who shrank from nothing, not even pillage and assassination. After taking part in the contests at Lacca and Pasco, Captain Aldao was sent to raise one of these bands and to act on his own responsibility, as circumstances should suggest. His own master, and within reach of no higher authority than himself, it can easily be conceived that his violence and unrestrained passions found plenty of victims among a timid people quite incapable of resistance. A characteristic incident soon happened. Aldao had determined to defend with his troop of Indians the bridge of Iscuchaca, but at the approach of a detachment of Spaniards, more than a thousand natives fled, thus losing their advantageous position, and without resistance delivering to the enemy an important post. Their furious leader, unable to prevent their flight, fell upon them as upon a flock of sheep, and did not cease slaying until a large heap of dead and wounded had fallen under the repeated strokes of his sword. However bloody might have been a contest at the bridge, and however deadly the fire of the Spaniards, fewer Indians would have fallen than thus lay on the ground, the victims of one man's anger.

The circumstances which occasioned the disbanding of San Martin's army, made it unnecessary for Aldao to remain longer in the mountains, and with the rank of lieutenant-colonel, he went to Lima, where fortune favored him at cards, until he had gained a large fortune, and then he left for Pasto. He there met a beautiful young girl of respectable family, with whom he became violently enamored, and who returned his passion. This was no passing fancy, but a deep, lasting feeling on both sides, only strengthened by the impossibility of a lawful union, which would ever be prevented by his priestly vows. Fortunately for him, she was unselfish enough to consent to be the mistress of a soldier whose epaulets could not conceal the stain of apostasy, and, leaving friends and country, she fled with him where the humiliation of her social position would be less known.

Aldao established himself at San Felipe, capital of the province of Aconcagua, where he became a merchant, and lived respectably; but the unfortunate pair were condemned to suffer the inevitable consequences of their false position, and the church which he had repudiated, would not quietly see him in the arms of another mistress. The curé Espinosa threatened to send him to Santiago to the tender mercies of the order he had abandoned, and finally forced him to remove to Mendoza, his native place, and carry there the scandal of his unlawful union. The church is ever bitter against those who have left her for social positions. If the monk Aldao could have married lawfully, perhaps his passions might have been moderated by the pleasures of home, and he might have been saved from the crimes of his after-life.

On recrossing the Andes, his reflections must have been strange, and anything but pleasant, for the mountain ridge which separated two provinces, was also a dividing line between the two phases of his existence: on one side he had been the chaplain, — the Dominican friar, — on the other, he was the Lieutenant-Colonel Felix Aldao, with an unwedded wife at his side. The people of Mendoza, who had been accustomed to see him with gown and rosary, would now see him with sword and epaulets, and women and children would point mockingly at " the Fraile," a name which came to be a more painful wound than any received in battle. He avoided society, and secretly nourished a sort of hatred for all mankind, which was the more bitter because suppressed.

On his arrival at Mendoza, in 1824, he took a farm at a little distance from the city, where he labored with commendable industry and intelligence, and where the only drawback to his happiness was the remembrance of the detested tie which still bound him to the church. In this retirement Aldao might have lived quietly to the end of his days, but unfortunately for himself and his country, echoes of arms and civil war once more resounded throughout the land, and he was drawn into that public life from which he was to escape only by death, loaded with crimes and pursued by endless maledictions.

The elements of destruction existing in the Argentine Republic were then in motion, and were soon to develop the cruel and despotic government which now crushes it. The brilliant but artificial government established by Rivadavia at Buenos Ayres, fascinated its immediate supporters, but provoked jealousies and opposition in the interior; divers ambitions were developing: the *Caudillos* [1] were soon to appear; parties were just forming; the envy excited by a rich, powerful city in her poorer neighbors, clamored for a confederation; Spanish prejudices caused many men to oppose all reform; the presidential government seemed to many a foreign domination; all was chaos; the clouds preceding the hurricane gathered darkly on the horizon, and as the terror of birds indicates a coming storm, so the general uneasiness of men's minds signified that some mighty commotion was at hand.

Suddenly the storm burst upon San Juan with the cry of "Viva la Religion!" The government of Car-

1 Country Chiefs.

ril was overthrown, and in less than twenty-four hours a fiddler had become a general, a lame cobbler was making laws, and a clown deciding the fate of a country. One Maradona, a pretended old nobleman, was found to give some show of decency to the plebeian mob ; and, unfortunately, deluded priests, believing it to be a question of religion, placed the cross at the head of this insurrection, — the beginning of the long series of crimes which brought the Republic to its present condition of barbarism. Two hundred citizens fled to Mendoza, and besought aid from the brave soldiers who had returned from Chili and Peru, Felix Aldao among the rest He hesitated, and asked himself why he should leave the asylum in which both his glory and his shame were hidden; but finally consented, and under the command of his brother José, marched to San Juan at the head of a company which obtained an easy victory over the plebeian crowd, without a leader or officers capable of directing its enthusiasm.

The Aldao brothers returned to Mendoza covered with laurels, and provided by their friends with money obtained by exorbitant contributions imposed upon their enemies. But the Aldaos had acquired in the expedition something more than fame and money, — the knowledge of their own power, — and formed a brotherly league for the purpose of obtaining their ends. All three were colonels, all brave, intelligent, and capable.

This triumvirate has exercised a most pernicious influence in the Argentine Republic, never yet fully appreciated. After reconquering Chili, San Martin sent the first regiment of the Andes to San Juan with orders to raise a company of dragoons, and then to join the army which was to invade Peru. But José and Francisco Aldao with other rebels, executed a military maneuver which deprived the army of this expected aid. Most of the officers were assassinated, and the two regiments, not having succeeded in occupying Mendoza, where Colonel Alvarado and other forces of the army were stationed, attempted a disastrous retreat to Tucuman, and dispersed with the shame of having deserted their banners.

The stragglers of the disbanded regiments, in passing through Rioja, met with a man already conspicuous in the provincial rebellions, and whose name was destined to become terrible in Argentine history. This gaucho with keen black eyes, and a pale face, almost covered with a thick, curly black beard, obtained from the deserters their arms. The dream of years was realized; Facundo Quiroga was in possession of arms, and provincial barbarism, the brutal passions of the multitude, plebeian ambitions and prejudices, the thirst for blood and pillage, had at last their partisan, their gaucho hero, their spirit personified. Facundo Quiroga had arms, and men would not be wanting; one cry from him resounding from forest to plain, would bring about him a thousand mounted gauchos.

Ah! when will an impartial history of the Argentine Republic be written? And when will its people be able, without fear of a tyrant, to read the terrible drama of the revolution, — the well-intentioned and brilliant, but chimerical government of Rivadavia; the power and brutal deeds of Facundo Quiroga; and the administration of Rosas, the great tyrant of the nineteenth century, who unconsciously revived the spirit of the Middle Ages, and the doctrine of equality armed with the knife of Danton and Robespierre. Had the defense of Montevideo gloriously ended the revolutionary period, we should have an epic poem in place of history, and in forty years should have passed through all the changes and elaborations which have been developed in Europe only with the lapse of many centuries. That we have made for ourselves a military reputation, witness Brazil, Chili, Peru, Bolivia, and the Indians to the south of us ; our victorious arms have been carried to the farthest extent of the continent. We have had our institutions, and contests of ideas and principles. And our future destiny is foretold in our numerous rivers, the boundless pasturage of our plains, our immense forests, and a climate favorable to the productions of the whole world. If we lack an intelligent population, let the people of Europe once feel that there is permanent peace and freedom in our country, and multitudes of emigrants would find their way to a land where success is sure. No, we are not lowest among Americans. Something is to result from this chaos ; either something surpassing the government of the United States of North America, or something a thousand times worse than that of Russia, — the Dark Ages returned, or political institutions superior to any yet known.

José and Francisco, after bringing disorder into the army which was to invade Peru, and exciting revolts in the interior, were taken prisoners and carried to Lima, where they would have received punishment for their misdeeds, had not the monk, chief of the mountain guerrillas, appeared and interceded for them with San Martin, urging as a consideration his own past services. Francisco, after the battle of Agacucho, in which he served under Bolivar, returned to Chili, where he was engaged by Rivadavia's agents to go to Mendoza and organize a force to dislodge Facundo Quiroga, who had taken possession of San Juan. For Quiroga, having heard something of the agitation among the Catholics, lost no time in raising a black flag with a red cross upon it, and the words, " Religion or Death!" though it is very certain that he did nothing for the benefit of religion anywhere, and equally true that violence and death constantly followed his footsteps. It is singular to see how these restless Caudillos looked for some pretense to disguise their vague, undefined ambition.

A letter addressed to Quiroga by one of his partisans contains this statement : " We can't do anything more with ' Religion or Death,' general, it no longer makes an impression ; *confederation* is the word for us now ; let us have a Constitution, and we will carry it at the point of the bayonet." Yet Quiroga was assassinated while endeavoring to pursuade the Unitarios to join him for the purpose of destroying Rosas and the Federals.

Francisco Aldao arrived at Mendoza with ten thousand dollars, which he had received beforehand for the enterprise against Quiroga ; but a consultation with his brothers caused him to change his mind, and keeping the money, he joined with them in forming the military trio from which Mendoza suffered so many outrages. From this moment the Aldaos labored secretly for the attainment of their own ends, the field being open to all unprincipled ambitions. They received an order to raise a regiment for the army of Brazil, and accepted it, with the intention of using the men for their own purpose.

Their ambition, however, met with an obstacle in the person of a creole negro. This slave, who early showed the talent not unfrequent in descendants of the African race, had been carefully educated by his owners, and was in condition to make use of his natural endowments when occasion required. He began his career as his master's assistant, and was rapidly promoted, until he became commander of a battalion, which brought him in contact with the chief politicians of the time. Barcala was not only one of the most distinguished characters of the revolution, but his reputation was untarnished, and this could be said of very few in those lawless days. He was a man of refined manners, tastes, and ideas, and his success was owing to his own merit. He never forgot his color and origin. He acquired his fame in history through his rare talent for organization, and the gift which he possessed in a high degree of conveying ideas to the masses; the lower classes were transformed by the magic of his power; and the officers and soldiers of his training were remarkable for their good behavior, decent dress, intelligence, and love of liberty. It was long before the impression made by Barcala in Mendoza was effaced; and in the revolution of 1840, against Rosas, a large battalion of infantry in Cordova still bore his name upon their banner, and resisted Rosas to the last.

He had been in Cordova in 1830, and had inspired its artisans and laborers with the love of liberty and equal-ality, in the broadest sense of these terms; and, though he was now dead, his ideas remained in the hearts of the people.

Obscure men who rise to power through the chances of social revolutions, never fail to persecute in others the intelligence and knowledge which they have not themselves; when the ignorant rule, civilization is brought down to their own level, and woe to those who rise above it, be it ever so little. In France, in 1793, the sovereign people guillotined those who could read and write as aristocrats; in the Argentine Republic, men of culture were called *savages*, and had their throats cut, and though the name seems mere irony, it is something more when applied by the assassin, knife in hand. The Caudillos of the interior rid their prov-inces of all lawyers, doctors, and men of letters; and Rosas pursued them even within the walls of the uni-versity and private schools. Those who were allowed to remain were such persons as could be useful in getting up a repetition of the government of Philip II. of Spain, and of the Inquisition.

Barcala felt himself to be a *gentleman*, and united a spotless reputation to great professional knowledge, and a talent for strategy which placed him among officers of the first rank. He made himself famous in the army of Brazil, and Paz and other officers of note re-garded him with a respect amounting to veneration. Quiroga, who shot all the officers made prisoners at Ciudadela, spared him — the only one who had fought until the last of his men were surrounded, and retreat was impossible. When offered his life on condition of serving under Quiroga, he accepted only with the understanding that he was not to fight against his own party; and in him Quiroga gained a whole army.

Such was the man whom the Aldaos wished to put out of their way; not a very difficult undertaking, since Lavalle, the Aldaos, and Barcala himself were to unite in an expedition to overthrow Albin Gutierrez, who had declared against the national government. Barcala and Lavalle marched to join the army against the empire, and the Aldaos remained to oppress the people, and give themselves up to the pleasures of dissipation.

The triumvirate had made use of all parties, and had served all parties in order to rid themselves of influential men. The revolution in favor of the national government having succeeded, they joined with Quiroga for the purpose of destroying it. The Constitution arranged by the Congress of 1826, was offered for acceptance to the provinces. The agents of this Congress were received in a rather singular manner by Quiroga in behalf of San Juan, which he then occupied. Two or three hides, stretched over lances stuck down in the middle of a clover field, formed a tent to protect this caliph of the faithful — this *divinely commissioned helper* — from the rays of the sun; here Facundo was lying upon a black cloak, dressed in a crimson *chiripa*, red cloth mantle, and untanned boots.

Dr. Zavaleta, Dean of the Cathedral, and agent of Congress, was received in this palace, and stood embarrassed in the presence of the commander, who neither moved nor looked at him, until he stammered a few words about his mission. Facundo then stretched out his hand, received the paper containing the Constitution, and wrote in the corner in scarcely legible characters, *"Despachado,"* and there was an end of the matter.[1]

In Mendoza the result was no better. The agent from Congress pathetically expatiated upon the evils existing in the Republic, conjured all patriots to unite under a constitution which would insure universal order and harmony of government ; but there was a threefold ambition to satisfy, so he made his touching speech with tears in his eyes in vain, and returned without having accomplished anything. The Constitution met with the same reception everywhere ; not from the people, who were allowed no voice in the matter, but from the Caudillos, who desired to retain for themselves entire liberty of action. The Constitution would have restrained them, whereas they required an open field for their ambitions, and pretexts for war, — religion, confederation, — anything to disguise the universal ambition. Thus the national government fell, and the celebrated Dorrego assumed the government of Buenos Ayres. The old Unitarios could not understand that Dorrego, with all his ambition and his intrigues, was nevertheless the only person who might have organized the Republic under a parliamentary form, and prevented it from being brought by Rosas under the rule of a cruel despotism which was to destroy all civilization and prosperity. Dorrego owed

---

[1] Subsequent information makes it certain that this scene was but a myth of the time, the only fact being that Facundo thus disposed of the Constitution sent to him.

his elevation to the parliamentary chamber and the press of the opposition party, and he would never have destroyed the powers which had defeated the former presidency; but all were overthrown when the gaucho of the pampas came into power, who understood little, and cared less for liberty and individual rights. It was his way to accomplish his ends by cutting men's throats; and on this principle the Republic is now governed.

The 1st of December, 1828, and the fatal victory of Navarro, taught the Caudillos their own power, and one and all prepared for the struggle — the Aldaos in Mendoza, and Facundo in the Llanos. A regiment of auxiliaries was put in training at Mendoza under command of the monk-colonel, whose fame was not yet so great as that of his brothers. As soldiers of the War of Independence, they knew what discipline can accomplish, and the auxiliaries, thoroughly equipped and trained, occupied the right wing in the famous battle of Tablada, in which eight hundred veterans of the national army, commanded by the able General Paz, left three thousand enemies dead, after a two days' fight. Of the regiment of auxiliaries, sixty-five survived, with their colonel, who was wounded in the side.

While this monk-colonel was confined at San Luis, by his wound, he amused himself by reading atheistical books, — an apparently insignificant fact, yet it would seem to prove that there was a struggle still going on in his conscience, of which he would fain have relieved himself. Quiroga, after the defeat, fled to the Llanos; Aldao naturally went back to his brothers. But many changes had taken place in his absence: a

division from San Juan marching to Cordova, revolted
on the way, and joined the Unitarios, who were sanguine of success, but unskilled in the art of war. The
two Aldaos then at Mendoza, pursued them, and after
a few marches and countermarches, conquered them
without firing a shot.

On returning to Mendoza, the victorious troops,
hearing of the victory at Tablada, revolted and threw
the power into the hands of the liberal party, which
showed no more prudence than it had done at San
Juan. These mistaken men persisted in immediately
establishing their long-desired constitutional forms, respect for life being their great maxim, and parliamentary discussion their means of action. Their enemies
took advantage of this infatuation to ridicule them, and
to endeavor again to overthrow their plans, while a
magnificent system of government was maturing under
the direction of General Albarado.

The brothers José and Francisco were planning
within their prison walls their reëstablishment in power;
while the monk presented himself in the neighborhood,
and with sixty men and the use of skillful intrigues,
opened a campaign against a government dependent
upon a fanatical people, two thousand men under arms,
and a man of reputation at its head. The prisoners
soon escaped, and the discussion of terms of conciliation
by the feeble government, gave time and resources to
the Aldaos. The die was cast, and the fate of Mendoza
was decided. A month was sufficient for the army to
be hemmed in, and even fired upon in the streets.

Facundo Quiroga sent several hundred gauchos from
Rioja to aid the three colonels of Mendoza, who had

assembled a considerable number of mountaineers. The government troops were exasperated at the inactivity in which they were kept by Albarado, and rebelled, insisting upon being led to battle. Finally the very sufferings of those who had felt the power of the Aldaos aroused them, and they went out to seek their enemies. In " el Pilar," of sad memory, they found themselves surrounded, not having taken a good position. In the evening twenty thousand shots were fired, and a hundred cannonades were discharged by the surrounded troops, and the next day the firing continued until twelve o'clock, yet they had not made their way out. The Aldaos knew that the ammunition was exhausted, and entrenched their men behind breast-works. Messages from Quiroga urged them to make no treaty, and to promise nothing. " We must," said he, "have as many enemies as possible to extort money from." But the people of Mendoza, hearing the incessant firing for two days, thought that by this time few survivors could remain, and the bereaved women ran through the streets entreating the priests and other influential persons to separate the combatants. A committee of priests approached the battle-field, selected neutral ground for a treaty, and it was agreed that all should submit to a government chosen by the people. The Aldaos must have laughed at the simplicity of their enemies, who were already conquered and prisoners, and yet maintained the proud bearing of free citizens. But Providence did not permit the farce to be enacted to the end, for it was to finish with a tragedy which filled even the actors with horror.

It was about half-past three in the afternoon when

the treaty was completed; the soldiers stacked their arms, officers collected in groups congratulating themselves upon getting out of the difficulty so easily. Francisco Aldao came into the enemy's camp, where he was cordially received, and in the lively conversation which arose, many a jest was exchanged by men who had formerly been friends. At this moment an emissary from the monk presented himself, and demanded unconditional surrender, under pain of death. Cries of indignation burst from all sides, and Francisco was loaded with the most bitter reproaches, but he said with quiet dignity, " Sirs, there is nothing in all this; Felix has just dined, that is all." And he repeated these words with a peculiar emphasis, at the same time sending an aide to inform Felix that he was there, and that the slightest manifestation on his part would be a violation of the treaty.

The alarm spread rapidly, however, the cry of treason arose throughout the camp, and the officers were in vain calling upon the men to form, when six cannon balls were fired directly into the group in the midst of which Francisco Aldao stood. If the cannonade had been a moment later, José Aldao also would have been there, for he was just on the point of starting, when he was surprised by the discharge, and exclaimed, " That is the work of Felix, — he is drunk ! " This was but too true, the monk was intoxicated, according to his usual afternoon custom ; only a few days before they had been obliged to keep him in bed to save him from some gaucho enemies while in this condition.

Confusion prevailed everywhere, and reached its height at the approach of the Auxiliaries of Don Felix,

and the Blues from San Juan. A moment after the
monk himself came into the camp, and seeing a dead
body lying upon a cannon wrapped in a cloak, a vague
presentiment induced him to command the face to be
uncovered; even then the fumes of the wine prevented
him from recognizing it, and his attendants tried to
make him withdraw, before he should perceive that it
was his brother; but he again demanded sternly,
" Who is it? " At the same instant he recognized
Francisco, and struck his head violently with his fist,
as if awakening out of a dream. Woe to the conquered! The carnage commenced, and he cried with
a hoarse voice to his men, " Slay! slay them! " while
he killed the defenseless prisoners about him. The
officers were all cut down or left wounded and mutilated, without arms, without hands. Day closed before
the butchery ceased, and the troops returned to the
city, but every shot which broke the silence of the
night, announced an assassination or the breaking open
of some door. When the following day dawned, the
pillage was still going on, and the sunlight revealed
the outrages of the night.

The actors in this frightful tragedy were themselves
stunned with the horror of their own work, and the
monk became aware of all that he had done, and the
death of his brother whom he had sacrificed. But he
was not a man to show his remorse, and if he felt any
he sought to stifle it by delivering himself up to intoxication and still further outrages. Thus the evil propensities which had been for a time under restraint,
broke forth again; and revenge for his brother's death
was an excuse for every excess. He had caused all

the officers to be put to death on that uncontested battle-field ; the next day he ordered the execution of all
the sergeants, and on the next the corporals. Every
time he became intoxicated his thirst for blood returned
with redoubled fury, and there are still persons alive
who heard him give orders for various assassinations,
with minute directions as to the manner in which they
were to be accomplished ; that at such a spot, at such
an hour, the legs of a certain victim were to be cut off ;
in another case the tongue was to be cut out, and in
another the face was to be so mutilated as not to be
recognized. Such deeds of barbarity were then un-
heard of and surpassed all imagination, but now they
are common enough, and Buenos Ayres, Tucuman,
Cordova, and Mendoza, have become familiar with still
greater atrocities. Terror had then paralyzed the people, and when Quiroga arrived, he found it easy to
obtain all the money he desired. There is still in existence an order which he drew upon the government
for the payment of his gaming debts ; for wherever he
went the silence imposed by the terror of his name was
only disturbed by rumors of punishments and executions for the purpose of obtaining means to carry on
his games at the card-table. Mendoza remained under
this evil influence, and a large army was prepared to
resist General Paz.

During the monk's rage for blood, his wife or mistress saved the lives of many victims. His brother
José, more considerate and more humane than himself,
also tried to appease his fury, but with each evening
came intoxication and unpremeditated outrages. From
this time Aldao lived in a state of continual alarm, em-

bittered by that horror of himself which was the only punishment he received in this world ; for while his less criminal brother José was assassinated, he died a natural death, feared and obeyed to the last. But Providence works in secret and he will surely meet his deserts.

A new army commenced another campaign against General Paz. Aldao had filled up the vacancies in his company of auxiliaries, and Facundo had gathered an undisciplined crowd of four or five thousand men. Aldao was accompanied by Don José Santos Ortiz, who was intrusted with the mission of trying to induce Quiroga to join with Paz in carrying on the war with Buenos Ayres, and it seems that Quiroga came near accepting the proposition. Paz on his part sent Major Pawnero,[1] a young man whose intelligence equaled his bravery, to make proposals of peace to Quiroga. But Quiroga's pride urged him to wipe out the mortification of his defeat at Tablado. The battle of Laguna Larga taught Quiroga that his heavy cavalry charges could not be always relied upon ; a simple maneuver of the infantry on the other side decided the victory, and Quiroga fled to Buenos Ayres, leaving on the field his infantry, artillery, and baggage. During the pursuit of the fugitives, a stout man whose weight had exhausted his horse, was overtaken and thrown down by a lance. A soldier was about to make an end of him, when he cried, " Do not kill me, it is important to the nation that I should be taken alive to General Paz. I am General Aldao."

An officer took charge of him as far as Cordova,

[1] Now candidate for the Vice-Presidency of the Republic, 1868. (ED.)

where a humiliating reception awaited him. Some officers from Mendoza, carried away by their desire for revenge, made him enter the town mounted upon a wretched animal, exposed to the insults of the people. " Wretch ! " they shouted, " thou hast brought destruction upon thy country ! " " I have also brought it much glory," replied the prisoner, with dignity, for the insults of his enemies had restored all his courage. He was then carried to prison, where he might reflect upon his past deeds in silence and solitude, and the retrospection became so intolerable that he excited the contempt of his jailers by his terror and childish exhibitions of alarm. He implored every one who came near him to tell him if anything was said about his death, and the ordinary noises about the prison filled him with fears, until at last he could no longer sleep at night, and never ceased his suspicious watch upon his jailers. Some priests undertook to reconcile him with the church, and whether through fear, or real repentance, he eagerly acceded to their propositions. One day while listening to Don José Santos Ortiz, he happened to look at a sentinel before his door, who knowing the terror he was constantly in, maliciously passed his hand across his own throat with a significant motion, and Aldao throwing the breviary from him, cried, " They will kill me to-day ! they will kill me ! "

His companion tried in vain to tranquillize him, by representing that he would have to be tried and legally condemned before he could be executed ; he only became the more agitated, saying, " Ah, you have not done what I have done ! " The soldier who had been famous for his bold, reckless audacity, did not dare to look death in the face, and showed the cowardice of a child.

In the mean time the people of Mendoza had again thrown off the yoke of the tyrants. Don José Aldao, unfortunately for himself, conceived the idea of escaping to the south, and trusting in the faith of the Indians; but the perfidious savages, having invited him and all his principal officers to a consultation, surrounded them; and though Don José succeeded in killing their chief, he and his friends, to the number of thirty, were all slain.

The people of Mendoza whom the monk Aldao had so terribly wronged, petitioned General Paz to deliver him up to them — and I mean the people in the largest sense of the word, for all had suffered by him more or less, and the craving for revenge seemed to be a disease which seized upon the whole community. No punishment could be invented severe enough for him; but at least a gallows should be erected for him in the field of Pilar, and it should be high enough for all the city to see him expire in the midst of their execrations. One committee after another was sent to Cordova to press their claim to the prisoner, as one connected in a peculiar manner with Mendoza, but General Paz was deaf to all these entreaties, and for the time there was still a chance that Aldao might some day escape from his prison.

The war recommenced about this time, and an accident which only an Argentine can understand, took General Paz from the head of his army. Having drawn up his men in a close column, he rode forward to a small eminence to reconnoitre, when, seeing a

company of mountaineers coming out of the woods
hard by, he supposed them to be some of his own troops
whom he had disguised as gauchos, and commanded an
aide to go and give them the necessary orders. The
aide obeyed unwillingly, being somewhat suspicious of
the new comers, and as he neared them was instantly
shot, while at the same moment Paz was caught in a
lasso, thrown from his horse, and was instantly in the
hands of his enemies. The army, deprived of the commander whose presence always insured victory, retreated to Tucuman, and sent into the city for the
prisoners.

A squadron of cuirassiers had formed in the square
at Cordova, in front of the state-prisons, from one of
which came frightful groans, breaking the silence of the
night, and exciting the compassion even of the oldest
veterans. The prisoner of Laguna Larga, the soldier
of the War of Independence, was on his knees, under
the influence of unmanly fear, groaning and sobbing
in the belief that these nocturnal preparations were for
his death; the officer who went in search of him found
him with a wafer, which he had consecrated, and held
in both hands as a protection against his executioners.
The prisoner, in his hour of need, had resumed his
priestly offices, and the theologians of the university
of Cordova had a long discussion upon the efficacy of
the consecration of the wafer as performed by him.
Being quieted with much difficulty, the miserable man
followed the army to Tucuman, and after the defeat at
Ciudadela, he accompanied the fugitives to Bolivia,
where they set him at liberty. Here ends one of the
most eventful periods in the life of Don Felix, the only
one of the trio then alive.

The battle of Ciudadela left the Republic once more at peace after the long previous struggle. The men who had been in favor of confederation had triumphed everywhere, from Buenos Ayres to Tucuman, and were now about to establish their form of government and to reconstruct the Republic. But instead of this, Facundo established a card-table in every city he visited; and with six hundred thousand dollars obtained by the year's conquests, went to Buenos Ayres to become the victim of another commander more astute than himself, who had determined to dispose of any man in the country who could in any way be his rival. The same indifference to the real interests of the people was manifested everywhere, and this state of things continued until 1840, though within the ten years Rosas established his power over the caudillos of the interior, while allowing them a nominal authority. The cities hoped than Facundo would reconstruct the Republic — a vain hope. They are now hoping that Rosas will be merciful to them if he succeeds in getting rid of his enemies.

Don Felix returned to Mendoza in 1832, and on his way through Rioja had an interview with Facundo, who had with him the noble Barcala. Aldao's first words were, " When are you going to shoot that negro ? " Quiroga frowned and seemed ill-pleased ; in fact he showed a haughty contempt for the monk, and wrote to the officers at Mendoza not to admit him into the army. But when Aldao presented himself, his personal influence was still too strong to be resisted, and the governor received him with offers of assistance, and bestowed upon him the title of commander-general of the frontier. He accepted the office, demanding at the

same time that his salary should be paid from the date
of his imprisonment at Tablado; he was evidently determined to secure for himself a comfortable and permanent establishment — the condition of the country
seeming to promise peace and quiet for the present.

He took up his quarters in one of the southern forts,
provided himself with a body-guard, and sent for a
coarse, ignorant woman, by the name of Dolores, with
whom he had become enamored in Rioja. Mendoza
had for some time witnessed the jealous rivalry of his
Lima mistress and this Dolores, and the latter being
finally victorious, her rival went back to Chili, leaving
two illegitimate children. An unfortunate influence
for the people was this utter disregard of morality —
vice in its most repugnant forms, — an apostate priest,
unchaste women, illegitimate children, whose illegal
birth was also sacreligious. Aldao omitted no cares for
his personal safety, and his body-guard never left him
for a moment, not even when he sat at the card-table;
and the fort from hall to cellar was one constant scene
of dissipation. Excitement became more and more
necessary to him, and when he visited the city he
ordered preparations for card playing as if it were a
regular part of public affairs. It is impossible to give
an idea of the degradation into which this man had
fallen, his debasing pleasures and entire forgetfulness
of business. It is true that neither the Aldaos nor
Quiroga ever really governed; they left to others the
labors of the administration, while they reserved for
themselves all the power.

Don Felix now governed Mendoza, through nominal
governors who dared not displease him in anything;

and his most casual remark uttered in his own fort, was enough to affect the government, and often became an absolute law. And this lasted for ten years, until constant intoxication brought his life to an end.

In 1832, Rosas prepared an expedition to the south, and invited the caudillos of the interior to coöperate with him for the protection of their respective frontiers, hoping by this means to make the pretext of an attack on the Indians cover an extensive military combination which he meant to use for his own elevation to power. Don Felix induced one tribe to attack another tribe, and deliver them prisoners to his troops; both tribes, however, united while on the way, and after putting to death sixty of the Mendoza soldiers, fled to the desert. Aldao followed and exterminated them, and this was all that was accomplished by the famous expedition; but Aldao made by it a valuable acquisition. Among the soldiers of his division was one Rodriguez, a man of great bravery, whom he took under his especial protection, and promoted to the command of a squadron. The monk was then becoming stout, incapable of action, and given up to intoxication, so that he would have been unable to sustain his power and reputation but for this Rodriguez, who, by proxy, still maintained the terror of his name.

Rosas having obtained absolute power in 1833, carefully studied the capacities of the various caudillos of the interior, that he might quietly bring them under submission; and this conquest of the provinces is one of the greatest acts of diplomacy accomplished by him. Soon afterwards he won over the auxiliaries of San Juan; had Quiroga put to death; got rid of his own tools, the Reinafés ; deposed Cullen, of Santa Fé, and then had him shot ; and made Benavides governor of San Juan in place of Yanzon. Barcala, the virtuous Barcala, was shot by the monk, who was now in the pay of Rosas. Brizuela, of Rioja, unrivaled for his brutality, was kept in command, notwithstanding the zeal of Benavides, his neighbor. Ibarra had quietly governed Santiago del Estero for eighteen years. In short, everything was arranged for the decline of the Republic into barbarism, when the despotic power of Rosas would be confirmed. Unfortunately there was no connected plan of resistance, no union, no leaders. Rosas had forbidden the passage of couriers throughout the interior, and the general want of confidence made any agreement between the cities impossible. The rebellion broke out, and the provinces joined in it one after another, but in the end were all forced to yield, paralyzed by the horrors of unheard-of outrages. Never was a revolution more universal or more ineffectual. Rosas would have lost his cause but for the weakness of his enemies.

Aldao together with Benavides now started on a campaign against Brizuela, who, unfortunately for the honor of their cause, had joined the patriots. It is hardly to be believed that a man in his position should make such a brute of himself as to remain intoxicated for six months at a time, without once seeing the light of day, or being for a moment in condition to receive the ambassadors from the different governors, or even Lavalle himself, who waited several days in vain for an audience. And Aldao behaved in the same way at San Luis, only not quite to the same extent.

The appearance of a small force commanded b
brave young Alvarez, caused the division of Bena
to disperse ; while the monk retreated, and by a rapid
march reached Mendoza in time to put down the rebellion of the 4th of November. The people looked
for nothing else than a repetition of the slaughter of
1829, but Aldao contented himself with some persecution and imposition of taxes. His rage for shedding
blood seemed to have ceased, and from this time no
such wholesale murders would have taken place in
Mendoza but for his disciples, who had profited but too
well by his former example.

Aldao again joined Benavides, and with him conquered Brizuela, both of them then taking up quarters
in Rioja, in order to intercept the army under Madrid,
which was approaching from the north.

One day the news came to San Juan that a division
from Tucuman was near at hand, and eight hundred
men went out to meet them, but were repulsed. Then
Acha, the immortal Acha, went with a handful of men
to meet the united forces of Benavides, Aldao, and
Lucero, amounting in all to twenty-five hundred men,
with four pieces of artillery ; and this battle of Angaco
is the one glorious event amidst the errors, failures,
and defeats of that period.

Acha's men were only about four hundred, little
disciplined, and unacquainted with the country, but to
make up for these disadvantages, he had with him a
number of truly patriotic young men of high standing
in the army, and their enthusiasm gave to the little
company the strength of double their number. As the
troops of the enemy quietly took their position, Acha

stood playing with a little switch, and with a smile which was habitual with him, pointed to the enemy and cried, "Rascals! now for real work!" The battle commenced, and a deadly firing was kept up for five long hours, the infantry of Benavides being within three yards of Acha's company; for Aldao had fled, leaving his companion to take care of himself. The young Alvarez, who was seriously wounded early in the contest, left a vacancy which could not be filled; and presently, when the men became discouraged and wavered in their resistance, he had his wound hastily bandaged and returned to his place, animating his soldiers by his eager enthusiasm, till they rushed again into the fight with redoubled ardor. As evening came on, all order seemed lost, and each man fought on his own account; little groups of cavalry, of ten, twelve, or twenty men, charged upon the enemy from all directions, and at last when the noise lessened somewhat, and the smoke of the powder cleared away, Acha found, not without some surprise, that he had won the day. With his usual smile, he congratulated his weary soldiers, saying, "Did I not say there would be some work worth seeing?" It is a pity that this remarkable man should have somewhat lessened his reputation by a foolish carelessness, which at last cost him his life. On the other hand, Benavides gained his reputation by an act of bravery which would have done honor to any general in the army.

The victory of Angaco might have been the means of saving the Republic, had Acha done justice to the bravery and self-possession of his enemy. Benavides, thus conquered by a handful of men, returned to San

Juan without showing the least discouragement, though his best officers had fallen, and all his stores were at the mercy of his victorious rival. He was retreating without haste to Mendoza, when he met a small reinforcement, and with this aid, little as it was, he conceived the possibility of a triumph, and determined to take immediate advantage of circumstances. Hastily returning, therefore, he attacked his unsuspecting conquerors, and after three days of vain resistance, took Acha himself prisoner, thus recovering all that he had lost, and winning as great renown as the battle of Angaco had given to his prisoner. When Madrid had been deprived of his vanguard, of the recruits which San Juan might have furnished, and of the chivalrous Acha,—a host within himself,—it was easy to strengthen the forces of Rosas under command of Pacheco. The battle of Rodeo del Medio was a corollary of the triumph at San Juan, and entirely owing to Benavides.

As to Aldao, his cowardly flight from the field of Angaco, had placed him in a humiliating position; all his former military fame seemed to have been transferred to Benavides, and in his own province he was regarded with open contempt. He made a journey to Buenos Ayres for the purpose of complaining to his master, and was rewarded by a magnificent reception. But this was followed by no attention from Rosas; he waited many months without obtaining an interview, and was then obliged to return to his own territory, which the army of Rosas had in the meantime despoiled of all implements of war. Henceforth Aldao had no other power than that obtained through Rodriguez and his band; this, however, was enough to enable him to

rule Mendoza, which had learned by years of oppression
to submit to him.   Rosas had placed all real power in
the hands of Benavides, whose prudence as well as
bravery enabled him to keep it.   The rivalry between
these two commanders was encouraged by Rosas, as it
insured his own safety.

Here ends the public career of Don Felix Aldao;
the rest of his life was only the gradual decay of a
constitution broken by dissipation and the hardships of
war, and to the end he was pursued by the scourge of
his own conscience and the maledictions of the people.

His harem had been increased by the acquisition of
new mistresses; and the immoralities and scandal of
his private life formed the common topic of conversation, where the shameful rivalry of these degraded
women was openly exposed; and they not only taunted
each other with their degradation, but laid violent hands
on one another in the streets.   And this state of things
was the more abominable because the administration
of the government was affected by it.   Neither justice
nor safety even was to be expected for those who
should happen to offend the reigning favorite of the
monk, and it was quickly known when a change of
dynasty had taken place in the seraglio.   Ladies of the
first families suffered outrageous punishments for not
treating these women with respect.   One young girl
was seated on a mule and whipped through the streets
for speaking slightingly of one of the mistresses; and
the principal inhabitants of Mendoza were compelled
to meet them at a ball, where the young men strove
for the honor of dancing with the coarse creature Dolores, who was the favorite at that time.   On the death

of one of the illegitimate children, Montero, the chief of the police, made the anouncement publicly, inviting the citizens to attend the funeral, and the principal men of the place bore the coffin, which was richly decorated and accompanied by the chief magistrates, who walked before and behind it, while a military procession followed.

When Acha and Benavides were fighting at San Juan, Montero conducted Dolores to the barracks at Mendoza, where she aided him in arousing the enthusiasm of the troops destined to march, by showing them Aldao's children, and calling upon them to support and aid their general. What a loss this general was to Rosas! Montero only could supply his place. Rosas needed just such men to maintain quiet in the provinces. All the governors had some peculiar qualities by which they served the ends of the man whose tools they were. Brizuela was a sponge with vast capacity for imbibing brandy, a sort of wine-bottle, who governed admirably in Rioja. Some left the people to take care of themselves while they got up cock-fights and races; others shut up the government offices and passed months without making a decree or using any administrative forms whatever; others let things slide on easily, tolerating everything, but an intelligent lawyer or judge. They all involuntarily agreed upon one point, the gradual disappearance of the public roads. Highwaymen became numerous, schools were closed, trade languished, the administration of justice was given up to stupid or ignorant men, the press was filled with nothing but fulsome praises of the "Restorator;" manners were fast declining towards barbarism, learning was despised, talent persecuted, and ignorance became a title to honor. And these governors did well in acting thus if they desired to remain in favor, for whoever showed any real capacity, or any interest in promoting the public welfare, was soon put out of the way. The Dictator had arisen to power through the barbarism of the people; and the poverty and ignorance of the provinces secured him from all dangerous opposition. The best governed of the cities scarcely perceived the gradual decline, for despotism, even under its most favorable circumstances, is for a people what phthisis is for the body; the patient feels no pain, eats, sleeps, and enjoys himself without care; it is only the physician who sees death surely approaching. Rosas assumed for himself the care of thinking for all; he must be the head, and the governors of the provinces the arms, hands, and feet, to execute his will; each member to be used, according to its capacity, for anything but thought in behalf of the Republic: the construction of the government was to be his own work.

The life of Felix Aldao was now drawing to a close. For a year before his death he was troubled with a cancer on his face, which eat into his nose and eyes, until he became partially blind; while the odor was so offensive that his companions at the card-table could hardly endure it. His temper did not improve with sickness, and he became so suspicious of the physicians who attended him that they were obliged to flee, feeling that their lives were in danger. During this year of illness no one dared to propose a temporary governor, for those unfortunate people had come to believe that the government belonged of right to the caudillos, and that it would be treason to question their capability, even when ill.   Aldao governed Mendoza to the last, and that without attending to anything but his own health.   As his death approached, he would not remain alone for a moment, tormented as he was by the terrors of his imagination, and a number of the citizens were obliged to take turns in watching with him.   One night he sprang from his bed and rushed in among them with a pair of pistols in his hands.   They without waiting to see that the wretched creature was a prey to his own fears, and not attacking them, fled out of the house and the town, and could with difficulty be induced to return the next day.   And these were the citizens of the Argentine Republic who had offended other states by their arrogant pride !   These were the people who had irritated Bolivar by their overbearing manners !   And now they stumbled over one another in their haste to run away from a sick monk !

At length, after months of acute suffering, the cancer caused the bursting of a vein, and the hemorrhage continued until he expired on the 18th of January — in retribution perhaps for the blood of the people which had flowed without stint at his command.   Some say that he went back to the church and died penitent, leaving a large part of his wealth to the Dominican order, to which he had belonged.   According to the obituary notices he made Rosas his testamentary executor; as the Roman proconsuls, dying in the provinces of the empire, used to leave their wealth to the emperor, together with the government of the provinces. These two contradictory statements prove at least one thing, that at his death there was still a question whether he was a monk or a general, but that matters little to him now. With the money acquired by oppressing the people of Mendoza, he left a home for each of his three families.

With so much that was bad, this man must have had some good qualities, for he had friends whose affection was never weakened by absence or death, and no one who inspired such devotion could be wholly bad. He was also beloved by his soldiers, many of whom remained with him for years. He was in the habit of sending large supplies of grain to the poor people south of Mendoza ; and whenever he learned of the arrival of the Chilian families who frequently emigrated to Mendoza, he supplied them with provisions until they could establish themselves. And, lastly, those who saw him intimately, say that he was extravagantly fond of his children, whose caresses were his greatest pleasure.

The family of Aldao is now represented by the acknowledged children of three women, some other natural children, and the legitimate offspring of his brother Don José. All the Aldaos had met with a tragic end, though that of Felix was the least so. All Mendoza followed his body to the church within which he was buried. That evening the Almeda was crowded with persons of both sexes ; until then, this promenade, the scene of much bloodshed when Pacheco was there, had been entirely unfrequented.

The only benefit which Mendoza received during the rule of this governor, was the settlement of its southern frontier by emigrants from Chili, who collected in villages under the protection of the fort of

San Carlos, the habitation of Aldao, who always encouraged this emigration.

Mendoza is now without a governor; it remains to be seen who will obtain possession of it. When Rosas heard that the monk was about to die, he sent a sister of his with her husband, who was physician and also secretary for Aldao. After his death, when the choice of a new governor was discussed, Rodriguez was in favor of the secretary, but the people preferred a native of the city.

I have now concluded my self-imposed task, with the fear of not having been sufficiently impartial; yet it is my misfortune if the facts are not strictly correct. I have carefully consulted both his friends and enemies, and the old soldiers who were with him at the beginning of his career. I have thrown aside all that seemed doubtful, and endeavored to moderate everything that was exaggerated. For the rest, the life of such a man, who took part in so many political changes, should be brought before the public by a more powerful pen than mine. The biography of these tools of a ruler, shows what means he employs, and the end at which he aims.

BIOGRAPHICAL SKETCH.

◆

DON DOMINGO F. SARMIENTO was born in 1811, the year after the Argentine Republic had achieved its independence of Spain, at San Juan, the capital of the province of that name, lying on the eastern skirts of the Andes. He was descended from two distinguished families that figured in the colonization, the Sarmientos and the Albarracines. The latter were descended from a Saracen chief, Al Ben Razin, who, in the middle of the twelfth century, conquered and gave name to a city, and founded a family which afterwards became Christian.

In 1846, Colonel Sarmiento went to see Arab life in the interior of Algiers; he found his family name familiar to the ears of the people, and was himself taken for an Arab, and told that he could easily be mistaken for one of the faithful. He was so ambitious as to emulate them in the wearing of their national garment, the bornoz; and in the exhilaration of the ride into the interior, under the Arab escort that the French commander had furnished him with, boasted that he could ride to the pyramids without halting. They took him at his word, and though the pyramids were not the goal sought, the feat nearly cost him his life; but the vigorous habits of his youth saved him. When he found himself in the tent of a Saracen chief, and looked about him to see the characteristic marks of Arab life, he was struck with amazement to find himself in the midst of surroundings so precisely like those of his native wild plains, that the conviction was brought forcibly home to him, that the gauchos of South America and the Arabs of Africa were one and the same people. It was a disheartening thought to him that he saw in these people one explanation of the difficulty of civilizing the engrafted population of those Spanish colonies, of which they were evidently the fountain-head, distilled through the Catholicism of Spain, and where, though they had perhaps lost the tradition of their origin, they had not lost the elements of *vis-inertiæ*, and repulsion to civilizing influences.

The Albarracines had the name of remarkable abilities, which had been transmitted from generation to generation, and in South America several distinguished writers were known among the Dominican friars that abounded in the family. Prelates and bishops, historians and logical writers were of the number, and they intermarried with a family of Oros, also of remarkable intellectual ability. The Oros, cousins of his mother, who were curates and friars of education, always had open house and hearts for the young Sarmiento, and their society helped to cultivate the faculties of the brilliant boy, in whom culminated the power of literary expression that had always marked the family. One of these able men, Don José de Oro, a clergyman, had much influence in the formation of his character. He had been chaplain of a regiment in San Martin's army.

After some patriotic efforts for his country in the

wars against the Spaniards in Chili, he had left society and retired to the mountainous region of San Luis, where his nephew, then a boy, followed him, and spent three years in the closest intellectual and affectionate intimacy, studying Latin, and listening to the historical and literary reminiscences of the holy man, who fed the active and open mind of the precocious boy with precious principles and a good store of miscellaneous knowledge. History and the polity of governments grew to be the passion of the young Sarmiento's soul. The appearance of Facundo Quiroga and his hordes in his native province and city had made a profound impression upon him, and with the disastrous history of the colonization and of the internal wars of his own country as a point of departure, and the influence of his uncle's keen and vigorous intellect and free and generous views, he was prepared for that remarkable career which has separated him from the body of his contemporaries in letters, in politics, in the consecration of his life.

But I will not anticipate. The earlier domestic history of his life was a still more remarkable preparation.

It is striking to see how great natures will mould even the most adverse circumstances. One can conceive of no circumstances more adverse to the growth of fine character than the isolated, provincial life of a Spanish colony, ruled by ecclesiastical domination, exercised over an uneducated mass like the remote descendants of Spaniards who have been cut off for two or three generations from means of improvement, and even from the knowledge of the world's progress. Yet here we find noble natures ready to respond to noble teachings.

Doña Paula Albarracine was the daughter of Don Cornelio Albarracine, who once owned half the valley of La Zonda, and troops of carts and mules, but died after being bedridden for twelve years, leaving to his fifteen children an inheritance of poverty and various portions of wild land. But I leave the son to describe his own mother.

PREFACE TO " THE RECOLLECTIONS OF A PROVINCE."

" The following pages are purely confidential, addressed to a hundred persons only, and dictated by personal considerations.

" In a letter written to a friend of my childhood, in 1832, I had the indiscretion to call Facundo Quiroga a bandit. All Argentines, both in Europe and America, now agree that it was a just epithet, but at that time my letter was shown to a bad priest, who was President of a Chamber of Representatives. It was read in full session, a sentence was decreed against me, and they had the meanness to put it into the hands of the offended one, who, meaner still than his flatterers, insulted my mother, calling her opprobrious names, and assured her that he should kill me when he pleased, and wherever I could be found. This event, which made it forever impossible for me to return to my country if God did not dispose events differently from what man purposed to do, was repeated sixteen years later with consequences apparently still more alarming. In May, 1843, I wrote another letter to an old benefactor, in which I committed the indiscretion (for which I honor myself,) of characterizing and judging the government of Rosas, according to the dictates of my conscience, and this letter, like that of 1832, was sent to the very man upon whom the judgment was pronounced. All my countrymen know what followed. The government of Buenos Ayres published the letter, made a requisition for me upon the government of Chili, and sent the diplomatic note and the letter with a circular to the confederate governors. The governor of Chili answered, Rosas replied, the circulars were repeated, the answers of the governors of the interior were received; the system of giving publicity to all those meannesses which disgrace the human race more than they can any government, was continued, and apparently the farce will go on without its being possible for any one to foresee the dénouement. The presses of all the neighboring countries have reproduced the publications of the government of Buenos Ayres, and in those thirty or more official notes, the name of D. F. Sarmiento has always been accompanied with the epithets, '*infamous, unclean, vile, savage,*' with variations such as, '*traitor, madman, contemptible, arrogant,*' etc. I am thus characterized by men who do not know me, before people who hear my name for the first time. The desire of every good man not to be despised, the aspiration of a patriot to preserve the esteem of his fellow citizens, have induced me to publish this little book, which I abandon to its fate. It is difficult to speak of one's self, one's own good qualities, without exciting contempt and attracting criticism, sometimes with good reason; but it is more difficult to consent to dishonor, and to let even one's own modesty conspire to one's injury, and I have not hesitated a moment which to choose between these opposite extremes."

THE HISTORY OF MY MOTHER.

"I feel an oppression of the heart when I approach the facts I am now to record. The mother is to the man the personification of Providence; is the living earth to which the heart clings as roots to the soil. All who have written of their family, have spoken with tenderness of their mother. St. Augustine lauded his so highly, that the Church placed her at his side upon the altars. Lamartine has said so much of his mother in his 'Confidences,' that human nature has been enriched with one of the most beautiful types of the mother known to history; a mother adorable in the beauty of her countenance, and endowed with a heart which seems to be an unfathomable abyss of goodness, love, and enthusiasm, to say nothing of gifts of supreme intelligence which created the soul of Lamartine, that last offshoot of the old aristocratic society which was transfigured under the maternal wing into the angel of peace, destined to announce to unquiet Europe the advent of the Republic.

" To the affections of the heart, there is no mother equal to the one who has presided over our own fate, but when pages like Lamartine's have been read, all mothers do not leave such an image sculptured upon the mind; mine however, God knows, is worthy the honors of apotheosis, and I should not have written these pages if the vigor of her mind had not inspired me to vindicate myself against the injustice of fate in these last years of her laborious life.

"My poor mother! On the night when I descended from Vesuvius, the fever of the emotions I had felt during the day gave me a horrible nightmare instead of the sleep which my agitated limbs needed. The flames of the volcano, and the darkness of the abyss, mingled I know not what of absurd in the terrified imagination, and on waking from those distracting dreams, one idea alone possessed me, tenacious and persistent as a real fact: my mother was dead! I wrote that night to my family; a fortnight after I bought a requiem mass in Rome, that the pensionists of Santa Rosa, my pupils, might sing it in her honor; and I made a vow, which I persevered in while I was under the

influence of those sad impressions, to present myself in my
country at some future day, and to say to Rosas and Benavides, and all my enemies (hangmen), 'You have had a
mother; I come to honor the memory of mine; make a
pause then in the brutalities of your policy; profane not
an act of filial piety. Let me tell all men who this poor
mother was that no longer exists;' — and as God lives, I
would have fulfilled it as I have fulfilled so many other
good vows, and as I will fulfill many others that I have made.
Happily, I have her here at my side, and she instructs
me in the events of other times unknown to me, forgotten
by all. At seventy-six years of age my mother has crossed
the Cordillera of the Andes to bid farewell to her son before descending to the tomb. This act alone may give an
idea of the moral energy of her character. Each family is
a poem, Lamartine has said, and mine is a sad, a luminous,
and a useful one, like those distant paper lanterns of the
hamlets, which serve to point the way to those who go
astray in the fields.

" My mother preserves scarcely any traces of a severe
and modest beauty, at this advanced age. Her lofty stature, her pronounced and bony form, her prominent cheek-
bones, the sign of decision and energy, are all the features
of her exterior that deserve notice, unless it may be the
prominent inequalities of her brow, so unusual in her sex.
She knew how to read and write in her youth, but lost
this facility from disuse in her old age. Her intellect has
been little cultivated, and is destitute of all adornment, but
so penetrating, that after listening to a class in grammar
which I was instructing, while combing her fleeces of wool
in the evening, she resolved all the difficulties which had
puzzled her daughters, giving the definitions of nouns and
verbs, tenses, and other accidents of speech, with rare sagacity and exactness. Apart from this, her soul, her con-

science were educated to a degree of elevation which the
loftiest knowledge could not attain by itself. I have been
able to study this rare moral beauty, by seeing its operation in circumstances so difficult, so diverse, and so oft-
repeated, without ever belying itself or losing its freshness
and purity, or temporizing with circumstances, which with
others would have sanctified the conceptions made so often
in daily life ; that here I would trace the genealogy of these
moral ideas which were the healthy atmosphere my soul
breathed while it was unfolding its powers at the domestic
hearth.

" I firmly believe in the transmission of moral aptitude
through the organization. I believe in the infusion of the
spirit of one man, into the spirit of another, by means of
speech and example. Those perverse mortals who rule
nations, infect the atmosphere with the breath of their
souls, and reproduce their own vices and defects. There
are nations who reveal the characters of those who rule
over them in all their acts; and the moral life of cultivated
and free nations, their monuments and their instruction,
preserve the maxims of great master-minds, and would
not have arrived at their actual degree of perfection, if a
particle of the spirit of Christ, for example, had not been
introduced by teaching and preaching into each one of
them, improving their moral natures. I wished to know
then who had educated my mother, and from her conversation, from citations of the sayings of others, and from her
general reminiscences, I have made out almost the whole
history of a man of God, whose memory lives in San Juan,
and whose doctrine is perpetuated more or less pure in
the hearts of our mothers.

" I am suspicious that this holy man knew his eighteenth
century, its Rosseau, its Feijoo,[1] and its philosophers as

1 Feijoo, whose real name was Benedict Jerom, was a Spanish Benedic-

well as he did the Holy Scriptures. Don José Castro had scarcely been named curate, when he wielded the lash of his censure and prohibition upon all the brutal practices of the Church, such as flagellations which inflamed the back with merciless whips, fanatics harnesssed with bridles who walked on four feet, even penitent arm crossings on Holy Week, and processions of the Saints, and mummeries which made their grimaces before the Holy Sacrament. He used his influence also to put to flight the belief in fairies, ghosts, jack-o'-lanterns, and various creations of other religious faiths interpolated into our own in all Christian nations. To this end he used not only ridicule, but from the cathedral made patient and scientific explanations of the natural phenomena which gave rise to these errors. His criticisms also upon the affairs of life, and popular criticisms made without that grossness of censure which is common in ordinary preachers, worked so much more salutary effects since they came accompanied by ridicule so full of wit as to raise a general laugh, in the church, he himself laughing till his eyes would fill with tears, adding new sallies, till the immense concourse of people, attracted by the delicious mirth of this comedy, relieved their hearts of every trace of ill-humor, and till the priest, having tranquilized all minds, would say, wiping his face, ' Come, children, we have laughed enough ; now lend me your attention. By the sign of the holy cross,' etc., and then came the text of the lesson of the day, followed by a stream of serene and placid light, moral, practical, easily-understood commentaries, applicable to all the exigencies of life. . . . My mother's religion is the most genuine version of the

tine monk, who attempted by his writings and example to correct and reform the vitiated religion and superstitious notions of his countrymen. This unusual boldness against the prejudices of the times proved very offensive to the Church, and the author was with difficulty saved from the horrors of the Inquisition.

religious idea of Don José Castro, and I will appeal to the practice of her whole life to explain that religious reform founded in an obscure province, where it is preserved in many privileged souls.

. . . "My mother has few seasons of devotion, but those she has reveal the affinities of her mind to certain illusions, if I may so express myself; for instance, to her relation to the saints in heaven. The Virgin de Dolores is her mother of God. St. Joseph the carpenter, is her Holy Patron Saint, and St. Domingo and St. Vincent Ferras, Dominican friars, bound by many ties to the affections of the family, her order of priesthood. God himself, through all the vicissitudes of her anxious life, has been the true Holy One of her devotion under the invocation of Providence. In this character God entered into all the acts of that laborious life, and was present every day seeing her contests with indigence, and witnessing her accomplishment of her duties. Providence rescued her from all her troubles by visible manifestations authenticated to her. . . . Sometimes she would call the whole family together, when she would give utterance to a supplication full of unction and fervor, a true prayer to God, the purest emanation of a soul which overflowed with thanksgiving for the smallest benefits vouchsafed to her; for it must be said, the Divine beneficence was very scantily meted out to her. I have never seen this profound faith in Providence belie itself for one moment, but ever ward off despair, moderate anxiety, and give to suffering and misery the august character of a holy virtue, practiced with the resignation of a martyr, who does not protest, who does not complain, but hopes always, feeling himself consciously sustained, supported, approved. I know no more religious soul, and yet I have seen no other Christian woman more regardless of religious ceremonies.

" The curate Castro counseled the mothers not to compromise the decorum of their social position, by going in shabby guise into the street to attend mass, it being proper for a family to present itself always in public with that apparel and decency required by its rank; and this precept my mother followed in her days of extreme poverty, with the modesty and dignity that always characterized her actions. These lessons of profound wisdom were a small part of that seed sown by the holy man, and fructified by the common sense and the moral sentiment upon which it fell in the heart of my mother.

" When a woman of twenty-three years she undertook a work not so much beyond her strength as beyond the usual conceptions of an unmarried maiden. The year before, there had been a great dearth of *anascotes*, (a kind of woolen stuff that resembles serge, much used for the garments of the religious orders,) and from the proceeds of her weaving, my mother had amassed a small sum of money. With that, and two peons of her aunts, the Irrazavales, she laid the foundations of the house she was to occupy on forming a new family. As these scanty earnings were hardly sufficient for so costly a work, she established her loom under one of the fig-trees which she had inherited in her portion of land, and from there, while throwing her shuttle, she assisted the workmen and their peons in building the little dwelling; sold the cloth she had made in the week on Saturdays, and paid the workmen with the fruit of her labor. In those times an industrious woman — and all were so, even those born and reared in opulence — could depend upon herself to provide for her necessities. Commerce had not pushed its products into the interior of America, nor had European manufactures cheapened productions then as now. A yard of unbleached linen cloth was then worth eight reals for the first quality, five for the ordinary quality, and four for a yard of anascote, the thread being thrown in. My mother wove twelve yards per week, which was the pattern for the dress of a friar, and received six dollars on Saturday, not without trespassing upon the night, to fill the quills with thread for the work of the following day. . . . The branches of industry carried on by my mother are so numerous and so various, that their enumeration would fatigue the memory with names which now signify nothing. . . .

" My family has preserved the reputation of industrial omniscience until my day, and the habit of laboring with her hands is an integral part of my mother's existence. We heard her exclaim at Aconcagua, in 1842, ' This is the first time in my life that I have sat down with folded hands ! ' And at seventy-six years of her age, it has been necessary, in order to prevent her falling into a decline, to invent occupations adapted to her impaired vision, among which are delicate handiwork for ornaments of ladies' dresses, and other superfluities.

" When her home was finished, she married Don José Clemente Sarmiento, my father, a genteel young man of a family which had fallen into decay like her own, and brought to him as a dowry, the chain of privations and miseries in which she passed long years of her life. My father was a man endowed with a thousand good qualities, which balanced others that without being evil, looked in another direction. Like my mother, he had been educated in the rude labors of that epoch, a workman on the paternal farm of La Bebida, a mule-driver in the carrier-trains. He was beautiful in countenance, and with an irresistible passion for the pleasures of youth, deficient in that mechanical constancy which makes fortunes. Inspired by the new ideas which had come in with the Revolution, he had an unconquerable hatred for material labor, unintellectually and rudely as he had been educated. I heard him say to the Presbyter Torres, speaking of me, ' O, no ! my son shall never take a spade in his hand !' And the education he gave me showed that it was a fixed idea that had its birth in his profoundly mistaken views of life. In the bosom of poverty, he reared me an *hidalgo*, and my hands exercised no other forces than those required by my plays and pastimes. My father had one hand made useless by a callus he had acquired in labor.

" When the Revolution of Independence came, his excitable imagination made him waste, in services lent to his country, the small acquisitions he had made. After seeing in 1812 the miseries of Belgrano's army, he returned to San Juan, and undertook to make a collection for the Mother Country, as he was accustomed to call it, which proved quite abundant, and by the suggestion of jealous enemies was denounced to the Municipality as an act of spoliation. When the authorities inquired into the subject, they were so well satisfied, that he was charged with carrying his patriotic offering to the army in person, and this event gave him ever after the sobriquet of ' Mother Country,' which, in his old age in Chili, was the origin of a calumny designed to injure his son.

" In 1817, he accompanied San Martin to Chili as an officer of militia in the mechanical service of the army, and from the field of battle of Chacabuco, he was dispatched to San Juan to carry the plausible news [1] of the triumph of the patriots. San Martin remembered him well in 1847,[2] and was much pleased to learn that I was his son.

" With these antecedents, my father passed his whole life in beginning speculations whose products were scat-

1 This news, true at the moment apparently, proved to be a fallacy.

2 In 1847 Colonel Sarmiento sought out San Martin in his French retreat.

tered in badly counseled moments. He worked with tenacity, and fell into discouragement; he again essayed his forces and struggled against every disadvantage, dissipating his energies in long journeys to other provinces, till after my arrival at manhood; and from that time he followed the fate of his son into camps, into banishment and emigration, watching over me like a guardian angel to avert if possible the dangers that threatened me.

"From this evil destiny of my father and the want of a persistent plan of action, the maintenance of the family fell, from the earliest period after marriage, upon the shoulders of my mother, my father only aiding her fruitful labors by occasional coöperation; and under the pressure of the want in which we were nurtured, I ever saw the shining light of that equanimity of mind, of that resignation armed with all the industrial means which she possessed, and of that confidence in Providence which was the best resource of her energetic soul against discouragement and despair. Winters came which the previous autumn had presaged would be scanty in the provision of the roots and dried fruits which were to meet the expenses, and like the pilot of an abandoned ship she prepared with solemn tranquillity to meet the storm. When the day of destitution came, her soul had braced itself to resignation by assiduous labor to meet the trial. She had wealthy relations; the parish curates were her brothers, but those brothers were ignorant of her sufferings. It would have derogated from the sanctity of the poverty which she combated with her labor, to have mitigated it by foreign intervention; it would have been asking quarter in those death-combats with her evil star.

"The fiesta of St. Peter was always celebrated by a splendid banquet given by our uncle the curate, and he knew the rights and the desire of the children of the family to participate in the festivities. Many times the curate asked, 'Why did I not see Domingo?' And to this day he supposes that it was obedience to my mother's orders, instead of poverty, which prevented our attendance.

"I must mention one more characteristic anecdote of my mother. She had a friend of her infancy from whom death separated her at the age of sixty. The two friends had always continued to visit each other, consecrating one whole day to the delight of fusing their families into one, and the same friendship has united the daughters of both. Her friend enjoyed the bounties of wealth, but on the day that my mother passed with her, our own servant went into the friend's kitchen to prepare all the food which we were to consume during the day, the protest of twenty years against the practice having never in the least changed my mother's firm and unalterable resolution, in order that the ineffable pleasure of seeing her friend should not be marred by the possible suspicion that she wished even for a day to lay aside the duty of sustaining her family, or to turn her face away from the inequalities of fortune. Thus was practised at the humble hearth of the family of which I made a part, the noble virtue of poverty. Happy are the poor who have had such a mother!"

"THE PATERNAL HEARTH."

"My mother's house, the fruit of her industry, whose sunburnt bricks and mud-walls might be computed in yards of linen, woven by her own hands to pay for its construction, has received in the course of the last few years some additions which confound it with other dwellings of a certain moderate rank. Its original form, however, is that to which the poetry of the heart clings, the indelible image which presents itself pertinaciously to my mind when I remember infant pleasures and pastimes, the hours of recreation after returning from school, the various places where whole hours and weeks were passed in ineffable beatitude, making mud saints to be worshipped when completed ; or armies of soldiers of the same paste, to feed my pride by the exercise of so much power.

"Towards the southern part of the little territory of thirty yards by forty, was the habitation of the family, divided into two apartments, one serving as a dormitory for our parents, and the large one for the hall of reception, with its lofty dais and cushions, remnant of the tradition of the Arab divan, preserved by the Spanish people. Two tables of the indestructible carob-tree (algarroba), which had passed down from hand to hand since the time when there was no other wood in San Juan but the carob-trees of the fields, and a few chairs of various structure, flanked the hall, while two great pictures in oil of San Domingo and San Vicente Ferrar, adorned the otherwise bare walls ; pictures shockingly painted, but most devoutly kept as heir-looms on account of their Dominican habit. At a short distance from the entrance door, the patriarchal fig-tree raised its deep green canopy, which even in my childhood shaded my mother's loom, whose strokes, and the noise of whose wheels, pedals, and shuttles, always waked us before sunrise, announcing that a new day had begun, and with it the necessity of providing for its wants by labor. Some branches of the fig-tree rubbed gently against the walls of the house, and heated by the reflection of the sun's rays, it anticipated the usual season, offering its mellow contribution of early figs to augment the rejoicing of the family on the 23d of November, my father's birthday. I linger with pleasure over these details, for saints and fig-tree were, at a later day, personages of a family drama in which colonial ideas struggled violently with more modern ones. Other industrial resources had their place on the narrow territory of twenty yards not occupied by the family mansion. Three orange-trees shed their fruit in autumn, their shade always. Under a corpulent peach-tree was a little pool of water for the solace of three or four geese, which multiplying, gave their contribution to the complicated and limited system of revenue, upon which reposed the existence of the family ; and as all these means were insufficient, there was a garden of esculents of the size of a scapulary, surrounded by a paling, to shelter it from the voracity of the goslings, and which produced such vegetables as enter into South American cookery, the whole sparkling and illuminated by groups of common flowers, a mulberry-colored rose-bush, and various other flowering shrubs. This was a sample of the exquisite economy of land in a Spanish colonial family, and also of the inexhaustible productions which the country people of Europe know how to extract from it. The manure of the fowls and the horse which my father rode, passed daily into use, to give new vigor to that little spot of land which never wearied of yielding its varied and luxuriant growths, and when I wished to suggest to my mother some views of rural economy culled from books, I was deservedly treated as a pedant in the presence of that science of culture, which was the favorite pleasure and occupation of her long life. Now, at seventy-six years of age, if she escapes us from within our dwelling, she is sure to be found propping up some drooping plants, responding to our objections with the violence of feeling that possesses her on seeing them so maltreated.

"Yet in that Noah's ark there was some little corner where were steeped and prepared the colors with which she dyed her webs, and a vat of bran, from whence issued every week a fair proportion of exquisitely white starch. In prosperous times was added to these the manufacture of candles made by the hand, some attempt at baking bread, which always resulted in failure, and a thousand rural operations, which it would be superfluous to enumerate. Such varied occupations were not without method, beginning in the morning with feeding the goslings, gathering the vegetables before they were wilted by the sun, and then establishing herself at her loom, which for long years was her chief occupation. I have in my possession the shuttle of algarroba, polished and blackened by years, which she had inherited from her mother, who received it from her grandmother, a humble relic of colonial life, embracing a period of about two hundred years, during which noble hands had thrown it almost unweariedly; and although one of my sisters has inherited from my mother the habit and the necessity of weaving, my covetousness has prevailed, and I am still the depository of this family jewel. It is a pity that I can never be rich and powerful enough to imitate that Persian king who continued to use the clay pottery which had served him in childhood, in order that he might not grow proud and despise poverty.

.   .   .   .

" Such was the domestic hearth near which I grew, and it is impossible that there should not be left, on a loyal nature, indelible impressions of morality, of industry, and of virtue, received in that sublime school in which the most laborious industry, the purest morality, dignity maintained in the midst of poverty, constancy, and resignation, divided all the hours. My sisters enjoyed the deserved reputation of being the most diligent and efficient girls in the whole province, and whatever feminine occupation required consummate skill, was always commended to these supreme artificers who could do everything which required patience and dexterity and very little money."

To complete this picture the author brings into

view two accessory personages, " La Toribia," a Zamba
domestic, " the key of the house, the right arm of her
mistress, the *bonne* who brought us all up, the cook,
the messenger, the huckstress, the washer and ironer,
the maid cf all work. She died young, nor was her
place ever filled, either in the domestic economy or in
the heart of my mother, for they were two friends,
mistress and maid, two fellow-laborers who discussed
together the means of maintaining the family, wrangled,
disputed, dissented, and each one then followed her
own opinion, both leading to the same end." The
other personage was " Na Cleme, the pauper that
hung upon the family, for my mother, like the Rigo-
leta of Sue, who never hoarded anything, had her
poor also, whom she helped to live by her scraps."
But the family servant and the family pauper, supposed by some to be a witch, and apparently of that
opinion herself, must be banished from our pages,
although the beneficent relations of the mother to them
add another trait to a noble portraiture.

" Our habitation remained as I have described it, until
the day when my two elder sisters arrived at the marriage-
able age, when an interior revolution began which cost two
years of debate, and showers of tears to my mother, on
finding herself conquered by a new world of ideas, habits,
and tastes, which were not those of the colonial existence,
of which she was the last and most finished type. The
first symptoms of those social revolutions operated by
human intelligence in the great foci of civilization are very
common and pass unperceived ; they extend through the
common people, insinuate themselves into ideas, and infil-
trate into the customs. The eighteenth century had glittered

over France, and undermined the ancient traditions, cooled off faith, and excited hatred and contempt for things hitherto venerated. Its political theories had overturned governments, unbound Spanish America, and opened its colonies to new customs and new habits of life. The time was coming when the industrious life of American women was to be looked upon disdainfully, and with an evil eye ; when French fashions were to prevail, and an anxiety for display in the multiplication and distribution of luxuries were to take possession of the domestic circle, when the dining-hour must be delayed from twelve o'clock to two or even four in the afternoon. Who does not know some of those good old people of the ancient stamp, who live, proud of their opulence, in an unencumbered apartment, furnished with four dusty leather chairs, the floor covered with spent cigars, and the table ornamented solely with an enormous inkstand, whose goose-quills, or perchance, condor-quills, are crystallized with dried ink. This was the general aspect, the family picture of colonial life. It is described in the novels of Scott and Dumas, and living proofs of it are still seen in Spain and in South America, the last of the old peoples who have been called upon to rejuvenate themselves. These ideas of regeneration and personal improvement, this impiety of the eighteenth century, entered, who would believe it, into the heads of my two elder sisters. Scarcely arrived at the age when woman feels that her existence is bound to society, which is the end and object of this existence, they began to aspire to new ideas of beauty, of taste, of comfort, which the atmosphere diffused by the revolution had wafted to them. The walls of the common sitting-room were smoothed and whitened anew ; a thing to which no reasonable opposition could be offered, but the mania extended to the destruction of the raised dais that occupied one side of the hall, with its carpet and its cushions, a divan as I said before, which came down to us from our Arabic ancestors, a privileged spot on which women alone were permitted to sit, and in whose spacious circumference, reclining upon ottomans, the visitors and hosts carried on their lively chit-chat, that indescribable medley of womanly talk.

" Why has the poetical dais been allowed to disappear from our houses, so convenient for sitting, so adequate for feminine repose, to substitute in its place, chairs, in which one by one or in rows, like soldiers in platoons, the eye reviews the company in our modern saloons ? But that dais expressed that man might not publicly approach the young ladies, talk freely, and mix freely with them, as our modern customs permit, and it was therefore repudiated by themselves, as easily as it had been formerly accepted as a privilege. The dais then yielded its place in the house to the more modern fashion of chairs, notwithstanding the feeble resistance of my mother, who enjoyed sitting upon one extreme of it in the morning to take her cup of maté, with her brazier and boiler of water on the lower step before her, or to reel her cottons or to fill her quills over night for the web of the following day. Not being accustomed to work upon a high seat, she was obliged to adopt the use of a carpet to supply the loss of the dais, which she lamented many long years.

" My sisters' spirit of innovation at last attacked sacred objects. I protest that I did not take part in this sacrilege which the poor little things committed, in obedience to the spirit of the time. Those two saints, so grand, so ancient, Santo Domingo and San Vicente Ferrar, decidedly marred the walls. If my mother could but consent that they should be taken down, and put into a sleeping-room, the little house would take a new aspect of modern and elegant refinement, for it was under the seducing form of good taste, that this iconoclastic impiety of the eighteenth century found its way into the house. Ah, what wounds that error dealt upon the bosom of Spanish America! The South American Colonies had been founded at an epoch when the Spanish fine arts showed proudly to Europe the pencils of Murillo, Velasquez, and Sambrano, as well as the swords of the Duke of Alva, the great captain, and of Cortez. The possession of Flanders added to its products those of Flemish engraving, which, painted in rough lineaments and crude colors the religious scenes which were the foundation of the national poetry. Murillo, in his early years, made innumerable virgins and saints for South America; the second-rate painters sent it whole lives of saints for the convents, the passion of Jesus Christ in immense galleries of pictures, and Flemish engraving, as now French lithography, put within reach of moderate fortunes the history of the Prodigal Son, and virgins and saints of as many types as the calendar furnishes. The walls of our ancestors' and fathers' apartments were tapestried with these images, and not rarely the practiced eye of an artist could discover some line of a master-hand in the midst of all this rubbish. But the revolution pointed its finger against the religious emblems. Ignorant and blind in its antipathies, it averted its eyes from painting which was Spanish, colonial, ancient, and irreconcilable with the new ideas. Devout families hid their pictures of the saints, not to show the bad taste of preserving them; and in San Juan, and other places, there were those who used the canvas for trowsers for their slaves. What treasures of art must have been lost by these stupid profanations in which all South America was an accomplice, for there was a period at which everywhere at once prevailed the fatal demolition of that luxuriant vegetation of the past artistic glory of Spain! European travellers, who passed through South America twenty years ago, collected at very low prices inestimable works of the best masters, which they found cast aside as useless lumber covered with dust and cobwebs; and when the day of the resurrection of the arts came to South America, when the bandage fell from the eyes of the people, the churches, the rising museums, and the amateurs found from time to time some picture of Murillo to expose to view, asking pardon for the injustice of which it had been the victim, now restored to public consideration, and to the lofty position which corresponded to its merits.

.   .   .   .

"The strife went on, therefore, between my poor mother, who loved her two Dominican saints as members of her family, and my young sisters who sacrificed the laws of the house to good appearances and the prejudices of the times. Every day, at all hours, under every pretext, the debate was renewed, some threatening glance was cast at the saints, as if to say, "you must leave your places vacant;" while my mother contemplated them with tender looks, exclaiming, "Poor saints! how badly they treat you when you harm no one!" But by this continuous battery, the ear became accustomed to the reproach, resistance was weaker every day, for if they were looked upon as indispensable objects of religion, it was not necessary that they should be in the parlor; the sleeping apartment was a much more appropriate place of worship, where their blessing could be invoked upon the very bed. As a family legacy, they were subject to the same arguments, while as an ornament they were in the worst taste; and from one concession to another, my mother's mind relented little by little, and one morning when her resistance would go no further than the wringing of her hands, when the guardian of that fortress returned from mass, her eyes expanded to see the bare walls where the great black patches had been before. My saints were then removed to the sleeping apartment, and to judge by their faces the change made no great impression upon them. My mother knelt weeping before them to ask their pardon by her prayers, remained out of humor and querulous all day, sad the following day, but resigned the next, till at last time and habit brought the balm which makes bearable the greatest misfortunes. This signal victory gave new animation to the spirit of reform, and after the divan and the saints, in an evil hour, the threatening glance fell upon the fig-tree that stood in the middle of the court-yard, discolored and knotty, by dint of dryness and old age. The matter being looked upon in this aspect, the fig-tree was condemned in the public conception : it sinned against all the rules of decorum and decency ; but with my mother it was an economical question which affected her, as well as one which deeply affected her heart. Ah ! would that the maturity of my own heart could have been anticipated and brought to her aid, but selfishness made me indifferent to her feelings, or weakly inclined me in her favor for the sake of the early figs ! They wished to separate her from that beloved companion in the flower of its life and strength. Ripe age wreathes associations around everything which surrounds us ; the domestic hearth is a living being ; a tree which we have seen planted, grow, and arrive at maturity, is a person endowed with life, which has acquired rights to existence that it reads in our hearts, and can accuse us as ingrates, and would leave remorse in the conscience if we should sacrifice without a legitimate reason. The sentence of the old fig-tree was discussed for two years, and its champion, wearied with the struggle, abandoned it to its fate ; but on making the preparations for its execution, the sentiments which had been outraged in her heart, glowed with new force, and she obstinately refused to permit the destruction of that witness and companion of her labors. One day, however, when the revocation of the permission had lost all its prestige, the blows of the hatchet upon the venerable trunk of the tree, and the rustling of the leaves shaken by the shock, the last sighs of the victim, were heard through the house. It was a sad, sad moment, a scene of mourning and repentance. The blows of the fig-slaying hatchet[1] also shook the heart of my mother; the tears rushed to her eyes, as the sap of the tree to the wound, and her sobs responded to the trembling of the leaves. Every new blow brought a new burst of grief, and my sister and I, repenting too late for having given such acute pain, burst into weeping, the only reparation now possible. The suspension of the work of destruction was ordered, as the family prepared to rush into the yard, and put a stop to the painful re-percussions of the hatchet upon my mother's heart. Two hours afterwards, the fig-tree lay prostrate upon the ground, displaying its hoary head as the fading leaves showed the knotty frame-work of that structure, which for so many years had lent its aid to the protection and sustenance of the family.

"After these great reforms, the humble habitation went on slowly and painfully enlarging itself. It fell to me to have the happiness of introducing one substantial change. On the border of our little homestead spot was a piece of ground my father had purchased in a moment of comparative ease. I was an apprentice in a small commercial establishment when sixteen years old. My first plans and economies had for their object the fencing in of this lot of territory, that it might be made productive to the family, and place it beyond the reach of indigence, although it

1 The Spanish word is *higuericida*, the fig-i-cidal.

could not make it pass out of the limits of poverty. My mother now had at her disposal a theatre worthy of her agricultural knowledge; to the decrepid fig-tree succeeded in her affections a hundred young trees, whose growth her maternal eye fostered. Hours of every day were consecrated to this plant and to that vine, upon which the family was in future to depend, for a portion of its sustenance.

" When I had accomplished this work, I could say in my joy at having produced such a result, *I saw that it was good*, and I was happy."

"MY EDUCATION.

" In a school, the details of which I have mentioned elsewhere,[1] and where I entered at five years of age, I remained nine years without having missed a single day, under any pretext, for my mother was there to see that I should fulfill my duty of punctuality, under the penalty of her indescribable severity. At five years of age, I read fluently, in a loud voice, with intonations and emphasis that only a complete comprehension of the subject could give, and so uncommon was this early skill at that period, that I was carried from house to house to display my reading, reaping a great harvest of cakes, embraces, and encomiums, which filled me with vanity."

In a letter to his uncle,[2] the illustrious Bishop of Cuyo, written after seeing Pompeii, our author describes himself again with much liveliness.

" I want your highness to do an act of justice in San Juan, seizing by the ear our cousin M. It was your illustrious highness who, when curate, put a little book into my hand, remarking to some one at the same time — I have

---

[1] In a work upon *Popular Education.*
[2] Taken from Travels in Europe, Africa, and America, in 1846-7.

not forgotten it, because I have not forgotten you — that at the age of four years I had the reputation of being the most troublesome and vociferous reader you had ever seen. The crude notions which I acquired by my habits of early reading, wandered a long time in my mind, like the clouds in space when they meet with no point of support to form a nucleus, till some little book which accident placed in my hands came to fill a vacuum, or some other, later, to explain a passage not well understood. I had many historical notions at that age, when the generality of children are thinking only of their plays; and now that I have visited Rome I have been able to recognize at first sight, by the image engraven in my memory from the earliest childhood, in which I passed hours poring over a Roman Guide Book, and which was the first book I owned, the monuments I met with. I do not know how nor when I read an account of the ruins of Pompeii, but not being able to keep to myself the novelty and wonder it excited, I attacked people in the street to tell them the portentous story. I told it thus to our cousin M., and instead of standing with open mouth as I had promised, he burst into a fit of laughter; and whenever he saw me where people were assembled, he made me tell the story of Pompeii for the general diversion. I have now seen that Pompeii which so preoccupied my childhood, and it reminds me of the incredulity of M."

From this digression we return to his little book.

" Apart from a natural faculty of comprehending what I read, I had a secret background of images of which the public was ignorant. My poor father, ignorant himself, but solicitous that his children should not be so, sharpened at home this rising thirst for knowledge, and made me read, without pity for my tender years, the ' Critical His-

tory of Spain,' in four volumes, the ' Desiderio and Electo,'
and other abominable books which I never turned to again,
but which left in my mind confused ideas of history, alle-
gories, fables, countries, and proper names. I owe thus to
my father that love of reading which has been the constant
occupation of my life, and although he could not give me
an education because of his poverty, he gave me by his paternal solicitude the powerful instrument by which I have
supplied the want through my own efforts, thus fulfilling
the most constant and earnest of his wishes.

"I never knew how to spin a top, to bat a ball, to fly a
kite, or had any inclination for such boyish sports. At
school I learned how to copy the knaves from cards, and
afterwards made a copy of San Martin on horseback, from
the paper lantern of a grocer, and from acquisition to acquisition, I succeeded, after ten years of perseverance, in
divining all the secrets of making caricatures. In a family
visit on one occasion, at the house of Doña Barbara Icaste,
I occupied the day in copying the face of a San Jeronimo,
and that type once acquired, I reproduced it distinctly in
the faces of all ages and sexes. My teacher, weary of
correcting me in this pastime, concluded by resigning himself to it, and respecting the instinctive mania. When I
had an opportunity to be instructed in drawing, the will
to perfect myself in it was unfortunately wanting. But later
in life I spread through my province a taste for that graphic
art, and under my direction or inspiration were formed half
a dozen artists, which San Juan now possesses. But that
taste was converted in my youth into one for sculpture,
which took two different forms, and I made saints and
soldiers, the two great objects of my childish fancy.

"My mother raised me with the persuasion that I should
be a clergyman, and the curate of San Juan, in imitation
of my uncle; and my father had visions for me of military

jackets, gold lace, sabres, and other accoutrements to match. Through my mother, I was to follow colonial vocations ; through my father, the ideas and preoccupations of that revolutionary epoch were infiltrated into me; and obeying these contradictory impulses, I passed my leisure hours in beatific contemplation of my 'mud saints, duly painted, leaving them in turn quiet in their niches to give battle in front of the house between two armies which my neighbors and I had been preparing for perhaps a month before by a large hoarding of wax balls, in order to thin out the bedaubed files of shapeless puppet soldiers.

" I should not relate these trifles if they had not, later in life, taken colossal forms and prefigured one of those remembered events which even at this day make me palpitate with glory and vanity. . . . In regard to my sacerdotal vocation, I assisted when a boy of thirteen at a pious chapel in the house of the humpbacked Rodriguez, capable of holding twenty persons, and endowed with a sacristy, belfry, and other requisites, with candlesticks, thuribles, and musical bells made by Don Javier Jofre's negro, Rufino, and of which we made an enormous consumption in pealings and processions. The chapel was consecrated to our family patron, St. Domingo, — I administering for two years the august dignity of Provincial of the order of Preachers, by acclamation of the chapter, and to the great edification of the devotees. The friars of the convent of St. Domingo came to hear me sing the mass in which I parodied my uncle, the curate, who sang very well, and I, being his acolyte, watched all the mechanism of the mass, not forgetting to mark the page in the missal in which were the gospel and epistle of the day, in order to reproduce them in perfection in my private mass.

"On Sunday afternoons, the Provincial transformed himself into the general-in-chief of an army of boys, and woe

to those who dared to make front to that rain of stones
which issued from the bosom of my phalanx."

I omit the details of the boyish battle our auto-
biographer describes, in which he showed the determination and pluck which have characterized all his
maturer acts. I omit it (his later ones were undertaken in better causes), fearing the publication of it
might not receive his sanction, though he amused himself and his " hundred friends " with the relation ; all
the personages engaged in it being probably well
known to them.

" This ends what I call the colonial history of my family.
What follows, is the slow and painful transition from one
mode of life to another, the life of the rising Republic, the
struggle of parties, civil war, proscription, and banishment.
To the family history succeeds as atmosphere and theatre
of action, the history of my native country. I succeed to
my progenitors, and I believe that by following my footsteps as those of another in that path, the curioso may linger
over the events which form the general picture, incidents
of the country known to all, objects of general interest, by
the examination of which, the items of my biography, val-
ueless for themselves, will serve as a thread of connection ;
for in my life, so destitute of aid, so full of contrarieties,
and yet so persevering in its aspiration for all that is noble
and elevated, may be seen depicted that unhappy South
America, agitating itself in its condition of nothingness,
making supreme efforts to unfold its wings, lacerating itself
at every attempt against the iron bars of the prison in
which it is chained.

" Strange emotions must indeed have agitated the souls
of our fathers in 1810. The twilight perspective of a new

epoch, liberty, independence — new words then — must have made their fibres tremble deliciously, powerfully excited their imaginations, and sent the blood rushing wildly through their hearts. That year, what anxiety, what happiness, what enthusiasm! There is a story of a king, who trembled like an aspen at the sight of a naked dagger, the effect of his mother's emotions when she carried him under her bosom, and in whose arms a man was stabbed. I was born in 1811, the ninth month after the 25th of May, and my father had thrown himself into the revolution, and my mother was agitated every day by the momentary news of the progress of the insurrection. Before I could speak plainly, they began to familiarize my eyes and my tongue with the alphabet, such was the eagerness with which the colonials who already felt themselves to be citizens fell to educating their children, as may be seen by the decrees of the gubernatorial junta and the other governments of that epoch.

" Full of this holy spirit, the government of San Juan, sent, in 1816, for some men from Buenos Ayres, worthy by their education and moral character to be teachers in Prussia, and on the opening of the school of La Patria, I passed immediately into the troop of four hundred children of all ages and conditions, who were eager to receive the only solid instruction which has been given amongst us in primary schools. The memory of Don Ignacio, and Don José Jenaro Rodriguez, still awaits the reparation due to their immense, their holy services; and I must not die until my country has fulfilled that sacred duty. The sentiment of equality was developed in our hearts by the epithet of Señor, which we were obliged to give each other without regard to condition or race; and by the morality of manners, stimulated by the example of the master; the oral lessons, and the punishments which were only severe and humiliating when inflicted for crimes. . . . When a pupil of the reading school, an elevated seat was constructed at the end of the hall, a sort of throne accessible by steps, and I was placed upon it with the name of ' FIRST CITIZEN.' Don Ignacio Rodriguez, who is still living, can tell if the seat was made for me. A youth named Domingo Moron succeeded me in that honorable place, and it afterwards fell into disuse. This circumstance and the consequent publicity acquired from that time, the praises of which I was always the object and the witness, must have contributed to give to my manners a character of fatuity of which I was not made aware until much later in life. From a child, I believed in my talents, as a rich man does in his money, or a soldier in his warlike deeds. Every one said so, and in nine years of school-life, there were not a dozen out of two thousand children who were before me in their capacity to learn, notwithstanding that at last I hated the school, as well as grammar, algebra, and arithmetic. My school morality also must have become slack by this eternal school-life, for I remember that I finally fell into disfavor with the master. . . .

" It is a deserved tribute to my mother to say that we were brought up in a holy horror of falsehood. I was always distinguished in school for exemplary veracity, and the masters rewarded it by proposing me as a model to others, praising me, and quoting me with encomiums, so that the purpose of being always truthful was deepened more and more in me; a purpose which has formed the foundation of my character, and to which all the acts of my life have testified.

" My school apprenticeship was concluded by one of those acts of injustice so frequent, from which I have guarded myself carefully whenever I have been in similar circumstances. Don Bernardino Rivadavia (then President), —

that unfortunate educator whose well-chosen plans were trampled under foot by the horses of Quiroga, Lopez, Rosas, and all the chiefs of the barbarous reaction movement, —summoned from each province six youths of known talents to be educated by the nation, in order that when their studies were concluded, they might return to their respective cities, to assume scientific professions and give lustre to their country. He asked that they should be from decent but poor families, and Don Ignacio Rodriguez came to my father to tell him that my name headed the list of chosen children whom the nation was about to take under its wing. But the covetousness of the rich interfered : lots were drawn ; all the city went to the registering, and a list of candidates was made out, and the election was made by ballot. Fortune was not the patron of my family, and I was not one of the six favored ones. What a day of sadness to my parents was that on which the fatal notice came to them ! My mother wept in silence ! My father buried his face in his hands.

" But the fate that had been unjust to me, was not so to the province, although it knew not how to take advantage, in later days, of the riches that were in preparation for it. The lot fell to Antonio Aberastain, as poor a boy as myself, endowed with remarkable talents, an iron application to study, and a moral sentiment which has made him a shining example to this day. No one knows better than I the depths of his character : we were friends from infancy ; I, his protegé in the adult school, when in 1836, we both arrived in San Juan, he from Buenos Ayres, I from Chili ; he began to lend me the support of his influence, to raise me in his arms every time the malicious envy of the village overwhelmed me with a wave of disfavor or jealousy, every time that the leveller vulgarity persisted in reducing me to the common herd. Supreme Judge of Doctor Alzadas, he was always there defending me against the rich young men who wished to throw obstacles in my path. I have owed to this good man, even the marrow of my bones. He was full of energy without the appearance of it, humble even to self-annihilation. To him, and to another man in Chili, I owed still later my own self-estimation, by the proofs they lavished upon me of theirs, both serving and upholding me more than a fortune could have done. The esteem of the good acts as galvanism. A glance of benevolence from them can say to Lazarus, ' Arise and walk!' I have never loved any one as I loved Aberastain; no man has left deeper traces of respect and admiration upon my heart.

"After he left San Juan, the Supreme Tribunal of Justice was administered by men without professional education, and often so unfit, poor fellows, that they would have been stupid mule-drivers. Ultimately the honorable House of Representatives declared that even in default of Sanjuanino advocates, no *foreigner* could be a judge, that is to say, no individual of another confederate province, and this legislative act shows the perversion of mind into which these people have fallen." [1]

On the occasion of laying the corner-stone of the " Sarmiento School " in San Juan, in 1864, — a splendid edifice built within the walls of an abandoned church, partly erected many years before, — Colonel Sarmiento thus speaks of the influence of school-days upon his life.

[1] In his biography of his friend, he relates that such was the common feeling of respect for Aberastain among his fellow-pupils in childhood, such his almost morbid conscientiousness, that he went by the soubriquet of " God-the-Father." We can hardly appreciate this Spanish custom of nicknaming, as we call it. In those communities, half the people are known by some fancy name growing out of personal or accidental or characteristic qualities.

" The inspiration to consecrate myself to the education
of the people, came to me here in my youth. My labor of
thirty years, that of serving the countries where I resided
with schools, turns now to its point of departure, to the very
simple idea of the importance of primary school education
over all other education, to insure the happiness of nations.
If I had been born in Buenos Ayres, or Cordova, or in
Santiago de Chili, the primary education of this part of the
country would not have arrived at this point when all are
striving for that end. I should have been preoccupied
with the brilliant university, and should have aspired to
its honors. But I was born and educated amidst the people of a province where there was no other education than
that of the public school, and the ' Escuela de la Patria '
was one of the first order, without a rival in any private
one, conducted by a man so respected by the people and
the government, that at that time the schoolmaster was
looked upon as one of the first magistrates of the province.
Observe, then, by what singular circumstances the school,
as an institution, was destined to acquire in my mind that
supreme importance which I have never ceased to give it ;
and how, at the close of my travels, I found in the United
States that the school occupied the same place as in San
Juan, and brought forth like results. The truth is, that the
first ideas in the child's mind keep the same relative position always, and however slightly they meet with confirmation, grow and develop, and determine the career in life.
If I should express all my thoughts, I should say that the
School of La Patria, in San Juan, associated in my mind
with the recollections of the only form of education with
which I was acquainted, went forth with me from this province, and accompanied me in all my wanderings. In Chili
it took the form of normal schools ; in Europe I connected
it with the study of legislation ; in the United States with

the spectacle of its wonderful results, of its temple school-houses, and of the prominent place it holds among the institutions of that country. In Buenos Ayres I reproduced it as a seed sown in propitious ground, and I return to do the same to-day in San Juan, by reëstablishing the School of La Patria, completed as an educational institution, and also as a democratic one, and I bring to it all the acquisitions made in my long and various travels. No longer confined to three halls that contained in all but three hundred pupils, we have here an edifice that will enable us to throw off the swaddling-clothes of infancy. To-day we lay the stone which consecrates to education these beginnings of an unfinished temple. And that you may see how advanced ideas have grown, I will repeat to you what I have replied to those who have wished this edifice kept to its first destination, and who yet abandoned it to sterility and destruction.

"At the corner of the next block, thirty steps from here, thirty years ago, I was a merchant's clerk, and here pursued my solitary studies. Even at that time, I saw that a spacious school-house might be erected within these walls, and with your assistance I now realize my thought after the delay of so many years.[1]

"Observe another class of ideas and events that deserve to be recorded. If the School of La Patria inspired me with this high estimation of primary education which has distinguished me from the generality of the men of my epoch, in my country, its excellence did not come of itself, nor from the advanced condition of the provinces. It was due to a respected family from Buenos Ayres whose head

[1] The citizens of San Juan, of all classes, contributed to the erection of the Sarmiento School, some by the produce of their farms and other labors, the ladies by theatrical exhibitions, concerts, fairs, and many liberal men by their money. It was erected within the ruins of an abandoned church.

was Don Ignacio Firmen Rodriguez, of venerated memory among Sanjuaninos, and whose image is to-day recalled to you by the foundation of a new school, the continuation of his work. I was asked at Buenos Ayres how it was possible that in the year 1818, so near our *middle ages*, we had schools and masters so advanced. This question was also put to me during my travels in America and Europe, after I found in Chili and even in Buenos Ayres itself, less advanced public schools than I had left here in my childhood, schools to be compared only with those of Germany and the United States.

" My master explained it to me in the last years of his life, feeling unwilling to accept all the eulogies with which my gratitude and my admiration sought to make his merits known. His explanation was that he had read Scotch treatises upon instruction, and had conformed himself to their principles. In fact, primary education in Scotland has been far superior to that of England, and this was proved from early times by its institutions and science. . . . . D. Ignacio, for thus he was always called, read, wrote, and ciphered perfectly. He dictated and sent to the press in Buenos Ayres, a grammar, an orthography, and a treatise upon arithmetic. Later, he taught algebra and some geography.

" One year I saw a book upon his table, which showed that he did not yet know Latin, and proposed to learn it.

" He was religious, which appeared less in ceremonies than in precepts, and explanations of the catechism, and especially in the frequent inculcation of the principles of morality.

" His special quality as a master was to inspire respect, and I ought to say that all education is vain in the presence of a deficiency of this quality as is the case in the generality of masters. To-day, for instance, there is not a single master in San Juan who possesses this primary qualification of his profession.

" In the absence of D. Ignacio, his influence, his shadow, I may say, presided over the school. A dull murmur of conversation might be heard ; but it did not come to be noisy, and never rose to a shout ; as soon as he was seen to pass by the window, that suppressed murmur began to subside and became silence, and this silence was never disturbed by any one in his presence ; there was no necessity of calling to order, to which our masters recur in vain. I preserve still the almost religious impression of this respect which he inspired in us all, without exception, a respect which we saw at home was mixed with love, and which accompanied us to adult years, although many of his pupils have occupied stations more exalted as to social position than his own.

"The sphere of his instruction was not very extensive, but as we only learn by having our intelligence developed, his mode of teaching went straight to the object, and whatever he taught we learned well, because he cultivated the thinking powers from the beginning. In San Juan there were fine readers taught by a new and easy method, long before they could be found in Chili, and the Sanjuaninos of those times were better spellers than there are to-day among the cultivated youth of Buenos Ayres.[1] At first he tried the system of emulation ; his pupils were Carthagenians and Romans ; but later he modified this system by giving to each pupil one opponent who always ended by being his best friend. At last he adopted Lancaster's method. But the system which he used to perfection was that of simultaneous recitation.

" He tried every system of punishments during the

[1] The Spanish language has been very much adulterated in South America. — Ed.

nine years that I was his pupil, according as his views improved, but he never deprived himself of the resource of corporal chastisement, in cases where he deemed it necessary.

"A thousand qualities distinguished this man from the generality of teachers, and established his superiority. Most of his teaching was oral, especially in grammar and arithmetic, and was reasoned out and duly exemplified.

"D. Ignacio has gone to his grave, but his spirit is enshrined in the hearts of a people who preserve the traditions of popular education. His pupils have diffused it, and San Juan and Buenos Ayres, by their improvements in education, testify to the service of the Rodriguez family of blessed memory.

"I have digressed into these details, although by so doing I have detained you too long, in order to rouse you to a great and noble effort. San Juan was the first Argentine province, as I have shown you, which after the revolution of independence elevated primary education to the highest grade of perfection possible at that epoch. From San Juan went forth the impulse which in these later days has stimulated two republics. San Juan owes it to herself to reëstablish the fame of her ancient school, and permit me to say, that it is the duty of my country and my compatriots to aid me in the full development of a system of common school education which shall put the seal upon the work of thirty years of my life."

"In regard to my education," he continues, "it may be said that fate intervened to dog my steps. I next went to the seminary of Loreto in Cordova, but was obliged to return without entering, for the revolution of Carita left me without a Latin teacher. In 1825, I began to study mathematics and surveying under M. Barreau, engineer of that province. Together we drew up the plan of the streets of Roji, Desemparados, and Santa Barbara, and from there round to the Pueblo Rajo, and I alone, my teacher having abandoned me, that of the Cathedral Santa Lucia and Legua. That same year I went to San Luis to continue with the clergyman Oro the education which the revolution of 1824 had interrupted. A year later I was summoned by the government to be sent to the College of the Moral Sciences, and arrived at San Juan, after having once refused to go, at the moment when the lancers of Facundo Quiroga appeared from the dusty wood, fluttering their sinister banners through the streets. The next year I entered a commercial house as a timid apprentice, — I, who had been educated by the presbyter Oro, in solitude which so develops the imagination, dreaming of congresses, war, glory, liberty, in short, of the Republic. I was sad for many days, and, like Franklin, whom his parents destined for a soap-boiler, but who was destined to rob the heavens of their lightnings, and tyrants of their sceptres, I 'took an aversion to the road that leads to fortune.' In my musings, in hours of idleness, I returned to the fields of San Luis, where I wandered through the woods with my Latin grammar in my hand studying *mascula sunt maribus*, and interrupting the repetition by throwing stones at the birds. I missed that sonorous voice which had for two whole years sounded in my ears, placid, friendly, moving my heart-strings, calling out my sentiments, elevating my mind. The reminiscences of that oral shower which fell every day upon my soul, presented themselves like the pictures of a book whose significance we comprehend by the action of the figures. Peoples, history, geography, religion, morals, politics, all these were annotated as in an index, but I missed the book, which gave the details, and I was alone in the world in the midst of parcels of condiments and pieces of chintz, which I was to measure out by the yard to those who came to buy them. But there must be books, I said, which treat specially of all things and teach them to children, and if one understands what he reads, he can learn them without the assistance of a master, — and I rushed to seek those books, and in that remote province, in that hour of taking my resolution, I found what I sought, such as I had conceived it, prepared by exiled patriots who wished well to America, and who had foreseen from London this necessity of South America to educate itself, and responding to my importunities had sent me the catechisms of Akermann which Don Tomas Rojo had introduced into San Juan. ' I have found it,' I could exclaim like Archimedes, for I had foreseen, sought and found those catechisms which later in the year 1829, I gave to Don Saturnino Laspiar for the education of his children.[1]   There was ancient history, and that Persia, and that Egypt, those Pyramids, and that Nile, of which the clergyman Oro had told me. I studied the history of Greece by heart, and then that of Rome, feeling myself to be successively Leonidas and Brutus, Aristides, Camillus, Harmodius, and Epaminondas ; and this while I was selling herbs and sugar, and making grimaces to those who came to draw me from my newly-discovered world where I wished to live.   In the mornings after sweeping the shop, I read, and as a certain Señora passed by on her way from church, and her eyes always fell, day after day, month after month, upon that boy, immovable, insensible to every disturbance, his eyes fixed upon a book, one day, shaking her head, she said to her family, ' That lad cannot be good — if those books were good he would not read them so eagerly !'

" From that time I read every book that fell into my

---

1 These were some young men whom the youthful Sarmiento taught to read, though much older than himself, and the sons of a wealthy man.

hands, without arrangement, with no other guide than the chance which brought them to me, or the knowledge I had acquired of their existence in the scanty libraries of San Juan. The first was the ' Life of Cicero' by Middleton, with very fine plates, and in that book I lived a long time with the Romans. If I had then had half the means of doing it, I should have studied law to make myself an advocate and defend causes like that distinguished orator who was the object of my passionate love. The second was the ' Life of Franklin,' and no book has ever done me more good. The ' Life of Franklin' was to me what ' Plutarch's Lives ' were to Rousseau, Henry IV., Madame Roland, and so many others. I felt myself to be Frank-lin, — and why not ? I was very poor like him, I studied like him, and following in his footsteps, I might one day come, like him, to be a *doctor ad honorem!* and to make myself a place in letters and American politics. The ' Life of Franklin' should be in every primary school. His example is so inspiring, the career he ran so glorious, that there would not be a boy at all well-inclined who would not try to be a little Franklin, through that noble tendency of the human mind to imitate models of perfec-tion that commend themselves to it. Holy aspirations of the young soul for the beautiful and the perfect ! Where among our books is the type, the practical possible model, which shall guide them? Our preachers propose to us the saints of heaven, that we may imitate their ascetic virtues and scourgings, but however well-intentioned a boy may be, he soon renounces the pretension to perform miracles, for the simple reason that those who counsel him to try it, do not perform any themselves."

It was at this time that he read the Bible with his uncle the presbyter Albarracin, Paley's " Natural

Theology and Evidences of Christianity," " The True Idea of the Holy See," and " Feijoo " (a Catholic writer who tried to reason away many of the superstitious observances of the Church, and came very near falling into the hands of the Inquisition for so doing). This completed that eminently religious and raisonnée education which had come to him from the cradle, transmitted from his mother to the schoolmaster, from his mentor Oro to the Presbyter Albarracin.

PUBLIC LIFE.

" At sixteen I entered prison, and came out of it with political opinions diametrically opposed to those of Silvio Pellico, to whom prisons taught the moral of resignation and self-annihilation. From the time ' My Prisons ' fell into my hands, I was inspired with a horror of that doctrine of moral discouragement which it went forth to preach through the world, and which was so acceptable to kings, who felt that they were threatened by the energy of their people. How would the human race have advanced, if in order to comprehend the interests of their country, men needed to have spiritual exercises in the dungeons of Spielberg, the Bastille, and Santos Lugares? Woe to the world if the Czar of Russia, the Emperor of Austria, or the tyrant Rosas conld teach morality to mankind! Silvio Pellico's book is the death of the soul, the morality of dungeons, the slow poison of degradation of mind. He and his book have happily passed away, and the world has gone on in spite of the cripples, paralytics, and valetudinarians whom political struggles have left.

" I was a shopkeeper by profession in 1827, and I do not remember whether I was also Cicero, Franklin, or Themistocles (it depends upon what book I was reading at the

time of the catastrophe), but I was told for the third time
to close my shop and mount guard in the character of en-
sign of militia, to which rank I had of late been promoted.
I was very much opposed to that guard, and over my own
signature I complained of the service, and used the expression, 'with which we are oppressed.' I was at once relieved of the guard, and summoned into the presence of
the colonel of the army of Chili, Don Manuel Quiroga,
then Governor of San Juan, who at the moment was taking
his ease, seated in the court-yard of the Government House.
This circumstance and my extreme youth (sixteen), naturally authorized the Governor, on speaking to me, to keep
his seat, and keep on his hat. But it was the first time I
had presented myself before one in authority. I was young,
ignorant of life, haughty by education, and perhaps by my
daily contact with Cæsar, Cicero, and other favorite personages, and as the Governor did not answer my respectful
salute, before answering his question, 'Is this your signature, sir?' I hurriedly lifted my hat, intentionally put it
on again, and answered resolutely, 'Yes, sir.'

"The dumb scene that followed would have perplexed
the spectator, doubting which was the chief and which the
subaltern, who were defying each other by their glances,
the eyes of each wide open and fixed upon each other; the
Governor endeavoring to make me cast down mine by the
flashes of anger that gleamed from his own, and I with
mine fixed unwinking, to make him understand that his
rage was aimed at a soul fortified against all intimidation.
I conquered, and in a transport of anger, he called an aide-
de-camp and sent me to prison.

"Friends flew to see me, among them Laspuir, now minister, who was very fond of me; he advised me to do what
he had always done, yield before difficulties. My father
came soon, and after I had told him the story, he said,

'You have done a foolish thing, but it is done ; now bear the consequences with courage.' The affair was followed up. I was asked if I had heard the government complained of. I answered, ' Yes, by many.' When asked for names, I said, ' Those who had spoken in my presence had not authorized me to communicate their opinions to the authorities.' They insisted ; I persisted ; they threatened me ; I held my tongue ; they abandoned the cause, and I was set at liberty.

" I was initiated thus by the authorities themselves into the party questions of the city ; into questions which divided the Republic, and it was not in Rome or in Greece that I was to seek for liberty and country, but there, in San Juan, in the horizon where the events opened that were preparing in the last days of Rivadavia's presidency. . . .

" At the fiesta of Pueblo Viejo, I fired a sky-rocket at the hoofs of a group of horses, and Colonel Quiroga, then ex-governor, came out from among the horsemen to maltreat me, attributing to malice prepense what was only a piece of folly. We had a wordy dispute, he on horseback, I on foot. He had a train of fifty horsemen, and I fixed my eyes upon him and his spirited horse to avoid being trampled upon, when I felt something touch me behind in a disagreeable and significant manner. I put my hand behind me, and touched — the barrel of a pistol, which was left in my hand. I was also at that instant the head of a phalanx, which had gathered in my defense. The Federal party, headed by Quiroga Carril, was on the point of a hand-to-hand encounter with the Unitario party, whom I served unconsciously at that moment. The ex-governor rode off, ·confounded by the mocking laughter he heard, and perhaps astonished at being a second time worsted in the presence of a boy who did not arrogantly give him provocation, nor timidly yield when once embarked in a bad undertaking. The next day I was a Unitario; a month later I knew the party questions in their very essence, knew their personages and their views, for from that moment I entered upon the voluminous study of opposing principles.

" When the war broke out, I gave into the hands of my aunt, Doña Angela, the shop I had in charge, enlisted with the troops which had risen in insurrection against Facundo Quiroga in the Quijadas, made the campaign of Jachel, found myself in the encounter at Tafin, escaped being taken prisoner with the carts and horses which I had previously taken in the Posito, under the order of Don Javier Angulo, fled with my father to Mendoza, where the very troops which had conquered us in San Juan had risen against the Aldaos, and shortly after was nominated adjutant."

He was subsequently an approved instructor of recruits, then second director of the Military Academy, to which office he was assigned for his knowledge of cavalry maneuvers and tactics, due to his peculiar habits of study. The campaign of Mendoza, which ended in the horrible tragedy of Pilar, brought on by the bad faith of Aldao, was to him the poetry, the idealization, the realization of his readings. He was only eighteen, a beardless youth, unknown to the world, but he lived in an ecstasy of enthusiasm, ready at any moment to be a hero, to sacrifice himself, or to die, in order to obtain the smallest result in the cause for which he fought, — which was liberty to all as well as to himself. He describes himself as fighting with " demoniac " zeal, the first in pursuit of guerillas, regardless of danger ; indeed, so beside himself, that at last his superior officer took away his rifle, as one takes a noisy trumpet from children, till they learn to do what they are bid.

These combats were in the streets of the city, and the conquerors in one were now prisoners in another. His father followed him everywhere like a tutelar angel, but was often unable to restrain his fanaticism. Indeed, on one occasion, when the noble Leprida most affectionately and earnestly, but in vain, endeavored to withdraw him from the combat, — the illustrious Leprida, President of that Congress of Tucuman, which declared the independence of Spanish rule, and before whom the most eminent men of the Republic bowed their heads, as before one of the fathers of their country, and who perished in that terrible massacre, — he also obliged his father to flee without him, who lingering too long on the road, almost beside himself with anxiety and shame for having preserved his own life by flight, was at last taken prisoner and carried to San Juan, where he escaped being shot only by a ransom of two thousand dollars. The young Sarmiento escaped many perils at that time — that of being shot by the order of his own government, from which he was saved by a noble foe, who carried him and other enthusiastic youths who were brought prisoners to him, to the shelter of his own roof, where he protected them at the risk of his own life; the peril of being shot in the barracks by three assassins instigated by Aldao, beside that of innumerable skirmishes and engagements. He says human nature never showed itself more unworthy to him than in that treacherous attack of the drunken friar, Aldao, upon a group of sixty officers, who had assembled after a truce had been agreed upon.

It was at that time that two hundred persons fell victims to the atrocities of Aldao, among whom were twenty of Sarmiento's own friends. But such is the elasticity of youth, that while a prisoner in his own house in Mendoza, to escape Aldao, an opportunity offering to study French with a soldier of Napoleon, who did not know Spanish nor the grammar of his own language, in six weeks from the beginning he had made such progress as to have translated twelve volumes.

He kept his books upon the dining-table (it was the sight of a French library in the place that had awakened his zeal), removed them at meal times, extinguished his candle at two in the morning, or when the reading absorbed him entirely, passed two or three days in succession, seated, with his dictionary by his side. Fourteen years afterward, on visiting France, he learned to pronounce the language.

It was after these events that with his family and those of the most prominent citizens of San Juan, he emigrated to Chili, to escape the fearful tyranny described in the work now published. At first he kept school in Los Andes, then was a shopkeeper in Pocuro, with a small capital provided by his family, afterwards a commercial clerk in Valparaiso, then majordomo of mines in Copiapo. While in Valparaiso, earning an ounce a month, he paid half of it to Rickard, the English professor, and two reals a week to the watchman of the ward, to wake him at two in the morning for his English studies. Saturday nights he passed without sleep, to eke out the leisure of Sunday. After he had taken lessons six weeks, Rickard told him that he only wanted the pronunciation, which he did not acquire, however, till very lately.

While majordomo of the Copiapo mines, he translated a volume a day of the sixty volumes of Sir Walter Scott's works, beside some other books. His reading in Valparaiso was very extensive, and these readings, enriched by several languages, spread out before him all the great discussions of philosophical, political, moral, and religious ideas, and to use his own expression, " opened the pores of his intelligence to imbibe them." When the labor of the mining day was over, he met, in a certain kitchen where they partook of refreshment, other Argentine majordomos, foremen, and laborers, exiles like himself, to discuss politics, and in the evenings assembled at the house of another, the only one who had a family establishment there, thus keeping up their habits of civilized life. At these reunions, in his miner's dress, — which consisted of doublet and hose, striped drawers, a red cap, and a broad sash, from which depended a purse capable of holding twenty-five pounds of sugar, but in which he always kept several bundles of tobacco, a dress he had assumed partly from fancy and partly from economy, — he was always the oracle to which all appealed for points of history, geography, or other book learning. Anecdotes are told of the astonishment of strangers at the little learned miner, who was supposed to be only a peon who had strayed into the company. Once, for want of the book, he recited a whole pamphlet he had written upon a plan for planting a colony on the Colorado River, and made converts too — for he was from his youth always eloquent upon the point of cultivating the soil. In the proper place we shall speak of his success in later life in showing to his countrymen the advantages of agriculture over cattle-growing. While at Copiapo it was his habit to entertain the miners by drawings of birds and animals, and he taught French to others, for those who knew less than himself were always objects of interest to him.

In 1836, he returned to San Juan, ill with a cerebral attack, destitute of resources, scarcely known to any one, for few old friends had yet returned from exile. A complicated operation in arithmetic, which the incompetent government needed, brought him again into notice, and after suffering many privations, he gradually took his place again with Cortinez, Aberastain, Quiroga Rosas, and Rodriguez, men of mark and education, worthy to figure in any part of South America. Together they founded a college for young ladies, in aid of which project he had written a forcible appeal for the education of women, and of which he was made director — and another for men, which was not allowed to succeed. The college for ladies lasted but two years, but left its mark upon the society of San Juan. A dramatic society and many public amusements that tended to cultivate and improve manners, were among the improvements made by these young men, stimulated by the undying zeal and executive ability of Sarmiento. Here, in the library of Quiroga Rosas, he found Villemain, and Schlegel ; in literature, Jouffroi, Lermennier, Guizot, Cousin; in philosophy, Tocqueville, and Pedro Leroux ; the " Encyclopedic Review," as synthesis of all opinions, Charles Didier, and a hundred other authors, whom he devoured with avidity. For two years these books furnished material for impassioned discussions between the friends, and in this school of philosophy, as he considered it, they talked over the new doctrines, attacked, defended, resisted, and were at last more or less conquered by them. Here his own mind, hitherto but a reflecting mirror of the ideas of others, began to move and march on. He now began to think clearly for himself on all subjects.

"The European mind," as he expresses it, " began to transfuse itself into the American mind, and I began to apply to the different circumstances of the two theatres of action the results at which I arrived.

"It was in 1837 that I learned Italian, in company with young Rawson,[1] whose talents had then begun to show themselves strikingly. Several years afterward, when editing the 'Mercurio' in Santiago de Chili, I familiarized myself with Portuguese, which is very easy. In Paris, still later, I shut myself up fifteen days with a German grammar and dictionary, and translated six pages to the satisfaction of an intelligent man who gave me lessons, that supreme effort leaving me an incomplete scholar, although I thought I had caught the structure of that rebellious idiom.

"I taught French to many persons for the sake of spreading good reading among them; and to sundry of my friends I taught it without giving them lessons. To put them in the path which I had trodden, I said, ' You must not fail to study — I am coming.' And when I saw their self-love fairly piqued, I gave them a few lessons upon the way to study for themselves.

"In all these efforts I always had in full activity the organ of instruction, and which was more cultivated in me than any other; educated by the living speech of the presbyter Oro, and the curate Albarracin, and always seeking the society of well-informed men, then and after-

[1] Late Secretary of State in the Republic.

wards my friends. Aberastain, Penero, Lopez, Alberdi, Gutierrez, Oro, Tejedor, Fragueiro, Montt, and many others, contributed, without knowing it, to develop my mind, transmitting their ideas to me, and giving me an opportunity to unfold my own as the complement to theirs.

" How are ideas formed ? I believe that in the mind of one who studies, it happens as in those inundations of rivers where the waters deposit little by little the particular solids washed down by them, and with which they fertilize the adjacent territory."

With the aid of the old friends whom he found in San Juan, he founded at this time a periodical called " La Zonda," which criticized village manners, promoted the spirit of enthusiasm, and would have been of incalculable benefit, if the government, which the periodical did not attack, had not felt a horrible apprehension of the light it was sending abroad.

" Out of this came my second imprisonment," he says, " for refusing to pay twenty-six dollars, of which in violation of the laws and decrees in force, the government proposed to rob me. Don Antonio Benavides (Governor), and Don Antonio Maradona (Minister), jointly and *in solidum* owe me twenty-six dollars every day that impends, and they shall pay me, as God lives, one or the other of them, sooner or later, the latter rather than the former, because a minister is put in his place to give counsel to the governor, who does not know so well the laws of his country, too self-willed to be restrained by laws, those frail barriers to his caprice, but which are insuperable through the respect their direct agents deserve among cultivated men. The governor of San Juan, wishing to free the province from the serious evils which might be brought upon it by the publication of a periodical which was edited by four men of letters competent to the task — that is, not wishing any one to examine his acts or enlighten public opinion, sent me word that the second number of 'La Zonda' was worth twelve dollars. I ordered the printer to draw so many dollars, and 'La Zonda' died of that suffocation."

One day he received a summons to appear before the governor, who asked him if he had obeyed the order to pay twenty-six dollars for the last number of "La Zonda." He replied that it was an illegal demand, and that he had had no official notice to pay it, for the messenger by whom it was sent, the printer, was not a legal messenger, and the law provided that no money should be required of writers, the publishers having the benefit of sales, in order to encourage publications. Finding him resolute in his refusal, Benavides threw him into prison. His friends visited him and advised him to yield the point, in order to save the college of which he was director. The aide-de-camp came to receive the money, and received a warrant against a merchant, accompanied by his own signature, by which Sarmiento was to recover in due time, in view of the law which was violated to his injury, the sum of which he was despoiled, with damages. Thus ended this affair, but he says, —

" My situation in San Juan became more and more thorny every day, as the political horizon became more and more charged with threatening clouds. Without any plan of life, without influence, repelling the idea of conspiracy, in coffee-houses, and assemblies, as well as in the presence of Benavides, I spoke my convictions with all the sincerity of my nature, and the suspicions of the government closed around me on every side like a cloud of flies buzzing in my ears.

"In 1839 an incident complicated the situation. The friar Aldao was defeated, and his instantaneous arrival in San Juan was announced. The few men who opposed the government feared for their lives. Dr. Aberastain was the only one who would not flee. I prevailed upon him to go, — I begged him to go, and he yielded to my request. I was the only one who knew Aldao well. I alone had been in Mendoza the spectator of atrocities of which two hundred unhappy persons, twenty of whom were my friends and companions, had been the victims. When they spoke to me of preparing for the intended flight, I gave reasons of convenience and duty which obliged me to remain in San Juan, to which they could but give assent. Aldao did not come, but the fears of the government and the rage of the new and hitherto unknown men into whose hands it had put arms, were concentrated upon me.

"At that time I made a supreme effort. I saw Maradona the ex-minister, the representatives of Sala, and as many men as could influence the mind of Benavides, in order that they might restrain him, if possible, from the abyss into which I saw him rushing — despotism, chieftainship, the overthrow of all the foundations on which society reposes. The growing tyrant sent for me.

" ' I know that you are conspiring, Don Domingo.'

" ' It is false, sir; I do not conspire.'

" ' You are influencing the Representatives.'

" ' Ah! that is another thing; your Excellency sees that there is no conspiracy. I have my right to apply to the magistrates and the representatives of the people, to prevent the calamities which your Excellency is preparing for the country. Your Excellency is alone, isolated, obstinate in carrying out your plan, and I am interested, that those who can and ought to do it, should restrain you in time.'

" ' Don Domingo, you will force me to take measures.'

" ' And what matters it ? '

" ' Severe ones.'

" ' And what matters it ? '

" ' You do not understand what I mean.'

" ' Yes, I understand — to shoot me, and what matters it ? '

" Benavides looked at me as if fascinated; and I protest that he could not see on my countenance any sign of boasting. I was inspired at that moment by the spirit of God. I was the representative of the rights of all, which were about to be trampled on. I saw in the countenance of Benavides symptoms of appreciation, of compassion, of respect, and I wished to respond to this movement of his soul.

" ' Sir,' I said, ' do not defile yourself with crime. When you can tolerate me no longer, banish me to Chili; in the mean time, remember that I must labor to restrain you, if possible, from the precipice over which ambition and unbridled passion are hurrying you,' and then I took my leave.

" Some days afterwards I was again summoned to the Governor's house.

" ' I have been convinced that you have received letters from Salta and the encampment of Brinuela.'

" ' Yes, sir ; and I was preparing to bring them to you.'

" ' I knew the papers had arrived, but I was ignorant,' he added angrily, ' that you wished to show them to me.'

" ' I had not made a fair copy of the representation I had made, with which to accompany them. Your Excellency has both now.'

" ' These proclamations are printed here.'

" ' You are mistaken, sir, they were printed in Salta.'

" ' There! do not deceive me.'

" ' I never deceive, sir. I repeat that they were printed in Salta. The press of San Juan has not this small capital; this other type, that ' ——

" Benavides insisted, sent for Galaburri the printer, and was convinced of his error.

" ' Give me this paper.'

" ' I will read it to you, sir ; it is in manuscript.'

" ' Read it, then.'

" I was silent.

" ' Read it.'

" ' Will your Excellency send away the Chief of Police, in whom I do not wish to place confidence.'

" And when he had gone out, while Benavides threw glances upon me that threatened death, as if I ought to pay for his bad education, which made him a third party, I read my *factum* in a clear expressive voice, pausing upon each conception that I wished to make salient, giving force to those ideas which I wished to make penetrate my auditor. When I had finished reading, which had put me into a state of exaltation, I raised my eyes, and read in the countenance of the chief — indifference! Not one single idea had penetrated his soul, nor had a suspicion arisen in it. His will and his ambition were a cuirass which defended his heart and his intellect.

" Benavides is a cold man ; and to this San Juan owes having been less abused than the other provinces. He has an excellent heart, and is tolerant ; envy has little part in his mind ; he is patient and tenacious. Afterwards I reflected that reason is impotent in a certain state of culture ; its edges are blunted and slip over those smooth and hardened surfaces. Like the generality of men in our countries, he

has no clear consciousness of law or of justice. I have
heard him say, candidly, that the province would never do
well till it had no lawyers, that his comrade Ibarra lived
tranquilly, and governed well, because he alone, in two
cases out of three, decided all causes. Rosas has his best
support in Benavides ; it is the force of inertia in exercise,
calling everything to be quiet and dead, without violence
and without parade. The province of San Juan is, with
the exception of La Rioja, San Luis, and some other cities,
one that has fallen lowest, because Benavides has im-
pressed upon it his materialism, his inertia, his abandon-
ment of all that constitutes public life, which is just what
despotism requires. The people eat, they sleep, they talk,
they laugh if they can, — and keep quiet, that in twenty
years hence, their sons may walk on four feet.

"Benavides had no minister then ; all the Federals
avoided him, and he alone, with the aid of his troops, carried on his insane designs. Thus men in power take the
name of the people to call themselves governments, after
they have degraded and abused them ! He had made one
Espinosa, a drunken Tucuman, though a valiant fellow, chief
of his forces ; and one Herrera, a Chilian bandit, taken out
of prison, and a comic actor whom I had hissed in the
theatre, were called into the service, the latter as captain ;
the Indian Saavedra, an assassin and highwayman, was
another. Juan Fernandez, a young man of good family who
had voluntarily descended into the rabble where he passed
his time in intoxication and gambling, the most despicable
and despised creature then in San Juan, was his aide-de-
camp. An Italian impostor, corrupt, clownish, and ignorant, was made mayor. Under the orders of these chiefs,
the scoriæ of society, many obscure young men of good
intentions, but ignorant and from the lowest orders of society, had been called into the service. Some of them,

even from that bad school, turned out good members
of society, however. Finally, I was summoned a fourth
time to the government house. This time I was prepared.
I knew that a terrible blow was to be inflicted, and that I
was the appointed victim. It was Sunday, and I had taken
leave of some friends at home half in jest and half in
earnest, and written down that my life was in danger. I
obeyed the summons, however, taking with me a servant
who could give information of my imprisonment should
that event occur. I met on the way one of my friends,
and resisted his prayers and supplications that I would not
present myself.

"'They are going to arrest you; everything is prepared.'

"'Let me alone; Benavides has sent for me by an
aide-de-camp, and I should be ashamed not to answer the
call.'

"They arrested me! And at oration, when the guard
presented itself that was to take me to the prison, the
noise of swords made my nerves thrill; there was a hum-
ming in my ears, and I was afraid! Death, which I believed my doom at that moment, looked to me sad, disgraceful, guilty; and I had not the courage to accept it in
that character. Nothing happened then, however, except
that I was fastened into my dungeon with shackles. The
days passed, and the mind habituated itself to conquer its
anxieties and disenchantment, as the eyes habituated themselves to the darkness. I was a passive victim, and except
my family, no one seemed to care for my fate. My cause
was no one's but my own. I suffered because I had been
indiscreet, because I had desired to attack the evil without
possessing the means to attack it; to material facts I opposed protests, and solitary abnegation, and the facts took
their own course in spite of me.

"On the night of the 17th of November, at two in the

morning, a group of horsemen parading in front of the prison, cried out, ' Death to the Unitarios.' So without antecedents was that cry, so coldly and composedly did it proceed out of the mouths of those who pronounced it, that it was evident that it was a thing arranged and agreed upon dispassionately. I understood perfectly that there was some design on foot. At four o'clock the same thing was repeated. I was awake, writing some foolish thing which kept me entertained. At dawn, an Andalusian was brought into the prison who pretended to be drunk, and in the midst of repartees and laughable jokes, designed to distract the attention of the sentinels, in passing me, making an evolution round another prisoner who was with me, he let fall short phrases — ' They are going to assassinate them. The troops are coming into the square ——. The commandant Espinosa is going to lance —— Señor Sarmiento ! —— Save yourself if you can !'

" This time I was equal to the situation. I sent home a boy, wrote to the bishop that he must not be frightened, and that he must try by his presence to save me; but the poor old man did just the contrary; he *was* frightened, and his legs would not hold him up. The troops came and formed in the square ; the boy who stood at the door of the dungeon in the character of a telegraph, communicated to me all the movements. Some cries were heard in the square, and there was much running of horses. I saw the lance of Espinosa pass by. There was a moment of silence, and soon eighty officers collected in a group near the prison, crying, ' Bring down the prisoners !' The officer of the guard came to me and ordered me to go out.

" ' By whose order ? '

" ' By Commandant Espinosa's.'

" ' I do not obey.'

" He then passed on to the next cell, and brought out

Oro and exhibited him. But on seeing him they cried, 'Come down! Not he! Sarmiento!'

"'Go then,' I said to myself, 'there is no way of getting excused here.' I went out and was saluted with a hurrah of threats and insults by men who did not know me, with the exception of two who had reason to detest me.

"'Come down! Come down! Crucify him.'

"'I do not obey! You have no right to send for me."

"'Officer of the guard, strike him down with your sword!'

"'Go down,' said the latter to me with his sword uplifted.

"'I do not obey,' I said, taking hold of the iron railing.

"'Go down!' and he struck me with his sword.

"'I do not obey,' I repeated quietly.

"'Give him the edge!' cried Espinosa, foaming with rage. 'If he stays up there, I will pierce him with my lance, Mr. officer of the guard.'

"'Go down, sir, for God's sake,' said the good official in a low voice, ashamed, in spite of himself, and half weeping; while he discharged blows upon me with his sword. 'I shall give you the edge, indeed I shall.'

"'Do what you please,' I said. 'I do not obey.'

" Some cries of alarm from two windows in the square from voices which were known to me, on seeing that sword rise and fall, had disturbed me a little. But I wished to die as I had lived, as I had sworn to live, without even willfully consenting to violence. Besides, I must humbly confess that I had a little stratagem in reserve. I had ascertained that Benavides was not in the square, and this datum had enabled me rapidly to arrange my plan of defense. The railing of the City Hall steps was really my table of safety. 'The troops have come to the square,' I said to myself. 'Now Benavides has a part in this affair, but he is not here, in order to refer this outrage to the Federal enthusiasm, as Rosas called the assassination of Mana, which he denounced as 'an atrocious license in a moment of profound and immense popular irritation.' The prison is in a straight line, a square and a half from Benavides' house. Sound runs so many leagues a minute, and to go two hundred and twenty-five yards required only a second of time. In vain would the Governor have wished to wash his hands of that anonymous outrage, for here was I in a high and respectable place to send the crime to its source and origin. The servants of Benavides' house, one of his scribes, and his aide-de-camp, ran on see-ing the sword glisten as it revolved in the air over my head, and one after another, as they ran into the house, shrieked, ' Sir! sir! they are killing Don Domingo!' I had then caught my cunning gaucho in his own net. Either he confessed himself an accomplice, or he would send the order to leave me in peace. Benavides had not courage at that time to take that responsibility ; my blood would have been distilling over his heart drop by drop all the rest of his life !

"When the furies who cried 'come down,' were con-vinced that I would not die under the hoofs of the horses, it being my pleasure to do that in a decent and clean place, ten or twelve rushed up the steps, and catching me in their arms, carried me down, at the moment when a dozen hussars whom Espinosa had sent for to despatch me, had arrived at the spot. But Espenosa wished to see my face and to terrify me. The comic actor whom I hissed in the theatre, made captain of the Confederacy, held his sword at my breast with his eyes fixed on Espinosa, ready at a signal to thrust it into me. The commandant whirled his lance and pricked me on my side, uttering blasphemies. I kept my countenance composed, stereotyped, just as I wished it to look after death. Espinosa pricked harder, but my countenance remained impassible, if I might judge by the rage it inspired him with, for recovering his lance, he gave me a horrible thrust. The blade was half a yard long and the width of a hand, and I preserved for many a day the scar which was left on my wrist by my effort in wresting it out of my side. Then the brute prepared to satiate his mocking rage. I, inspired by the sentiment of self-preservation, and calculating that it was time for Benavides' aide-de-camp to arrive, raised my hand over my head and said imperiously, ' Listen! Commandant,' and as he lent his attention, I turned round, thrust myself under the gallery to get round the other side of the horses, and as I arrived at the end they fell upon me. I warded off a cloud of bayonets with both hands, and at that moment the Governor's aide arrived with orders to suspend the farce, consenting only that they should shave me, as they had done to many others. If he had not permitted some punishment, Espinosa would have wholly lost the dominion of his passions, and I should not have had sufficient coolness to pull off the mask under which Benavides wished to hide himself. They put me into the lowest dungeon, and then occurred a scene which doubled the terror of the people : my mother and two of my sisters defied the guards, ascended the steps; they were seen to go in and out of the empty cells, then descended like a vision, and rushed to the house of Benavides to demand the son, the brother! O, the agonies that despotism inflicts !

" What passed next many know, but it was not I who supplicated or gave satisfaction! for on no day of that trial did I belie the severity of my principles nor did my spirit flag again. One thing in regard to this event I will

record here for the benefit of those who despair of due
punishment being meted out to crimes committed with
impunity ten years ago. The perpetrators of that bloody
farce, *all* without one exception, have died a bloody death.
A fatal ball struck Espinosa at Angaco. Acha, coming
suddenly into the street one dark night, fired a few shots
out of mere wantonness into the square, and the comic
actor, who hoped for Espinosa's signal to stab me, fell
dead from his horse ; the Indian Saavedra, who had given
me a thrust, was assassinated. And the crippled gaucho
Fernandez, who wallowed in drunkenness and dissipation,
if he yet lives, it is to show who was the Governor's adjutant in those days of madness and infamy. Like my
mother, I believe in Providence ; and Bàrcena, Gaetan,
Salomon, and all the Mashorqueros (thugs) assassinated by
each other, or sentenced by him who had put the dagger
into their hands, devoured by remorse, desperation, delirium, and the contempt of men, tormented by epilepsy or
wasted by consumption, have made me hope yet for
the end which will adjust all things. Rosas is already in
despair ! His body is a skeleton, trembling and disjointed.
The venom of his soul is corroding the vase which holds it,
and you will soon hear it crack, that his putrescent existence may give place to the rehabilitation of morality and
justice, and to the sentiments of humanity compromised
for so many years. Woe, then, to those who have not re-
pented of their crimes ! The greatest punishment that
can be inflicted upon them is to live, and I wish to inflict
upon all, without exception, this punishment.

" My residence of four years in San Juan — and this is the
only epoch of my adult life that I have resided in my own
country — was a continuous and obstinate combat. I, like
others, wished to elevate myself, and the least concession
on my part would have opened to me the door to the

administration of Benavides, and to a place in his army. He desired it, and in the beginning had a great esteem for me; but I wished to rise in the world without sinning against morality or committing crimes against liberty and civilization. Public balls, societies, masquerades, theatres, I was always at the head of; to the growing ignorance I opposed colleges; to the crime of governing without law or justice I replied with a periodical; against the attempt to suppress such a publication illegally, I gave my person to the prison; against the holding of extraordinary powers I advocated by speech and writing the right of petitioning the representatives in order to make them fulfill their duty; to intimidation I opposed firmness and contempt; to the knife of the 18th of November, an impassible countenance, and patience under mocking impositions and ignoble deceit. Everything that is evil has been said of me, and some evil has been believed of me in San Juan; but no one has ever doubted my honor or my patriotism, and I appeal for the truth of this to the testimony of those who have chosen to call themselves my enemies. I lived honorably, making an efficient workman by means of some rudiments of practical geometry and the art of drawing up plans which I acquired in my childhood. Forced by want of lawyers, I defended some causes; and when Dr. Aberastain was supreme judge of Alzada, and my intimate friend, I lost before his tribunal the two most important ones. If this does not testify to my legal capacity, it at least shows the incorruptibility of the judge."

The next day, on passing through the baths of Zonda into exile, and turning his back upon all the comforts and pleasures of life, he wrote with a piece of charcoal, with the hand covered with the scars of his late encounter, that noble protest which he quotes in the prologue to " Civilization and Barbarism " —

" *On ne tue pas les idées !* "

An English writer says of this : —

" Let those acquainted with Señor Sarmiento say whether he has fulfilled his mission. There is in these few words a satire which tells volumes. It brands his enemies with ignorance, at the same time that it is extremely ludicrous and cutting. It is not too much to say that less interesting anecdotes than this have appeared in D'Israeli's ' Curiosities of Literature.' " [1]

Again he emigrated to Chili, thought seriously of establishing himself there, and had the intention of opening a college, but one of his compatriots dissuaded him from it, and facilitated his writing for the periodic press. By way of experiment, he sent from Santiago to the only journal of Chili, the " Valparaiso Mercury," an anonymous article signed " A Lieutenant of Artillery," upon the battle of Chacabuco, which attracted notice in literary and political society by its freshness of style and elevation of thought.

A mutual jealousy of each other's glory has always prevailed among the States of South America, occasioned by their efforts to establish themselves as distinct nations, with more definite limits than any previously suggested by their geography or by the history of their war for independence. This jealousy has often led to the perversion of history, and, at the time we are considering, Chili had well-nigh erased from her records the glorious name of San Martin, and thrust into the background the share of the Argentines in the battles of Chacabuco and Maypo, which decided the establishment of Chilian independence.

[1] *River Plate Magazine*, No. 3, page 151.

The above-mentioned article upon the first of these battles, followed by another upon the second, roused the generous sentiments of the people by its pathos, and earnestly appealed to the justice of the generation then in full enjoyment of the fruits of the great deeds whose contemporaries had of necessity received wounds as well as gifts from the rough hands of war. So timely was this appeal in behalf of a just claim to renown obscured by prejudice and malice, that it gained for its author, hitherto without a name, in two senses, a position in the unfamiliar theatre in which he had thus appeared, and for General San Martin the rank and pay of Captain-General that very year, and subsequently the tokens of gratitude due from a nation to its liberators, visible to-day in the equestrian statue erected to his memory in the finest boulevard of Santiago, facing the Andes and surrounded by the poplars which he himself had planted.

The party which was in the Chilian government at this time asked through one of the secretaries the concurrence of Señor Sarmiento at the approaching election. The first words Don Manuel Montt[1] said to him, were, "Ideas, sir, have no country." From that moment they understood each other. I wish I had space to delineate the character of Don Manuel Montt. "My meeting him in the path of my life," says Señor Sarmiento, in speaking of this gentleman, "gave a new phase to my existence, and if it attains any noble ends, I shall owe it to his aid opportunely tendered."

By request he took the editorship of the "Mercurio," which he successfully çarried through the political campaign of that year, and he also founded and

1 Then Minister of State in Chili.

edited the "Nacional" in Santiago. Of course, such vigorous articles as he wrote upon all subjects provoked opposition. Even South American apathy was stung into repartee, and he needed all the steadiness and calmness of his friend Montt to enable him to bear the abuse that the "Revista Catolica" and the "Seminario" heaped upon him, but out of this strife came many improvements.

In 1841, at the end of the electoral campaign which secured the triumph of their candidate, he took leave of Don Manuel Montt and the editorship of the "Mercurio" and the "Nacional," to return to fight the battles of his country. Montt opposed his intention, assuring him that there was no safety there for him ; that the situation of Colonel La Madrid, who was bravely opposing Rosas, was very critical. But, for that very reason, Señor Sarmiento's resolution was irrevocable. He was determined to offer the aid of his arm in that cause, and furnished with a warm letter of introduction to La Madrid from the Argentine Commission in Chili, who well knew the value of his assistance, and accompanied by three other compatriots, he set out on foot to surmount the Andes and join the General at Mendoza. After the fearful passage of the mountain summits was effected, through the peculiar and repeated dangers incident to such regions, on descending the eastern side, his rencontre with his countrymen was as distressing as unexpected. He and his little party saw afar off, like blots upon the interminable wastes of snow, groups of fleeing soldiers, and looking at each other in dismay, they could only exclaim, "Routed!" and seen from afar by the fugitives, the latter repeated the word "routed," across the snows.

At the foot of the Vacas, a lofty summit, they found, in a small hut, the first detachment from Mendoza, and other squads arrived from time to time during the day from the battle-ground of *La Cienega del Medio*, finding no shelter but that of the rocks, and no food but what each one had brought for himself. Toward night came the rear-guard with La Madrid himself, accompanied by Alvarez and the other chiefs. Many others having been decapitated at Uspellata, among whom were the Commandant Sagraña and six other chiefs. Hundreds had taken refuge in the mountains, and of these, many were youths of the first families of Buenos Ayres and the northern Argentine Provinces, who had volunteered with patriotic enthusiasm to resist the tyrant Rosas. Not a moment was to be lost if he would save the lives of his countrymen. Señor Sarmiento and his companions, without waiting to take rest, retraced their steps over the giant heights to Aconcagua.

At *Los Andes*, the first town on the other side of the mountains, Señor Sarmïento established himself in the house of a friend, and for twelve hours, with another friend for his secretary, brought into requisition his executive abilities, so often tested in his adventurous life. That very afternoon he sought, contracted for, and despatched twelve mountain laborers to the aid of the exhausted fugitives, purchased, collected, and despatched six loads of substantial comforts, sent an express to the Argentine Commission at Santiago to put them in motion ; wrote to Don Manuel Montt, the minister, asking for government aid, physicians, and other help ; a letter to certain friends that they might

appeal to public charity ; one to the director of the
theatre, to give an entertainment for their benefit, and
an article to the " Mercurio " of Valparaiso to alarm
the whole country and awake compassion. When the
assistance he had so quickly collected was on the way,
and the various couriers despatched with the letters,
and his purse emptied to the last *maravedi*, he was
obliged to seek repose, for he had *run* down the mountains from *Los Ojos de Agua* to *Los Andes* without resting from his previous ascent. Within two days he
received replies from General las Heras and his friends
Gana, Zapata, and Quiroga Rosas, which do honor to
themselves as well as to him. In three days sufficient
food, medicines, physicians, etc., etc., for a thousand
men, were on their way over the giant heights.

The danger of the transit was increased by threats
of an approaching storm. Those conversant with the
Andes knew by the heavy clouds, always more dangerous than the frozen snows, and on this day, unusually
dark and lowering, that it would be of more than ordinary violence. It was easy after the first day to calculate
how many out of the thousand would be frozen before
succor could reach them. The sublime but heart-
rending spectacle of the gently falling snow that
covered every rock and quenched every fire that was
kindled, chilled the hopes of the relieving party, but
no one turned back. After three days of suffering,
seven of the fugitives had perished, and many others
had lost their limbs by frost before the physicians got
to the foot of the Cordilleras. An Argentine artist
has immortalized upon canvas the scene in which the
first Chilian broke the snow on arriving at the spot.

The heat and shelter of the hut had saved three hundred, a leaning rock had sheltered another hundred, and their *ponchos*, by confining the warmth to their bodies, had saved the rest. But they were nearly starved. Among the refugees was the famous El Chacho, who had succeeded Facundo Quiroga in the chieftainship of the peasantry. He had thrown himself on the side of General La Madrid against Rosas, but had contributed not a little to the loss of the battle by his rashness and want of discipline. He did not know, when his life was then saved by the aid of Señor Sarmiento, that twenty years later he and his hordes would be annihilated by that same deliverer. Like other peasant chiefs, El Chacho, who mingled in all the disputes of the country, sometimes took one side, sometimes the other, and was now a dangerouse nemy, and now a dangerous friend, according as his caprices led him. Señor Sarmiento somewhere likens this chieftain to the *Radies* of Arabia, who receive from every new government some privilege or post, said government shutting its eyes to the risk of treachery should self-interest interpose its claims.

Señor Sarmiento was thus thrown back upon Chili, and his first reception in Santiago was a sad chill over a doubly exiled heart. He was charged through the press with having complained of the hardness of some of the people while he eulogized the generosity of others to his unfortunate countrymen, and then of improper use of the scanty funds he had collected for their necessities. The man who made the charge was not a compatriot, nor had he contributed, nor did he know how the money was appropriated, and must have invented the slander with what Mr. Sarmiento called the "most exquisite evil intention." General Las Heras answered the charge and vindicated him, "but for a long time," he says, "I was frightened by that gratuitous and spontaneous act of depravity, and frozen by it as if a jar of cold water had been poured over me."

He soon resumed the editorship of the "Mercurio," and one of the most active, most agitated, and most fruitful phases of his life — fruitful to himself and to others — ensued. Every interest of society responded to his touch.

He endeavored to organize primary instruction for the people — an idea that had never dawned upon the Chilian mind.

The proposition for a popular tax for education was well received, but there was no thought of any other appropriation of it than to educate the upper classes with it! Señor Sarmiento put the new idea into actual operation for *the people*. The newspaper he established was the first ever edited in Santiago, the residence of learned and literary Chilians. He wrote the first spelling-book in which the correct sounds of the Spanish alphabet were given, and which was afterwards printed in the United States and illustrated with vignettes ; banished from the schools such books as " The Temporal and Eternal," " The Pains of Hell," and others of a similar character, fit only to mislead the minds of youth and imbue them with false ideas, and replaced them with " The Life of Jesus Christ," " Morality in Deed and Life," " The Conscience of a Child," " The Life of Franklin," " The Why, or the Science of Things," etc., etc. He presented to the university of Chili the first paper upon orthography that ever saw the light in Spanish America, where the language had become sadly corrupted ; founded the " Monitor for Schools," a large periodical in which he treated in a masterly manner the most difficult questions upon popular education, stimulating the teachers and defending them against arbitrary acts and stupid decrees. This periodical he wished to call by a more comprehensive title, which should commend it to the perusal of all classes, of literary men as well as of schoolmasters, but this was thought too pretentious by the government, in whose name everything was done, without rendering any credit to the real author of books or measures, because indeed he was a foreigner! Not till long after he left the country, when the editorship of this valuable work was resumed after an interval of many years, was his name ever publicly mentioned in connection with it. This tardy recognition saved the credit of the country, but Señor Sarmiento did not have its aid in the difficult days when he made bricks without straw.

It was at this period, 1842, that he founded the first Normal School that was opened on this side the Atlantic. For three years he directed it in person, and it is remarkable to observe, that unaided and alone he thought out and put in practice all those methods of instruction most approved by advanced minds at the present day. Indeed, it was living instruction such as we can hardly boast in our days of text books, when the mine from which the teaching is done is not always in the mind of the teacher. Señor Sarmiento had few text-books, nor did he need them. Everything he taught was practically illustrated and embellished from the vast stores of his varied acquirements.

Don José Suarez, his Chilian biographer, describes his methods of instruction minutely. He dwells much upon his moral influence, which was of the noblest kind. He says of him in this relation : —

"Sarmiento always treated us as friends, inspiring us with that respectful confidence which makes a superior so dear. He was always ready to favor us and to help us in our misfortunes ; he often despoiled himself of his own garments to give them to his pupils, the greater part of whom were poor. He often invited us to accompany him in his afternoon walks in order to give us importance in the eyes of others, and to comfort our hearts by encouragement. It was my happiness often to accompany him to the Convent of la Dominica, and to other places. He always gave us his arm in these walks. When he returned from Europe in 1847, he who traces these remembrances, on the occasion of visiting him at his place of residence, was presented with all the etiquette of fashion, and as if he were a distinguished man, to the Minister of the Interior, Don Manuel Montt, who had come to welcome him home. In our career of schoolmaster, we do not remember that the hand of so distinguished a Chilian ever touched our humble one as on that occasion. We had previously been presented to the Señor General Las-Heras, Dr. Ocampo, and other Argentines of importance, who visited Sarmiento. He treated his pupils thus, not because we were individually worthy of the honor, but to give importance to our profession, then humiliated, calumniated, and despised.[1] But he himself, in spite of his

[1] Not ten years before the foundation of the Normal School, the Cour

learning and his influential relatives, was called by the
disdainful epithets of *clerk* and *schoolmaster*, and was insulted every day to his face by the supercilious Chilians,
my compatriots ! "

Don José is partially right in saying this.   In
1843 he founded and edited the periodical called " El
Progreso," the first paper that had ever been printed
in Santiago de Chili, the residence of learned Chilians.
He also edited the " Argentine Herald," in behalf of
his countrymen, unjustly abused by Rosas.   Envy,
jealousy, hatred, prejudice, and ill-will were his portion for a long time, growing out of his active effort
to ameliorate evils.   Rival papers heaped abuses upon
him ; he was sensitive to blame ; his patriotic heart
was doubly sore with the repeated and apparently in-
curable miseries of his country ; the word *foreigner*,
when applied to him, was a dagger in a heart like his
that was ready to toil for his adopted country as if it
were his own.   The impetuosity of his nature was not
yet softened even into apparent concession to a present
evil.   He was unceremonious in speaking the truth,
and the truth is the sharpest of swords to the evil
disposed or the apathetic.   There was no peace for
any one in his sphere who stood in the way of the reforms which he felt to be vital to the very existence of
civilized society, certainly to the continuance of free
governments in those unhappy countries.   He did not
make personal attacks, but the strife of pens waxed

of Santiago had condemned a robber who had stolen the candelabra of the
Virgin in the Church of San Merced, " to serve as a schoolmaster in
Copiapo for the term of three years," as they would have condemned him
to be whipped or to labor in the Penitentiary.

hot, and such was the exasperation of his mind that one day, as he describes it, —

"It touched upon delirium; I was frantic, demented, and conceived the sublime idea of castigating all Chili; declaring it ungrateful, infamous, vile. I wrote I know not what diatribe, put my name to it, and carried it to the press of 'el Progreso,' giving it directly into the hands of the compositors. I then returned home in silence, loaded my pistols, and awaited the explosion of the mine I had laid for my own destruction, but I felt avenged, and satisfied that I had achieved a great act of justice. Nations, I said to myself, may be criminal, and are so at times, and there is no judge who can punish them adequately but their own tyrants or their own writers. I complained of the President, of Montt, of the Viales, in order that no one should escape my justice; and to the writers and the public in general I told horrible, humiliating truths, enough to rouse the indignation of a whole city, till beside itself with anger it should demand the head of the audacious one who could so insult it.

"From this certain danger I was saved by the kindness of Don Jacobo Vial, to whom the frightened compositors had shown my manuscript. Don Antonio came to my house looking very sad, and spoke to me in the gentle and compassionate voice with which one is wont to address a lunatic. No sign of displeasure or of resentment appeared in his countenance.

"'Don Domingo,' he said, 'the printers have shown me the article you left with them this morning.'

"'I hear you.'

"'Have you considered the consequences?'

"'Perfectly,' looking at my pistols.

"'It is useless.'

"'I know it; leave me in peace!'

" ' Has Lopez seen it ? '

" ' No.'

" Don Antonio took his hat and went to Lopez and to the minister, to advise Don Manuel Montt of what I had done. Lopez came and made me consent that he should see the article, and erase some words. This was at three in the afternoon ; at twelve that night, Don Antonio brought me a note from Lopez in which he told me that he had given up erasing words, for this was making concessions ; that if I insisted upon publishing the article in spite of the disapprobation of my friends, I should immediately take a post-chaise and escape to Valparaiso.

" Lopez, with his usual sagacity, had touched the chord that would make me yield. First, he did not oppose me arbitrarily, because that will not answer with the demented. Secondly, he disapproved of me, and that made an impression. Thirdly, he showed me that it would be weakness to soften my phrases, and he knew I would not consent to show weakness. Fourth, he pointed out to me what way to flee, and this humbled me. No. I did not understand the thing thus ; if I wounded them to the death I would stay and take the consequences.

" The pillow came to bring me its counsels, if not slumber. Very early the next day the minister sent for me ; he spoke to me of indifferent things, of the Normal School, of I know not what common topics. At last he circumspectly touched the wound, enforcing himself by applying the balsam and pointing out to me how many persons esteemed me and treated me with distinction in compensation for these vulgar injuries which had no evil consequences. I replied ; was very exalted in my reply, then paused, and at the moment when I was about to lose all the respect due to the minister and the friend, the door was opened by Don Miguel de la Barra, who either by accident or intention, arrived at the precise moment to prevent a scandal.

" Thus that Chili which I wished to dress in state's prison garments (ensambenitar), to display its crimes more surely to the public gaze, showed me at the very moment virtues worthy of respect, a delicacy and infinite toleration, and proofs of sympathy and appreciation which made the suicide I had prepared for myself wholly unjustifiable. From that time the public and the writer understood each other reciprocally. That learnt to be tolerant, and to do justice to good intentions, and I habituated myself to look at it as a necessary part of my existence, and neither to fear its anger nor to provoke it. I am now unanimously acknowledged to be a good and loyal Chilian. But woe to him who persisted in calling me a *foreigner !* It was safer for him to emigrate to California."

In 1845 he wrote the lives of the Presbyter Balmaceda, of Colonel Pereira, of the Senator Gaudarillas, of Facundo Quiroga (three editions of the latter were published, and though proscribed by Rosas, together with his other works, was largely read in the Republic), the life of the priest Castro y Barros, and of General San Martin. At this epoch he united with the celebrated Garcia del Rivera, in the editorship of the " Museum of both Americas."

Don Manuel Montt saved Señor Sarmiento more than once from rash acts. When he gave up the editorship of the " Progreso " the first time, because he could not bear the criticisms upon it, he said to him in his quiet, commanding way, " You must write a book upon what you wish, and confound them;" thus restoring him to his own self-reliance. When he thought of going to Bolivar, under whom he had been promised place, Montt decidedly opposed it; he told him it would look like a defeat (for he had again resigned the post of public writer to escape persecution); he said Bolivar's cause was like a game of cards — "and did you not think of going to Europe?" The European expedition was decided upon, and when he took leave of his friend, the latter said to him, "You will return to your own country according to present appearances; if you ever wish to return to Chili, you shall take any place you wish. Undeceive yourself; these enmities which trouble you are wholly upon the surface. No one despises you, many esteem you."

"Such a statesman," to use the words of Señor Sarmiento, in speaking of this true and appreciative friend, whose words on their first meeting were, "Sir, ideas are of no country," "can, like Deucalion, make men out of stones. In Europe his letters followed me everywhere, even more constantly than those of my own family, and in every one was a suggestion of some point to be studied, or a hope that I should do such or such a thing, which hope was a sure indication that I would do it."

Colonel Sarmiento's "Travels in Europe, Algiers, and America," are full of lively pictures of all that is most interesting and instructive to observe in other lands. He studied not only education, but legislation, and all the nations he visited seemed to yield up to his well-prepared inspection the secret of their being for evil or for good. In France he saw and conversed with Thiers, Guizot, and Humboldt, and was made a member of the Historical Society. He visited Spain at the moment when the Duke of Montpensier entered Madrid to marry the Infanta. The Spanish nation were averse to this marriage, and though they treated the Duke with courtesy and offered him no insult, it was easy to see their want of sympathy. The ancient splendors of the national customs were invoked to cover this wound to their national pride. Royal bull-fights, which always take the Spanish people off their feet, were instituted with the most gorgeous displays, and the spectacles brought out all the Argentine poetry and the native brilliancy of our author's pen.

Señor Sarmiento's insight into the sorrows and evils of Spain was undoubtedly such as few travellers were prepared to exercise, and he saw very plainly that the Spain of to-day was the Spain of three centuries ago. More interesting to him than all the remains and the momentary resuscitation of ancient splendor, was his interview with Cobden in Barcelona, which he must describe in his own words, for the impulse it gave to his life and labors was very great, giving him a method which he has since used with great effect to breathe the breath of life into the apathetic children of the Spanish colony, that incubus upon the souls of men.

COBDEN.

" *Barcelona.* Here I have had the felicity of being presented to Cobden, the great English agitator, and I assure you that after Napoleon there is no man I so much wished to see. You know the long struggle of the league against the corn-laws in England, a glorious struggle of ratiocination, discussion, speech, and will, which unrooted the English aristocracy, sapping at the base its power over the land, which it possesses by the right of primogeniture, and leaving it alive, that it may bleed to death by degrees, make itself one with the people, and yield its power without violence when its weakened hands can no longer manage it. Since the days of Jesus Christ, this simple method of propagating a doctrine by the mere use of speech, had not been put in practice. The Catholics who came after Christ continued preaching, it is true, but from time to time they burned their opponents, and the wars of religion have inundated the earth with blood. The principles of liberty had not till now gone forth from that sad soil, liberty and the guillotine, emancipation of the people and conquest. Cobden rehabilitated ancient preaching, the apostleship without the martyrdom. Some millions of pounds sterling, collected by subscription, supported that war of words for eight years. Nine million tracts did those batteries of logic and argument throw out in 1843, alone, and some two thousand meetings as sham-fights, and sixteen monster-meetings, field battles that threw into the shade by the brilliancy of their results the useless ones of Jena, Austerlitz, and Marengo, ended in delivering up the keys of the English parliament to Cobden, who dictated from that Kremlin to the aristocracy the capitulation which suffered it to remain with its baggage, ammunition, flags, and positions, provided it would let as much wheat enter England as the people needed for bread. With Cobden began a new era for the world; the word again made itself flesh, producing of itself alone the greatest effects, and henceforth when men wish to know if it is possible to destroy an abuse protected by power, defended by riches, rank, and corruption, when they ask if there is any hope of overthrowing such abuse by means of persevering efforts and sacrifices, the name of Cobden will be remembered, and the work will be undertaken.

" You imagine Cobden a lively, caustic O'Connell, an enthusiast, ardent in politics, rapid, startling in reply? How you deceive yourself, my poor Victorino! He is perfectly simple, fastidious like an Englishman, calm as an axiom, cold, vulgar, if I may so express it, like all great truths. We were friends in two hours; we talked alone almost all night; he related to me his adventures, his struggles; he showed me his mode of action, the strategy of his speech, the little stories with which it was necessary to entertain the people that they might not go to sleep as they listened to him. He lamented the almost insuperable difficulty which the masses offer by their incapacity of comprehending and their prejudices. He gave me a card by which I could find him in Manchester, and we did not separate till we reached the door of my hotel, I overwhelmed with happiness, humbled by such greatness and such simplicity, meditating upon means so noble and results so gigantic. I did not sleep that night. I was in a fever. It seemed to me that war was about to become ridiculous when that system of aggregation of wills and juxtaposition of masses could be so generalized and put into practice to destroy abuses, governments, laws, and institutions.

" What more simple thing! To-day we are two, to-morrow four, next year a thousand, publicly united in the same design. The government will resist? It is because we are not many, because many more remain in favor of the abuse. Then let the preaching come on, and the pamphlets, the daily papers, the association, the league. The Government and the Chambers know the day and the hour in which they are conquered, — and yield! Go and plant such a beautiful system in America!

" Cobden had destroyed, or attacked before commencing his specific work, all the great principles on which the science of the government reposed. The *European equi-librium* (balance of power), declared him a maniac, thus to perplex the ministers by mixing up foreign affairs with theirs. The colonies were the only means of furnishing employment to the younger sons of the lords. The com-mercial balance was the *résumé* of ignorance in political economy, and politics, with all its pretensions of science, was the charlatanism of dunces and blackguards ; protec-tion of natural industry an innocent means of stealing money on the wing, ruining the consumer, and turning the protected manufacturer into the street. For all these truths, hitherto considered fundamental, he substituted good sense, the common sense of all men, more fit to judge than the interested science of lords and ministers."

In Spain, Señor Sarmiento was made a member of the Literary Society of Professors, and published in Madrid a paper against the projected expedition of General Flores, whose object it was to found a mon-archy in South America, of which the natural son of Queen Christina was to be the head. This document opened many eyes by its exhaustive investigation of the subject. The expedition was given up.

In England, Señor Sarmiento found the English reprint of Mr. Mann's Report of his educational tour in Europe. He came to the United States after his own more extended one, sought out Mr. Mann, and become acquainted, through his aid, with the common-school system of Massachusetts, which on his return to Chili he introduced there with great effect. He em-bodied his observations upon education in Europe and America in a noble work on "Popular Education."

When in Paris he had studied the art of silk-culture

under the elder Mundo, the first authority in the world, and on his return to Chili he founded the "American Silk-growing Society," for whose use he introduced at his own expense the best machines and other utensils, seeds, and books known in Europe.

In 1849 he began the publication of " La Cronica," a periodical which contains the only authentic collection of documents in South America upon the subject of immigration, a cause which he had industriously promoted since 1839, when his attention first became fixed upon its advantages. On each one of the topics he treated, a law was proposed, and even Rosas established a periodical in Mendoza to combat it. Rosas could hardly have been punished more effectually for his ill-treatment of Señor Sarmiento than he unceasingly was by the liberal views of government and the intense activity of that patriotic gentleman. It was at this time that the grateful letter he wrote to his old friend and deliverer Ramirez, grateful for past services and confident of continued friendship, but which contained his characterization of Rosas, was shown by that apostate friend to the tyrant, thus perpetuating his banishment indefinitely.

In 1850 he wrote " Argiropolis, or the Capital of the Confederate States," in which he proposed a new capital instead of Buenos Ayres ; and the " Recollections of a Province."

In 1851 he published the " South America," another periodical, and his " Travels ; " also a " Memorial of German Emigration," which was reviewed and highly commended by Dr. Wappaus, professor of geography and statistics in the University of Gottingen.

BUENOS AYRES.

Thus prepared, and matured by study, experience, travels in foreign lands, and years of beneficent action in a true cosmopolitan spirit, he left Chili in 1851 with the present President, Colonel Mitre, and the present General Paunero, to incorporate himself in the army of General Urquiza, who was about to open the campaign against Rosas. The battle of Caseros, which disposed of Rosas, took place on the third of February, 1852, and Señor, now Colonel Sarmiento, had the pleasure of writing a description of it upon the tyrant's own table with the tyrant's own pen. Six days after, he left Urquiza's army, for he saw that that old servant of Rosas meant no good to the country, but purposed to make himself a tyrant in Rosas' place. Durqué had been made President, who fell in with Urquiza's plans. The event proved that his prophecy was right, though Urquiza was not wholly successful.

He left a note for Urquiza, in which he told him it was his profound conviction that he was entering upon a thorny path, dissipating sooner or later, but not less fatally, the glory which for a moment had hung round his name.

Colonel Sarmiento returned to Chili, this time a voluntary exile. He went by way of Rio Janeiro, and passed a few weeks in close intimacy with its enlightened Emperor, who had read and admired his works and received him with much distinction. The Emperor had made an alliance with the Republic, to which he had formerly been opposed, and wished to converse with Colonel Sarmiento upon its status and its prospects.

In October, 1852, he wrote a pamphlet upon San Juan, its men, and its acts in the regeneration of the Republic ; the restoration of Benavides and the peoples' conduct towards him. When elected by San Juan Deputy to the National Congress, which office he declined, he published a letter to General Urquiza giving his reasons, and subsequently a pamphlet entitled " Convention of Sanatuolas de los Arreyos," in which he treats of the condition of the government in the Republic and the reactionary policy of Buenos Ayres. In 1853 he began to publish the second volume of " The Cronica," a political and literary periodical, and also his " Commentary on the Constitution of the Argentine Republic," with numerous documents illustrative of the text. In the following year he published a letter to the electors of Buenos Ayres, who had chosen him for their deputy, an appointment which he did not accept.

He finally took up his residence in Buenos Ayres as a private citizen. In that year he was nominated Deputy to Congress from Tucuman, but did not accept the nomination for some political reasons. In 1857 he solicited and obtained the direction of the department of schools, and was also made Councillor of the Municipality of Buenos Ayres, Durqué being still President. The difficulties which he encountered in carrying out his purpose of introducing the North American system of common schools into Buenos Ayres as a starting-point, are described in a very graphic and lively manner in a letter to the Señora Juana Manso, too long for insertion here. Three ministries went out, which made the acceptance of his bill the *sine qua non* of their acceptance of the ministry, but after waiting and working a year in the most indefatigable and persevering manner, and allowing himself to be the subject of much abuse, he succeeded in setting the matter in operation, in the midst of intestine political difficulties of various kinds, invasion by the Indians, attempts at usurpation, and capture of the city by warlike and ambitious chiefs, and various modes of opposition to his views. A resolution had been offered to appropriate 600 dollars in gold to set in motion all the schools of Buenos Ayres! He succeeded at last in obtaining $127,000, and erected a splendid building called the Model School, which was afterwards emulated in another parish of the city. Monsieur Banvard, the architect of school-houses in France, said there was not in all France such architecture, such apparatus, and such luxury of appliances consecrated to the education of the people. The furniture and apparatus were procured in the United States. In 1860, when he left Buenos Ayres, there were 17,279 children in the schools. The Señora Manso had written him in 1864, that since his departure the number had decreased by five thousand. To this he replies, that by the natural increase the number should then have been 35,000, instead of 12,450, as she reports : —

"I assure you," he says, "that the revelation of so sad a fact has killed me, and I am tempted to leave behind me useless honors of position, and present myself again to the provincial government of Buenos Ayres, saying to it, ' Give me the department of schools — this is all the future of the Republic.' . . . ' The United States, with their schools from the beginning, as a basis, have accomplished doubtless, in one century, what all humanity has been doing and undoing in six thousand years of history! THE SOVEREIGN PEOPLE!

"I bid you adieu sadly. Write, combat, resist. Agitate the waves of a dead sea, whose surface tends to become hardened with the crust of impurities which escape from its depths, the Spanish colony, the tradition of Rosas, cows, cows, cows! Men, people, nation, republic, future!

"They write me from San Juan that on the twenty-fifth of May, if not before, they shall open the Sarmiento School, a continuation and reflection of the impulse given in Buenos Ayres. It is a monumental structure which would be considered a good one in Boston or New York, capacious enough to hold 1,700 children. But I much fear that it is a body without a soul. The provinces take their inspiration from the capitals. When they throw stones at the elections in Buenos Ayres, it is *bon ton* to stab each other in Rosario. When the attendance of children in the schools diminishes in cultivated Buenos Ayres, in *a whole Buenos Ayres*, as they say in the provinces, the children in the mountains will be born dumb so as not to learn to spell."

In 1858, after the Model School-house was finished and opened, and while enthusiasm was at its height about the schools, Señor Sarmiento was elected Senator of the State and Province of Buenos Ayres. He then proposed in his seat that the lands which Rosas had usurped, worth a million dollars, should be devoted to the erection of school-houses throughout the province, and a line of splendid structures is now seen stretching out into the pampas. While Senator, he also proposed many other bills which finally received the sanction of law. One was a sentence of impeach-

ment against Rosas. Another was the adoption of the
metrical system of weights and measures ; also, a law
of election by ballots, like that of New York and
Maine, voters being previously registered. The adoption of the Commercial Code, which he brought up
three successive years till he was successful ; a law to
punish printed *slanders* against individuals, and the
law which transformed the district of Chivilcoi from
barren pampas to a paradise of cultivated farms, were
others.

It was in 1859, as we learn from the " Diario of the
Sessions of Buenos Ayres, 1860," that General Urquiza, then general-in-chief of the army of Buenos
Ayres, made another attempt to usurp the government. Colonel Sarmiento had been made chief-of-
staff of the army of reserve. Urquiza was resisted
at Cepada, where, however, he gained a partial victory, the citizens losing their infantry and artillery.
But they fled back to the city to defend it, for em-
boldened by apparent success, Urquiza had dared to
besiege it. He was kept at bay, however, and still
holding the city in terror, listened to proposals for a
treaty which had been made to the government in
1858 by Colonel Sarmiento and others, ex-officially.
These were for two conventions, one to be held at
Buenos Ayres to make amendments to the Constitution, and also a national convention, at which said
amendments should be discussed and either ratified or
rejected. Urquiza now accepted them on three conditions. One of these was to reincorporate into the
army all the soldiers who had been dismissed from it
for whatever cause. This included the creatures of

Rosas; another was that the actual governor, Dr. Alsini, should be deposed. The force in the city was sufficient to defend it, but there was a panic, and the estancieros (landed proprietors) and cattle-growers feared it would be lost; some intriguers were in the legislature, and taking advantage of the panic, they wished to depose the governor to please Urquiza, whom they feared.

Colonel Sarmiento, who was still Senator, was absent from his seat at the moment, visiting one of the forts. He entered the antechamber of the Senate just as it had sent the requisition to the Governor to resign. He demanded the floor, but the President of the Senate did not grant it; he persisted in demanding it, and the *sixth* time, in spite of much opposition and exclamations, such as, " we are all agreed," he obtained it. He then said that he did not propose to them to revoke what they had done; it was too late for that, and might endanger the situation in the presence of the enemy, but he wished his name to be recorded as protesting against the act, which he designated as a crime; and he also proposed that the assembly that had destroyed the executive power should nominate another, and not leave them without a government. The latter was assented to, but the former was objected to as *against the rules.* It was put to a vote, and eight joined him in the protest. When the votes were counted, eleven voted for it, and that being a majority, their honor was saved, and the eighth of November is ever remembered as a nefarious day. In the afternoon they saw their error.

The result of the treaty was the meeting of both

conventions. Colonel Sarmiento had much influence in both, and was largely instrumental in bringing about the desired results, one of which was to incorporate the province of Buenos Ayres into the Confederacy. He also made a speech in this Convention of Buenos Ayres, in opposition to the proposition to have a state religion, and perfect practical toleration was declared to every form of opinion. There are now, thanks to him, as many Protestant as Catholic churches. This was agreeable to the instincts of Buenos Ayres, which had always manifested a liberal spirit in this respect. It needed only the word of a master-spirit to settle the question forever. The speech was printed at the time.

The debates of this deliberative assembly have been published, and from the elevation of the ideas expressed in them, and from their matter as a model of parliamentary tactics, they bear a character which has gained for them the reputation of being the most important documents of the kind extant. Colonel Sarmiento took the most important part in them. It has been said by his friends and biographers, that the most able of his speeches were made in secret session. It was ever his aim to moderate the spirit of reform, while he was the rock upon which were shattered the attempts of a wavering majority to resist every change. The general tendency of his propositions was to assimilate the Argentine Constitution to that of the United States.

Although in other respects an innovator, he dreaded the introduction of any variation from the original, for fear, as he said, " that a stream of blood might escape through any opening left in the machinery of government by the omission of some wheel, the purpose of which, through inexperience, had not been appreciated." This doctrine was maintained in all his writings and speeches, and any departure from it in practice has been attended by the same penalties that attached to what he calls " French novelties," current in all parts of South America.

This debate, marked by the conflict of such opposite parties, ideas, and interests, was closed with the proclamation of the Union by Colonel Sarmiento, as a member of the Convention, under the endeared name of the United *Provinces* of the Rio de la Plata. The measure was ratified by acclamation, all members of the Convention, including the President, rising to their feet, an example followed by the throng of spectators, under the enthusiasm awakened by this sublime movement of generous self-sacrifice. If it is borne in mind that the subsequent Convention of Santa Fé was divided by passions even more highly inflamed, that it ended with a similar scene of acclamation, and that its proceedings are allowed to have been influenced to a still greater degree by the counsels of Colonel Sarmiento, it will certainly be admitted that his invariable ardor in the support of his principles must have been regulated by kindly feeling and by an unusual power of carrying a required point and exercising, at the same time, a conciliatory influence upon opposing minds.

In the interval between these two Conventions, occurred another scene of so noble a character, as to compensate for many others which have disfigured the history of the same period by the hatred and violence displayed in them. This occasion presented the spectacle of the reconciliation of enemies whose inveterate hostility had been exercised both by the strife of reproaches and recriminations in the press, and by actual warfare in the field. On the day of which we speak, the multitude of a hundred thousand souls assembled upon the Mole of Buenos Ayres, was traversed by the government carriage containing Generals Urquiza and Mitre, President Durqué, and Colonel Sarmiento, in his capacity of minister, to which place he had been elevated, — these men, the principal antagonists in the long contest which had lately ceased, cordially embraced each other in the presence of the people and deposited their former hatred upon the altar of the common interests of their country. No more touching or humanizing scene was ever witnessed by any people, nor has the reconciliation of political enemies ever been more sincere. Yet they were again to meet upon the field of battle only a year later, impelled by a current of events which it was not granted them to control, and by the errors committed by each of the hostile parties.

The next eight years after this victory was achieved over apathy and ignorance, and after General Urquiza had retired to Entre Rios, his native province, were very eventful to the Republic, and the changes wrought and the improvements made, were due in the largest measure to the energy of Colonel Sarmiento. His various writings upon education, the report to the Chilian government upon the results of his mission to Europe and North America, his reports upon the state of public instruction in Buenos Ayres, the educational census taken in Chili, San Juan, and Buenos Ayres, his able work on popular education, and a series of occasional pamphlets upon similar topics, were but the heralds of deeds in which the spirit was to be embodied. While holding in succession the offices of senator, minister, and chief of staff, he founded and edited the " Annals of Education," with the object of disseminating information and exciting interest in his measures for the education of the people. He induced some of the best men in the city to take the personal supervision of the schools, and he regarded as his most important work, great as was his reputation as a writer, his " Progressive Method of Reading," which the government had stereotyped with vignettes in the United States. In Tucuman, Salta, and La Rioja, the symbol of a crossed pen and sword is employed in memory of him.

But his influence and his activity were by no means confined to educational labors, unless his practical illustrations of beneficent legislation may be looked upon as the highest branch of it. The tendency of the public administration bore the marks of his ripe age, and of the official training he had undergone in Chili in the service of a government accused of erring on the side of an excessive exercise of its authority by the people of countries which are ever wavering between the Scylla of despotism and the Charybdis of anarchy. He somewhere quotes Mr. Webster's speech before the Supreme Court of Rhode Island, in the case of Dorr, condemned to perpetual imprisonment for his share in the insurrection of Rhode Island. Mr. Webster says, —

" Is it not obvious enough, that men cannot get together and count themselves, and say they are so many hundreds and so many thousands, and judge of their own qualifications, and call themselves the people, and set up a government? Why, another set of men, forty miles off on the same day, with the same propriety, with as good qualifications, and in as large numbers, may meet and set up another government; one may meet at Newport and another at Chepachet, and both may call themselves the people. What is this but anarchy? What liberty is there here but a tumultuary, tempestuous, violent, stormy liberty, a sort of South American liberty, without power except in its spasms, a liberty supported by arms to-day, crushed by arms to-morrow? Is that *our* liberty? "

And holding up these forcible words Colonel Sarmiento adds, —

" If the liberal party in South America which has been overthrown by more than one tyrant, beholds itself in this terrible mirror, will it not turn away its face from the unsightly image? "

Both in Chili and in Buenos Ayres, Colonel Sarmiento has been noted, even by his adversaries, for his inclination to limit the injurious extension attempted to be given to the rights of the people. On his first appearance in the Chilian press, when he had it in his power to choose between the political parties of the country, both of which solicited his support, he decided in favor of that which proposed, while applying liberal ideas to public action, to aim at the stability of the power which was to represent them. Twenty years have since elapsed, and no tyrant has appeared in

Chili, although the doings of the government have not always been justifiable.

He followed the same course in the Argentine Republic. On the one hand he opposed the mutilated confederation that excluded Buenos Ayres, which was but a disguise for the old method of arbitrary rule by partisan leaders, and on the other he inclined to the incorporation of this estate, although the people were yet unfamiliar with the use of the liberties it had gained.

His influence in the city became in innumerable ways very conspicuous. When he entered upon his duties as Senator, the galleries, which had been accustomed to control the debates by hisses and applauses, designed to produce disturbance, and disorderly conduct, covered the amphitheatre with pasquinades against the new Senator. Three years later, the same area was the scene of the heated debates of the Provincial Convention, assembled to propose reforms in the Federal Constitution, — those remarkable debates already alluded to. The reader will look in vain for an instance of applause, still less of disorder, on the part of the listeners to these speeches, the excitement attending which was confined to the Convention itself. The eager multitude of spectators held their breath to listen to the debate ; and the fifty members of the Convention, animated as were their contests with each other, were treated with a religious respect which made them seem true *Patres Conscripti*. To what was this change due? Simply to the influence of one man, who through the press, by spoken discourses, and by legal measures, had taught the persons who were present at the ses-

sions of the legislature that they were not the people,
and that it was ruinous to the Republic for them to
taint the atmosphere of absolute liberty, which the
representative of the people should breathe, by expressing their own crude opinions in the sanctuary of the
law. On the withdrawal of that salutary and restrain-
ing influence, it is reported that Buenos Ayres became
again the theatre of that tumultuous and stormy liberty
of which Webster spoke, and which gives other nations
such cause for scandal. It was the same spirit which
impelled him on more than half a dozen occasions, to
maintain from his place in the Senate the rights of the
executive authority against the encroachments of the
legislature ; and to one governor, who had summoned
to his audience-chamber the leaders of various factions,
in order to advise with them upon the nomination of a
minister, he said, as appears from subsequent speeches
in the Senate, the following prophetic words: " In less
than a year we shall have to go and pick up from the
rubbish of the streets the fragments of the executive
power which our governors are throwing away, one
after the other, for want of courage enough to perform
their duties."

A year had not elapsed, when, in the presence of
the enemy, on November 8, 1859, this same governor
was deposed by the coalition in the legislature already
described, which was led astray by the fear of some,
the ill-will of others, and perhaps the treason of a very
small number.

While member of a senatorial commission, Colonel
Sarmiento proposed a new law for the regulation of
elections, designed to cure the constantly recurring

defects of the one then in operation, as well as to close
the door against the shameless frauds, and to punish
the violence prevalent at the elections of Buenos
Ayres, by furnishing definitions of these illegal actions.
Buenos Ayres would have spared itself many days of
disgrace and disturbance by the prompt passage of this
law, which was agreed to by the Senate, but owing to
its very perfection, was indefinitely postponed in the
House of Representatives, an evidence of oversight in
not making the legal use of rights the basis of liberty,
which that body had afterwards reason to deplore.

In every form this far-seeing patriot had warred
against the nomadic life of the cattle-grower, which
was an insurmountable barrier to the improvement of
the rural districts.   After two years' discussion he succeeded in getting permission from the government to
survey and lay out in small farms, in the North American mode, an extensive tract which was in possession of
squatters, and these farms he sold cheaply, in part to
the squatters themselves, and in part to emigrants from
other lands.   He personally superintended laying out
the squares with broad streets, and planting them
with trees, which grow as if by magic on the rich
pampa lands whose native growth is only rich grass,
that feeds countless herds of cattle without any labor
to the owners.   This survey was made in Chivilcoi in
1858, and last year, a railroad was completed to it
from Buenos Ayres.   On the occasion of opening the
station, many persons accompanied the Governor to
witness the ceremony, and all were amazed beyond
expression to see the spectacle.   It was a Chicago in
the desert, as Colonel Sarmiento has expressed it.   For

the first time within the life of one man, was a region
in South America so transformed. It contained a
church which Colonel Sarmiento had dedicated, a beautiful public school-house, for the front of which he had
induced a native artist to carve a marble group of
Christ blessing the children, and which was raised to
its place on the same festival, with an eloquent address;
a bank of discount ; various private schools, and a fine
railroad station. Where the industrial movement is
most conspicuous, at this railroad station, the only
square called for a living man bears the name of Sarmiento. The 25th of May (the anniversary of their
successful battle against Spanish rule), the 9th of July
(their independence day), Washington, and Lincoln;
Moreno and Belgrave (generals of the war of independence) ; Florencio Varela, the first martyr assassinated by Rosas, and Echevarria, the poet, give names
to the other squares.

At the three days' banquet of the festival, the name
of Sarmiento was toasted from one end of the long
tables to the other, by the representatives of every
public interest, each of which he had fostered ; and
subsequently thousands poured out to see with their
own eyes how a little enterprise could make the desert
blossom as the rose. In a land where cows were the
chief object of interest, milk could not be supplied for
the cities or even for the country, and the art of butter-
making was lost ! To this day it is imported, and is
one of the most expensive articles of luxury. Cereals
and vegetables are now brought to Buenos Ayres from
Chivilcoi, as well as from the Isles of the Parana, a
South American Venice, which by Colonel Sarmiento's

means have been redeemed from the waters and made the source of millions of revenue to the owners.

Thirty-nine individuals possessed the lands of Chivilcoi in 1858 ; now twenty thousand happy, prosperous farming people occupy the country, and enjoy all the conveniences of civilized life. There are no immense fortunes made, but great riches are distributed to all, and are increasing rapidly and wonderfully.

The cultivation of the Isles of the Parana, another enterprise of our author, resulted as brilliantly as the surveying of land in Chivilcoi. He often escaped from the burning debates of the Chambers, the press, and the schools, to the enchanting region at the mouth of the Parana, which is a delta of thirty miles by twenty, of islands, of a fertility unexampled perhaps in the world. In sailing up those channels bordered with the most luxuriant natural vegetation, he saw with the eye of a San Juan agriculturist, that if redeemed from the waters, they might become a source of immense wealth to the province. It did not take long for a brilliant thought to come to a white heat in his mind, and securing to himself from government the right to take possession of them, he seized his most romantic pen, and began to kindle the public with descriptions of their beauty, and of their immense agricultural future, if they could be cultivated judiciously — already a rural Venice whose canals Nature had supplied. By hundreds people put their hands to the work of clearing the rubbish, planting trees on the borders of the channels, etc. Dr. Francia, the tyrant of Paraguay, spent four hundred thousand francs in the enterprise. Not only Colonel Sarmiento, but all the persons interested, lived in a state of ecstasy, navigating their boats from island to island, enjoying the primitive and unsurpassed scenery, and scattering seed on the earth just snatched from the dominion of the waters. They had what he describes as a " frantic vegetation," for the territory was inundated every fifteen days, though only for a few hours at a time, so that everything that was planted was choked by the natural grasses, stimulated by the cultivation to unwonted growth. The result to those engaged in the undertaking was utter ruin at the end of two years. But at the end of five years, the aspect of the canals was one of magical beauty; they were planted with poplar-trees for leagues and leagues, and barques of all descriptions were navigating them, receiving the showers of peaches that fell from the trees for miles together. Finding the spot so humid, he consummated his labors by sending a courier to Chili for a species of osier for basket-making, and presented a twig to every planter. Now, millions of money are made by it, and they have cause to remember the speech which he made on the occasion, prophesying the riches that would accrue from this development of their industry, but which was then made the subject of ridicule. There is perhaps no place in the world so picturesque or of such dreamlike beauty as these channels bordered with trees. They are the delight of all the dwellers upon the River La Plata.

After immense opposition, Colonel Sarmiento succeeded in carrying a railroad from San Fernando, on the mainland opposite the islands, to Buenos Ayres, by which fruits, vegetables, and timber, are transported to its markets. As a reward for his labors, he enjoys the life-right of a perpetual seat in the railroad trains, while thousands are enriching themselves with the fruits of his enterprise.

One disgraceful feature of the recent mutilated Confederation was the perpetuation in the provinces of the rule of irresponsible and irremovable chieftains. Benavides, for sixteen years a supporter of Rosas, went on as a supporter of Urquiza, after the fight of Caseros. To suppress insurrections among the people, Urquiza had to interfere by force in 1852, not to secure to San Juan "a republican form of government" in accordance with the Federal constitution, but violently to impose upon it the rule of its old master. In 1857 he made an unsuccessful attempt to reëstablish him again; and he interfered in 1858 to punish the community for the death of Benavides, who had been taken prisoner, and had lost his life in an affray occasioned by an attempt to rescue him.

Instead of avoiding direct conflict with this obstinate resistance, the national government, which Urquiza actually controlled, sent a governor to San Juan, who had been previously known only by his violent conduct and his vices, to serve as a sort of executioner. The result which might have been expected, soon followed in a terrible outbreak, during which the band of outsiders sent to torment the people perished at their hands.

Colonel Sarmiento, then Minister of State at Buenos Ayres, was informed of the first symptoms of this outbreak by a message sent him by his friend, the irreproachable and venerable Dr. Aberastain, and he availed himself of the information to urge with earnestness upon the President and upon General Urquiza the importance of saving the Republic from a day of mourning, by removing Virasoro, their recent gubernatorial appointee.

On the 16th of November, they published a joint letter, signed also by the Governor of Buenos Ayres, which at last gained what had been so anxiously solicited; but on the very day that President Durqué revoked the appointment, Virasoro fell in a frightful conflict with the rebellious people.

A commission was despatched to San Juan, for the purpose of pacifying the disturbance, but while on its way, the old hostility of faction poisoned the minds of its members, and under the influence of General Urquiza, then living apart on his own estates, who tampered with the forces that passed by his residence, it became the instrument of a bloody revenge. Among other victims, Dr. Aberastain, who had been made governor after the fall of Virasoro, was cruelly and uselessly sacrificed in a horrible massacre, among hundreds of other victims, by that very Saa, who within a year has again headed an insurrection in the western provinces.

Everything was again thrown into confusion, and on the receipt of the news, Colonel Sarmiento withdrew from the ministry, as his continuance in office would have misled the public as to the nature of the resolutions forced upon the government of Buenos Ayres, for circumstances made it seem the personal interest of the minister that this war should be made, while in fact the contest which he fain would have averted, had already become inevitable. At this time he also refused the embassy to the United States, because he would not receive from the hands of the President the bribe of $14,000 with which he tempted him to withdraw his resignation.

The battle of Pavon terminated these unhappy consequences of an evil which a conciliatory policy had failed to subdue. Urquiza was routed, the national government was dissolved, and as it was expedient for an army to be sent into the interior, to secure and increase the results of the victory, Colonel Sarmiento was made commander-in-chief and official representative of the political views of his party. A pamphlet written by him describes this campaign, which began with the rout of a force entrenched behind the Carcaraña.

In pursuance of the operations of the war, and having captured two pieces of artillery from San Juan at San Luis, he was the first to reach the city of Mendoza, on January 1, 1862, attended by the victorious troops of Buenos Ayres. Proceeding at once to San Juan, he met with the reception to be looked for from the people of his birthplace upon their release from so long a series of disasters endured in behalf of a cause whose triumph had demanded a sacrifice of which they were the victims, as well as the generous sympathy thus awakened in Buenos Ayres ; for it is positively known that it was the odium of the San Juan massacres that solved the difficulties previously insuperable either by political combinations, treaties, or battles. On January 11, he celebrated, as governor of the province, an office to which the general voice had called him, the obsequies of the illustrious men who had fallen in those massacres, and thenceforward zealously availed himself of the means just placed in his hands to abate the evil effects of so many years of confusion.

The many years he had spent in connection with the Chilian administration, at that time farther advanced in the path of progress than any other to be found in South America, his many travels, his steady devotion to public life, all made him worthy of a wider field of usefulness than that afforded by an interior province. But the moral importance of a community which had undergone such trials, and the liberal instincts it had always shown, were enough to make amends for its scanty population in lending importance to his labors. An era of tranquillity in the interior followed the storms of the past, while new sources of disturbance made their appearance in the capital.

He availed himself rather of the deference with which he was regarded, than of his official power, to render acceptable various reforms in administration and in the collection of revenue, setting on foot, also, some public works, while the people, but for him, would have been disinclined to any changes. A Topographical Department, entrusted to European engineers, was employed in the work of mapping and surveying the country, a work required by a method of agriculture dependent on canals for irrigation. The map of the province has since been lithographed.

Public education, as was to be expected, received a great impulse, in the foundation of a college for advanced studies, the nucleus of a future university ; a high school for children of each sex, and primary schools in each ward, parish, or department. Upon the foundations of an abandoned church in the city, the building devoted to educational purposes was at once begun, of which former mention was made. The following public enterprises also deserve notice: a normal farm, for the promotion and improvement of agricultural art; a large cemetery which was urgently required by public decency, the old one being overcrowded; a public promenade, shaded by groups of trees, with iron benches beneath them; numerous repairs of existing structures; the paving of two leagues of streets; the construction of bridges of quarried marble over the canals, etc.; and the opening of straight roads thirty yards wide between the departments, to facilitate the wagon traffic.

He endeavored to bring back the refinements of cultivated society to a province so remote and which had been so exposed to conditions detrimental to progress, by the observance of public ceremonies and festivities on such occasions as the laying of corner-stones of new buildings, at the opening of various new works, and by military parades, all photographed at the time, in all of which were employed the forms, ornaments, and symbols used for such purposes by all civilized nations. The halcyon days of his short rule must have seemed after their late misfortunes like a dream of the night.

In his first addresses to the provincial legislature, he proposed the development of the mining interest; for San Juan, an oasis in the desert of the Travesias, as the barren region around the province is called, is full of mining wealth. Three years had passed in fruitless endeavors to extract the silver which showed itself in numerous localities throughout the province.

Mr. Rickard was sent for from Chili, and, after an examination of the principal mining districts, he made a report of them favorable enough to encourage the formation of a mining company, with a capital of a hundred thousand dollars in gold ; and when the stock was subscribed for, he went to England for materials, machinery, and workmen, stopping at Buenos Ayres to obtain more subscriptions and assistance from the government. No more fortunate choice of an agent could have been made. Mr. Rickard not only fulfilled all the objects of his expedition, but enlisted English capital in the enterprise, by publishing his " Mining Journey across the Andes," which made the public familiar with the name of the new mining district and other public works (trabajos publicos). A Review was established at the same time to keep the public informed of the results of the undertaking.

If the richness and permanence of these mines, and the skillful method of working them which have been adopted, answer the well-grounded hopes which have been formed of them, it is supposed that their shares will soon be quoted at the London Exchange, and the " Mining Journal " will inform the world of their products. Facing the central chain of the Andes, five thousand feet above the sea-level, in the beautiful and cultivated valley of Colingasta, enhancing the grandeur of one of the most superb views among the mountains, arise the columns of smoke emitted from the lofty chimney of the Smelting and Amalgamating Works of the San Juan Mining Company, situated near the mines of Fontal and of Castaño, which are connected with the plain by a cart-road, and offer an inexhaustible stock of metallic wealth to English capital and metallurgical science. Mr. Rickard has bought up all the stock in order to extend the enterprise by the introduction of more capital.

It will soon be known whether these mineral districts, with their thousands of argentiferous veins, can rival the mines of Mexico or Potosi in richness and productiveness.

But all this fair promise of peace and progress was disturbed and saddened from the outset by the incursions of banditti which distracted the neighboring provinces, and were carried even to the gates of San Juan, which thus found itself threatened with ruin while it was intent upon paving its streets and making bridges and roads. On January 1, 1863, a letter conveying the compliments of the season was sent to the Governor of San Juan by one of the ministers of the general government, containing the expression, " We are sailing over a sea of flowers." Another minister stated on March 22, " We have never enjoyed a period of greater good fortune ; at peace, as we are, with all the world, and on friendly terms with Urquiza and El Chacho." These dreams of a government which, owing to its location at one extremity and in the most civilized part of the Republic, had fallen into a false security, were dispelled by the fight of La Punta del Agua, which happened ten days later, on the 2d of April. On this occasion, no political pretext was assigned for their plundering inroads by the troops of horsemen coming from the open country of La Rioja, San Luis, and Cordova, and headed by El Chacho, a leader who had been used to making war on the towns with impunity under all the successive governments, for thirty years past. The national government entrusted to the Governor of San Juan the suppression of these disturbances, assigning to the duty the National Guard of San Juan and Mendoza, a battalion of regulars, and the First Regiment of the Line, commanded by Colonel Sanders, who was famous for having received up to that time fifty-one wounds from knife, bullet, lance, rapier, and sword.

Governor Sarmiento received his appointment to the direction of these military operations on the 8th of April. He had been informed on the 6th of an invasion of Mendoza by adventurers crossing from Chili in his rear. This intelligence, and the outbreak of insurrection in all directions, made the instructions he had received useless and inapplicable, and forced him to rely upon the inspiration of the moment, and to act as the facts of the case required.

Seventeen military expeditions were successively despatched from San Juan, towards the south, east, and north. The conflict of April 2 in San Luis was followed by several others: one in Mendoza, April 13; one in La Rioja, May 21; one in the Playas de Cordova, June 29; one in the Chanar, between the last-named provinces, July 8; one in the Bajo Hondo, between San Juan and La Rioja, August 14, and a final and decisive engagement at Causete, near the gate of the city of San Juan, on October 29. The Argentine montonera, although everywhere beaten, continually reappeared, unexpectedly threatening the place they supposed to be weakest, and mocking the vigilance of the armies in pursuit of them.

Eight hours after his entrance into the rural departments of San Juan, El Chacho had been routed and was in flight towards the desert, trusting to that and to the speed of his horses for his safety ; but this time he failed to find in it the security which had enabled him to laugh at the pursuit of regular troops for thirty years. The author of " Civilization and Barbarism," who has given us so lively a description of the warfare of the pampas, had, in this instance, departed from his ordinary course, and pursued the brigand with such energy as to surprise him in his last fastness, where he was seized and executed.

The want of space forbids the insertion of the story of his capture, which did credit to the skill and military tactics of the commander.

While governor of San Juan, upon the invasion of the province, he twice placed it in a state of siege under a proclamation of martial law. This course was unjustly and imprudently disapproved by the national government, and singular to relate, the two persons suspected of dealings with the insurgents, who were released from imprisonment by the national authorities, met the melancholy fate of obscure deaths in inglorious combats such as too often occur in those unhappy countries, — domestic broils involving whole hecatombs of lives.

Upon the capture, arms in hand, of Clavero, one of the ringleaders of the insurrection of Mendoza, a place subjected by the President himself to the control of Governor Sarmiento, commander-in-chief, he was tried before a council of war and condemned to death. The sentence, according to rule, was referred to the

commander-in-chief. Governor Sarmiento felt convinced that he judged aright in sanctioning it, but the
national government, ignorant till long after of the
actual occurrences connected with this series of operations, failed to do justice to the director of this complicated and obstinate warfare, until information was
received of the decisive affair at Causete. Clavero
was set at liberty. At this day, government sees its
mistake. In speaking of this, transaction, Colonel
Sarmiento again quotes Webster in his able speech
about martial law and its occasional necessity, and in
his "Life of Abraham Lincoln," dwells with much
force upon that statesman's action in circumstances not
wholly unlike those in which he then took part. He
wrote several articles at the time upon the question of
state rights which arose out of all these circumstances,
which were afterwards published in the "Nacional" at
Buenos Ayres, and still later reproduced in a pamphlet
entitled "The State of Siege according to Dr. Rawson," who was Secretary of State.[1]

The future of San Juan became secure upon the disappearance of El Chacho, who had plundered it more
than once during his residence in the neighborhood
and since the organization of its mining wealth had set
it on the road to wealth.

The National Government again applied to Congress
for authority to appoint the Governor of San Juan to
the diplomatic mission to the United States.

---

[1] At this moment, 1868, a change of cabinet has thrown Dr. Rawson out
of this position, and Colonel Sarmiento has been appointed Secretary of
State by the present administration, but he declines to take the place in
this last hour of its existence.

After resigning his office of Governor, with the view of accepting this appointment, he went to Chili to execute a similar mission, for he was made ambassador both to that country and to Peru at the same time.

He took occasion, while at Valparaiso, to protest against the unprecedented conduct of Admiral Pinzon in seizing the Chincha Islands. This protest was couched in concise language, which clearly indicated, however, how the principles of international law had in this instance been trampled under foot. A still greater sensation was occasioned in Chili and in Peru by his address to the President of the Chilian Republic upon presenting his credentials, due, perhaps, to the expressive phrases in which this discourse recalled the glories of the War of Independence against Spain, the common glory of Peru, Chili, and the United Provinces.

Colonel Sarmiento's resignation of the government of San Juan, gives occasion for the remark that his principles have made themselves manifest throughout his public career by the repeated withdrawal from situations of personal advantage whenever his retention of them would have interfered with a public interest or a sound political principle.

When sixteen years old, he had quitted the management of a prosperous establishment to join an army which took the field against Facundo Quiroga; in 1842 he gave up the high position won in Chili by his writings, to attach himself to another Argentine army. In 1851 he did the same, to join the final war against Rosas. After being disappointed in the ability and disposition of General Urquiza, the commander of the expedition against Rosas, to give a settled or a better government, he alone of all his countrymen withdrew entirely from the scene of operations, as has been before mentioned, in order neither to countenance by his presence the evil rule he foresaw, nor to attempt a forcible resistance to it.

In 1855 he had twice declined a seat in the Congress, because he could not take it consistently with his principles, preferring to establish himself in Buenos Ayres without any public office, and contend alone against the then mutilated confederation. In 1861 he refused the embassy to the United States for kindred reasons, and again withdrew from the ministry on learning the news of the violent proceedings at San Juan and the consequent death of his friend, Dr. Aberastain.

Before his departure from the Argentine Republic, the attention of the world had been called to the United States and its public men by our civil war, and by European attempts to introduce monarchy into Mexico. He still watches the political struggle with the deepest interest and the eye of a philosopher and a legislator, from whom we may learn much. A letter addressed of late to Senator Sumner on the occasion of the suspension of the Department of Education, may well put to shame the backwardness of our National Congress in reference to that cause whose neglected claims are the strongest possible comment upon the superficial education of our people.[1]

From Chili he went to Peru. During his stay in Lima he was invited by the plenipotentiaries sent to the South American Congress, to which he had never

[1] See Appendix.

been accredited by his government, to take part in its deliberations, and give it the benefit of his knowledge. He assisted in drawing up the treaties of alliance agreed to by the accredited plenipotentiaries, and did much to couch the alliance in such terms as would least impair the sovereignty of each State.

The Chilian press has preserved the memory of several remarkable predictions of Colonel Sarmiento in respect to the consequences of political conditions whose significance his sagacity enabled him to penetrate with remarkable insight, as the events proved.

In September, 1847, he assured Señor Carbello, the Chilian Minister Plenipotentiary at Washington, of the close approach of the French Revolution which took place in February, 1848, at which latter time he had returned from his travels, and was again in Chili, whence he wrote, in March, before any tidings could have reached Chili, inquiring for the details of an event that he was confident had happened. His prediction of the present condition of the United States, published last winter in " The Commonwealth," deserved to stand side by side with those prophecies which Mr. Sumner collected in his striking article in " The Atlantic." At that time he traversed the United States from end to end, saw its growing prosperity with a fresh eye, — fresh from the apathy of South America and Spain; fresh from the complicated conditions of the most advanced countries of Europe, where he had detected the clogs in the machinery of despotic and indeed of all monarchical or *personal* governments. He also detected the flaws in our country, and saw where liberty was travestied by the continued existence of slavery, but looking through all these obstacles he confidently predicted that in twenty years this would be the Great Republic of the world, and command the respect of all nations, possessing vitality enough to cure its own internal sores. It is still more remarkable to find a passage in his travels wherein, speaking of the division of the religious world into sects, he recognizes the principles of Roger Williams into whose spirit he intelligently enters, and prophesies that America is a land where eventually all sects will be merged in a pure practice of Christianity which shall repudiate all discordant forms and show the spectacle of a religious nation in which only the principles of Christianity shall be recognized without its forms.

Perhaps the most remarkable instance of his foresight was his celebrated letter to General Urquiza in 1860, in which he told him that a year later he should require him to answer for the consequences of that invasion of San Juan which ended in the death of Dr. Aberastain. In 1861, and as it happened on the same day of the same month, while moving on San Juan with an army, he addressed a letter from Villanueva to General Urquiza, who had been just defeated at Pavon, to remind him of his former letter which had been justified by the event.

During his late residence in the United States, Colonel Sarmiento has given all his leisure time to the subject of education and to the preparation of papers descriptive of American industry and American progress, and of valuable works, to send home to his country.

An able " Life of Lincoln," compiled from the best

authorities then known, and made up largely of his best and most effective speeches, taken as far back as the debates upon the Mexican war, and prefaced by a very instructive Introduction, he has printed and sent to South America, offering it "in unlimited quantities" if they will but read it. The skill with which he made prominent in it, topics upon which South America needed instruction, was very marked. The burst of sympathy which followed in the Argentine Republic, the death of our beloved President, was quite touching, and has been but little known and appreciated here. They too observed public mourning for the event, and their hearts were opened to receive the instruction his life and death afforded. Indeed the interest with which they watch our career is very worthy of note, and the noble speech and defense of our country made by Hector Florence Varela, one of the most accomplished of their citizens, at the Peace Congress in Geneva in 1867, a speech for which General Dix sent him an official note of thanks,[1] show how intelligent is their appreciation.

His book entitled "The Schools the Basis of the Prosperity of the United States," is a large work, containing a mine of information and wisdom. Many of its papers are descriptive of South American wants, to which the remedy is pointed out in others upon North American prosperity. This book is highly spoken of by Mr. Laboulaye, as well as by the best patriots and literary men of South America who have had the good fortune to read it; but an edition of a thousand copies,

[1] The speech and the note have been published in the April number of the *Boston Radical*.

which Colonel Sarmiento sent home for distribution, was stored in the government house, which shortly after was burnt down with all its treasures, books, and archives.   Only a few individuals, who knew the edition was there, and insisted upon having copies, obtained the books.   The catastrophe seems almost symbolic of the disasters that ever and anon befall the devoted Republic, which from time to time rises phœnix-like from its own ashes, and after having vainly fluttered its wings for a flight into the empyrean, falls back to earth with broken pinion.   May it prove of immortal vigor in the end, like the patriot educator, who never tires of scattering the good seed broadcast, sure that in the nature of things it is indestructible ; that a little vegetation will first spring up and cover the naked rock, disintegrating the surface by striking its slender roots, and this will make a richer bed for the next seed to fall upon, till at last the desert shall blossom as the rose.   What undying faith in principles is needed to keep alive even such indomitable energies !

When Colonel Sarmiento was in Europe in 1847, he was solicited to make the " Revue des Deux Mondes " answer to its name by his own contributions to it.   He did not accept the offer, but the last publication he has undertaken is a Review of his own called " Ambas Americas," or " The Two Americas," in which he purposes to embody all the current educational literature and improvements of the time.   He has sent home a large edition of the first number to be distributed not only in his own Republic but in the sister Republics.   Many of these are hardly yet acquainted with the movement set on foot in Chili and the Argentine Republic thirty years ago. In such portions of the country, the education of the people as a people has never yet been contemplated, and this very able Review will give the first intimation of such a plan to many of them. He hopes for assistance from this country to enrich his work.

His able coadjutor, La Señora Juana Manso, inspired by his example, still continues in her able editorship of the "Common-School Annals," founded many years since by Colonel Sarmiento. She is resolved that her compatriots shall not want for the best theories upon every branch of the subject. In one of her last issues, speaking of this last effort of Colonel Sarmiento, she joyfully exclaims, "the giant is on his feet again!" Like Antæus of old, when he falls to the earth, he rebounds from it with new motives for exertion, and apparently with new powers of execution. The foundation and execution of the "Ambas Americas" was the first effort which Colonel Sarmiento made after hearing of the death of his noble and only son in the Paraguayan war. The thought of what the sixty thousand children of the Republic needed drew him out of his deep sadness for that immeasurable and irreparable loss, for his son was a young man of the finest promise, spoken of by his eulogists as the "hope of the nation," the "coming man," the "idol of society," and young as he was (but twenty-one), "the intelligent and pure patriot" to whose future career the most experienced men of his country looked with expectation and confidence. He was educated by his father from earliest infancy, and was just about to graduate at

the University of Buenos Ayres, when the call to
fight for liberty and his country snatched him from his
studies.   The motives of the allies in that war were
not conquest, for they mutually agreed not to occupy
Paraguay, but simply to dethrone the tyrant and
restore the country to its enslaved people.[1]   The motive of young Captain Sarmiento and his Lieutenant
Paz who fell on the same field of battle, and were
brought home and buried together in the tomb of the
martyred Varela, by request of his sons, was as pure
as those which actuated our noblest young men to fight
for the liberty of *all*, as well as in defense of their
country.

At the instance of his government, which consisted
of his personal as well as political friends, who thought
his mind might be temporarily diverted from his sorrows by a change of scene, Colonel Sarmiento visited
the French Exposition in 1867, and was present at the
awarding of medals to his countrymen for their superior wools.

Such are the principal events in the life of a statesman of South America, of which we have known so
little.   Perhaps they have many more men of merit,
for in his works we meet the names of many who have
been distinguished, and of whom he speaks in terms of
high respect, such as the Generals of the War of Independence, Puyrredon, San Martin, and Las Heras,
statesmen like Don Manuel Montt, ex-president of
Chili, the celebrated litterateur Bello, the virtuous

[1] It is not clearly understood in this country that the object of Lopez,
tyrant of Paraguay, was not to found or defend a republic, but to found an
empire extending over Entrerios, Corrientes, and Uruguay.

Aberastain, "a Cato assassinated in another Utica," Dr. Velez, the author of the "Codes of Law," of which M. Laboulaye says it is the most advanced work on that subject in the world, with many other personages too numerous to name and of whom nothing is known here. But none of them have had the opportunity, like the subject of this sketch, to acquire that knowledge which, when well directed, serves to change radically the condition of a nation. Even the circumstance of not having received that kind of education which is given in universities may have served to' preserve his mind free from those leading-strings of national tradition which often becomes a second nature in the individual, destroying all originality and perpetuating errors of opinion. A man who has contended with barbarism in South America, and has studied the sources of the development of other nations, during residence therein, must have acquired by practice and by comparison, rich materials for thought, and a fund of ideas of no common order. That of diffusing education among the people, from which nothing has distracted him for thirty years, neither war nor exile, the poverty of his private life, nor the seductions of exalted position, has given a special character to his life. The present minister of the government of Buenos Ayres, speaking of education, in his report to the legislature of this year, says, " We cannot speak of education without naming Colonel Sarmiento;" and this saying will be often repeated in different parts of South America, for his new Review, the "Ambas Americas," a work specially designed to impart to the southern hemisphere the knowledge and the ideas that have been acquired in the northern, will spread the knowledge of his character and efforts, as well as of his great theme, Popular Education.

It may be said of him in reference to the subject of education, as was said of a contemporary by Plutarch, " He is more than an echo of Socrates in the practice of morality, he is even a disciple." Who like him has during a long life pursued the one aim of saving a nation from decay by proposing to rouse the dormant moral sentiments of the human soul?

Will his example be followed in his own country? He has had so little encouragement in his laborious career that it had been feared few would be found to follow him in a path so bristling with difficulties, but the present sympathy of his countrymen, whom a great calamity has waked from their long apathy, inspires better hopes.

It is but justice to do so much honor to his country, as to say, that by what we have seen of the correspondence of " Ambas Americas," and through the political articles of the New York papers, it is evident that there are everywhere some who appreciate the true value of his labors, and there is a party there that understands how much it might be benefited by putting the reins of government into such able and experienced hands. " It is like the judgment of posterity," one letter says, " this opinion that is held to-day of the same ideas and efforts which ten years ago met with such resistance."

In countries so little experienced in republican practices as South America must be, the material facts of an election are not always the expression of the most dominant opinion of the best minds, but rather of the accidental influences of the moment. It is therefore doubtful whether Colonel Sarmiento, being so far from the theatre of party movements, can effectually serve his country otherwise than by his advice or his writings, but that they are now esteemed worthy of consideration there, is a powerful stimulus to his perseverance in his life-long work.

APPENDIX.

———◆———

To Mr. Senator Sumner, —

Honorable Sir, — Encouraged by the distinction with which you have been kind enough to favor me, I take the liberty of submitting to your enlightened consideration a few observations upon a subject which will soon be brought before the Senate, and in whose favorable selection not only the United States, but republican principles everywhere, and the civilization of the popular masses are deeply interested. I have heard that the discontinuance of the National Department of Education has been resolved upon, and if the measure is definitely carried, such action will in my judgment produce a deplorable reaction against the growing interest inspired of late by universal education.

For statesmen like yourself, my suggestions would have little value, if I should pretend to propose new plans upon subjects on which North Americans are so far in advance of other nations. But it may be of some use to know the impressions made upon other peoples, and my feelings in this special case would be, as it were, the expression of their common aspirations. I can speak for South America, where twenty or thirty millions of human beings are agitated by a chaos of revolutions, which conduce to nothing, *because certain elements of government are wanting*, and I have recently visited Europe, where I conversed with eminent men upon the salutary moral influence which the United States are beginning to exercise.

When Europe recovered from its surprise and wonder at the happy issue of the past civil war, and at the triumph of republican institutions, — among all the causes incomprehensible at a distance, which had brought about this result, it discerned one alone clearly, and that was that behind Lincoln, Congress, and Grant, was *a people that could read and write*.

The Republic now presents itself to those who do not despair of liberty in the world, with the *school* as the basis of its Constitution. To the political economist, the North American School, which creates the *producer*, is a sufficient explanation of the prodigious development of wealth ; and in view of the governments themselves, the sudden appearance of the United States and of Prussia as great nations, is closely allied to their systems of universal education. England and France have showed of late that they have profited by the lesson, taking more interest than formerly in the diffusion of education. This is the clear influence exercised by American institutions in their most acceptable forms.

Mr. Laboulaye, the distinguished French professor who has done so much to make North American institutions known in Europe, not long ago presented to the workmen of Lyons the portraiture of Horace Mann as the only man comparable to Washington in the part which he took in the definitive and enduring organization of American democracy. But in the greater part of the world to-day, if the influence and efficacy of North American institutions of education are known by their results, very few if any have an idea of their mode of operation, or of their organization. In England, reports, data, and ideas are frequently sought from the United States, and I am acquainted with the fact that the ex-minister Ratazzi, desiring to organize a vast system of education in Italy, lamented that he had not within reach the precise documents which could explain the systems that have given such happy results in the United States, the only country which can serve as a guide in this respect. The speech of the Hon. Mr. Garfield in the House of Representatives in favor of the creation of the National Department of Education, has been reproduced in the presses of South America as a stimulus toward adopting the same measure, and another of Professor Wickersham, of Pennsylvania, has had the same currency in France and South America.

If the United States, then, owe an account to the human race of their own experience and progress in certain respects which are important to the well-being and improvement of mankind, just as they received from England and from human thought many of the principal benefits of government, a means of transmitting the knowledge would hereby have been established, and the National Department of Education would have fulfilled that useful function, beside the special object for which it was created. It would have come to be, as it were, the Department of International and Foreign Educational Relations, and its reports and data would, when collected, have been a fountain of information, not only for the Southern States, but other nations, for even if a Report of Massachusetts or New York Schools can be obtained in Europe, such documents, by their purely provincial character, are wanting in the authority which the seal of the United States would give to those of a National Department. The great inequality with which education is actually distributed in the United States, and which it was the confessed object of the said Department to regulate, would have given an opportunity to see the work of diffusion, and the application of means, as well as the desired results.

With some diffidence, I will venture to make one observation with respect to the United States themselves. The greatest antagonism between the Southern States and the Northern, has come, in my judgment, from the Southern following the same plan as that of ancient society in Europe and South America, and the Northern advancing in new and peculiar paths. The system of education in the South, limited to universities and colleges, was that of England, France, Spain, Italy, and the South America of to-day, leaving the majority of the people without intellectual preparation and development. The visible sign of the advanced North American system of government is the *Common School*, and if ever the South shows the same *visible sign*, its regeneration will be secured.

For the Republicans of Europe and South America, the North Americans have added a new organism of government in the COMMON SCHOOL, thus solving a grave difficulty which the ancient Republics could not solve. The North American Republic is a government which under a *written* Constitution is carried on by *written* speech. Athens, Rome, Venice, Florence, were republican cities (or city republics) governing by word of mouth from the Forum. Washington is only the desk on which the laws are written and where the reasons are given for the law, which on the following day the people in California, Chicago, or Richmond, read *written*. Hence the Republic to-day is in extension indefinitely dilatable, as the people govern from their residence, be it in Egypt, in Capua, or in Greece, because they can read that which is sent to them *written*. If, then, Republican institutions are to be diffused throughout the world, patriots, instead of making revolutions, would begin by founding common schools, in imitation of the United States, as the cement of the future Constitutions. If Protestantism, by requiring the Christian to know how to read, in order to put into his hands the Bible, has so much aided by this means alone, the development and improvement of the human race, the SCHOOL of the American Republic will make useless the ancient aristocracies and the modern repressive governments, by suppressing the popular incapacity and its legitimate fruits — revolutions.

You will understand why, with these ideas and hopes, I deplore the suppression of the *National Department of Education*, which proposes to be a guide at home and abroad to the laggards of the South in the United States, and would have been a Pharos to the other nations, in the new path marked out by the North. So persuaded was I of the beneficent influence which this department was destined to execute, that I attended the meetings of Superintendents of Schools in Washington and Indianopolis to add my voice to it, and established a Spanish Educational Review [1] in order to make known at large in South America the important data which this public office would furnish. If the preservation of the National Department of Education does not interest you much for practical results in the South, which have not yet been put to the proof, I think you cannot be indifferent to the ad-

[1] *Ambas Americas.*

vantage that other nations would reap from its labors — nations as my own in the dark upon the mode of operation of the American Common School system. May the hope of benefiting millions, and of ameliorating the condition of the human race everywhere, induce you to rekindle and keep forever burning the torch which is to diffuse that light.

I have the honor to subscribe myself, etc.,

D. F. SARMIENTO.

ERRATA.

Page 30th, line 1st, for *Christian* read *Chilian.*

" " line 16th, for *Ariste* read *Triste.*

" 130th, line 2d from below, for *crisis social* read *social crisis.*

" 136th, line 9th, for *fifty-foot soldiers* read *fifty foot-soldiers.*

" 248th, line 4th, for *Agacucho* read *Ayacucho.*

" 255th, line 1st, for *mountaineers* read *montoneros.*

" 262d, line 1st, for *mountaineers* read *montoneros.*

" 264th, line 17th, for *sacreligious* read *sacrilegious.*

" 276th, lines 4th and 5th from below, for *pyramids* read *desert of Sahara.*

Page 284th, line 13th, for *cathedral* read *pulpit.*

" 308th, line 1st from below, strike out *Doctor.*

" 321st, line 8th, for *Jachel* read *Jachal.*

" 322d, lines 6th and 8th, for *Leprida* read *Laprida.*

" 323d, lines 3d and 8th from below, for *Rickard* read *Richard.*

" 327th, lines 12th and 13th from below, for *Antonio* read *Nazario.*

" 330th, line 7th from below, for *Brinuela* read *Brizuela.*

" 343d, line 9th, for *Uspellata* read *Huspellata.*

" " line 10th, for *Sagrana* read *Lagrano.*

" 345th, line 15th from below, for *Radies* read *Kadies.*

" 353d, lines 1st and 5th, for *Bolivar* read *Bolivia.*

" " " " for *under whom* read *where.*

" 359th, line 16th from below, for *Durqué* read *Durqui.*

" 360th, line 8th, for *Sanatuolas* read *San Nicolas.*

" " " from below, for *Durqué* read *Durqui.*

" 367th, line 9th, for *Durqué* read *Durqui.*

" 373d, line 15th, for *Belgrave* read *Belgrano.*

" 374th, line 3d from below, for *Dr. Francia, the tyrant of Paraguay spent,* read *From France were sent.*

Page 374th, line 2d from below, for *in* read *to foster.*

" 378th, line 16th, for *Commander-in-chief* read *Chief-of-staff.*

" 385th, line 1st, for *Commander-in-chief* read *President.*